ANOTHER DAWN ANOTHER

The true story of Warrant Officer Tre
a veteran rear gunner in RAF Bomt
World War Two.

Foxtrot Finals [courtesy Alex Hamilton GAvA]

*Trevor Bowyer's Medals: Distinguished Flying Cross,
1939-45 Star, Aircrew Europe Star, Africa Star,
Defence Medal, 1939-45 War Medal,
Imperial Service Medal, Air Gunners' brevet*

Kenneth JS Ballantyne

1

First published in Great Britain in 2009
Revised and reprinted in 2010
Revised and reprinted in 2011
Revised and reprinted in 2012

by Laundry Cottage Books, Laundry Cottage
Shawbirch Road,
Admaston, Wellington, Shropshire. TF5 0AD

Tel: 01952 – 223931

Email: cenneach@westcoast13.wanadoo.co.uk

Website: www.laundrycottagebooks.co.uk

MMIX © Kenneth JS Ballantyne

ISBN 978-0-9550601-3-7

The right of Kenneth JS Ballantyne to be
identified as the author of this work has been asserted
by him in accordance with the Copyright,
Designs and Patents Act 1988.

All rights reserved. No part of this publication may be
reproduced, stored in a retrieval system, or transmitted
in any form or by any means, electronic, mechanical,
photocopying, recording or otherwise or in any
circumstances or in any country without the prior
written permission of Kenneth JS Ballantyne or the
Executors of his Estate.

An environmentally friendly book, typeset, printed and bound in England
by www.printondemand-worldwide.com

This book is made entirely of chain-of-custody materials

Titles published by
Laundry Cottage Books

All the Things You Are by Kenneth Ballantyne
ISBN 978-0-9550601-4-4

"Twelve previously untold stories of World War 2 including the Women's Land Army, WRNS, a WAAF, an Arnhem paratrooper and a shipwreck survivor in this revealing and often humorous book."

Another Dawn Another Dusk by Kenneth Ballantyne
ISBN 978-0-9550601-3-7

The Journey by Kenneth Ballantyne
ISBN 978-0-9550601-1-3

The D-Day Dodger by Albert F Darlington
ISBN 978-0-9550601-2-0

"The autobiography of a young infantry soldier in North Africa and Italy during World War 2."

Bibliography

A Bridge Too Far, Cornelius Ryan; Wordsworth Editions Ltd, 1999

A Drop in the Ocean [The Goldfish Club], J French and J B Smith; published by Leo Cooper

A Lighter Shade of Blue, ACM Sir Christopher Foxley-Norris; Ian Allen Ltd, 1978

Bomber Crew, John Sweetman; Abacus

Boys at War, Russell Margerison; Northway Publications

Donitz and the Wolf Packs, Bernard Edwards; Arms & Armour

Flypast Magazine, November 1996

Halifax & Wellington, Bowyer & Van Ishoven; The Promotional Reprint Co Ltd

Jump For It! [The Caterpillar Club], Gerald Bowman; published Evans Bros Ltd., 1955 and Pan Books Ltd., 1957

Malta Convoy, Shankland and Hunter; published by Fontana/Collins, 1973

More or Less, Kenneth More; Hodder & Stoughton

Night Mail, WH Auden

Operations Record Book No.61 Squadron

Operations Record Book No.70 Squadron

Private James Stokes by Paul F Wilson

Rear Gunner, Ron Smith, DFM; Goodall Publications Ltd

Shropshire Airfields, Toby Neal; Langrish Caiger Publications

Survival at Stalag IVB, Tony Vercoe; McFarland & Co Inc

Tail End Charlie's Story, H James Flowers

Tail Gunner, Chan Chandler, DFC*; Airlife Classic

The Bomber Command War Diaries, Middlebrook & Everitt; Midland Publishing Ltd

The Battle of Britain & The Blitz, Editor Nigel Fountain; Michael O'Mara Books Ltd

The British Travelling Post Office, Peter Johnson; Ian Allen Ltd

The Dambuster Who Cracked the Dam, Arthur G Thorning; Pen & Sword Books Ltd;

Thundering Through the Clear Air, Derek Brammer; Tucann Books

Voices in the Air, Edited by Laddie Lucas; Arrow Books

Acknowledgements

I am deeply indebted to the many people who have made the telling of Trevor Bowyer's life story possible, in particular his son Neville, who contacted me and asked me to write his father's story and then provided me with so many of the biographical details, experiences, family photographs, service record and, most valuable of all, a copy of that treasured possession of all aircrew, the logbook.

A huge thank you is also due to veterans of No.50 and 61 Squadrons, H James Flowers, Reg Payne, Ted Beswick, Bernard Fitch, Jimmie Flint and Sir Michael Beetham, all of whom are former Lancaster bomber aircrew and who have shared with me their memories and experiences of operational life during the war years and at RAF Skellingthorpe in particular. I am especially grateful to all of them for showing so much interest in this work and giving me their time and unreserved consent to use their own material and personal photographs. My additional thanks are due to Reg Payne for kindly allowing me to reproduce some of his many paintings, particularly *Dawn Landings* which I used for the cover of this book.

I am also extremely grateful to Ray Morris of Newtown in Wales, formerly Sgt Fitter Ray Morris 937114, of No.252 Squadron for the help, information and photographs which he has provided to me about living and fighting an air war in the desert of North Africa. Without his help it would have been much more difficult to piece together the strands of Trevor's time with No.70 Squadron at Abu Sueir.

My thanks also go to the following people for their consent to use their photographs and material in this book: Peter Jackson and his father Wallace, Lynn Forsyth, Julie Adney and the family of Blake Turner, Adele Badiali, the artist Alex Hamilton, GAvA for his kind permission to reproduce his paintings of *Foxtrot Finals* and *Strike in the Aegean*, the Chief Executive of the National Memorial Arboretum for his kind consent to reproduce the image of the National Memorial, Arthur Atkinson, Trevor's wireless operator on No.61 Squadron and to Derek Brammer, former Secretary of No.50/61 Squadrons Association for his invaluable advice and immeasurable knowledge of Lincoln, Skellingthorpe and the two Squadrons.

My grateful thanks also go to Rob Davis for his kind permission to reproduce the story about the barmaid and the aircrew on pages 212/213 from his very informative and comprehensive website, part of which is specific to RAF Bomber Command 1939-45. Rob's website can be found at www.elsham.pwp.blueyonder.co.uk.

My thanks are also due to all those who have kindly uploaded photographs on to the internet to be shared by us all and in particular the owners of the pictures on pages 44, 83-84, 88, 95, 99, 138, 328 (bottom) and 331 (top).

All remaining photographs are from my own collection.

I am also indebted to Sue Browning of Sue Browning, Editing and Proofreading for kindly correcting my punctuation, grammar and spelling, and for guiding the flow of this story through the pitfalls of creative writing, and my apologies to her for tinkering with it afterwards.

Last, but certainly not least, my special thanks to my wife Elaine, without whose continuing help and support this story would not have been written and published.

Kenneth Ballantyne

Dedication

This book is dedicated to all the men and women of RAF Bomber Command and the Middle East Air Force who fought so bravely during every day of World War Two, at home and abroad, between 1939 and 1945 to keep our country free. None shall ever be forgotten.

Bomber Command crest

"Through these portals go the bravest of men: always frightened but never afraid."
No.83 Squadron RAF Scampton, Lincolnshire

Memorial stone in Lincoln Cathedral

*Trevor John Bowyer at twenty-five taken at Mindel
& Faraday, 34/36 Oxford Street, London in 1939
[Neville Bowyer collection]*

Preface

"The fighters are our salvation but the bombers alone provide the means of victory."
Winston S Churchill, September 1940.

The trouble with youth is that it thinks that it will always be young and that the elderly have always been old. It has probably always been that way but equally always untrue. Take a moment to step back and look at the elderly man you see in front of you and reflect upon what he has seen and what he has done to give you your freedom. He too was young once: when he was just eighteen years of age, he volunteered to go to war for you; he joined an RAF bomber crew and went to face some of the most terrifying combat conditions and experiences of the war. Night after night he put his life on the line and flew out against an enemy determined to kill him. He used up more of his bank account of courage in a week than you will ever get the chance to do in a lifetime. He didn't think of himself as being brave, just doing a job of work, but brave he most certainly was; they all were, that generation of men and women who gave their youth for those of us who have come afterwards.

There was no post-traumatic stress syndrome counselling after he had seen two Lancaster bombers collide and explode a few yards away, in an instant killing fourteen of his comrades; no time to get over the loss of a close friend whom he had seen plummet to his death beneath a burning parachute; there was another mission, another job to be done the next night. One week's leave in six, if he was still alive to take it, that was his respite. Danger, death and destruction were his world when he was a young man, younger than you are now. Maybe he was good at his job, or maybe just lucky; most likely both and so he survived, but 55,573 young men, nearly half the total strength of Bomber Command, did not survive. Put into context, that was a lower survival chance than a British infantry officer on the Western Front in the Great War. Every aircrew member was a volunteer; you didn't get posted to Bomber Command, you asked to go.

I have written this book through the eyes of rear gunner Trevor Bowyer and, with the help of some of his contemporaries, have tried to tell just a little part of the Bomber Command story during World War Two and more particularly, of the crews who flew the aircraft.

The British bombing strategy of German-occupied Europe during the Second World War has been analysed and discussed, criticised and maligned for over fifty years, often by those who offer nothing but the counsel of perfection drawn from the wisdom of hindsight. Sir Arthur Harris, Bomber Harris, as he became known after the war, has been largely held responsible for the strategy and particularly that part of it known as area bombing, the bombing of cities rather than specific targets, but, as so often in politics, he was made the scapegoat of his political masters whose strategy it really was.

The raid on Dresden has been the focus of most debate but this, like the policy of area bombing, was devised by the War Cabinet and carried out upon Churchill's orders, himself a great advocate of the policy. In July 1940 Churchill wrote privately, *"When I look round to see how we can win this war there is only one sure path... and that is an absolutely devastating, exterminating attack by very heavy bombers from this country upon the Nazi homeland."*

In 1940 Britain stood alone. Its army had been defeated in Europe, and whilst most of the men had been saved at Dunkirk and ports along the Atlantic coast, their equipment and weapons had been left behind. The Royal Navy was occupied either in the Far East or protecting the vital convoy route across the Atlantic from America and Canada: only the RAF was capable of taking the war to the Germans. The Battle of Britain had saved the country from invasion for the time being, winning the war was another matter altogether.

Long-range bombing of German targets was the only way to take the war to the enemy, but in the early years, at night, in poor weather conditions, with primitive navigational equipment and no heavy bombers, only 30 per cent of aircraft were hitting within five miles of the target. Area bombing was approved by the Cabinet, ordered by the Air Ministry, and Arthur Harris was appointed to carry out the strategy. Whether it worked as conceived is a matter of genuine debate. However, what is not in doubt is that it forced the Germans to devote around a million men and 55,000 anti-aircraft guns to the protection of their homeland, troops and weapons which otherwise would have been used on the Russian Front or to repel the invasion of Europe in June 1944. In addition, fighter production was prioritised at the expense of bomber production, thereby significantly reducing the opportunity for the Nazis to be in a position to make a further attempt upon the invasion of Britain.

Although the attacks upon German cities remain the best-known activity of Bomber Command it had many other roles during the war, including the support of the retreating British Expeditionary Force [BEF] to Dunkirk, flying in the obsolescent, slow, lightly armed Fairey Battle, the 'flying coffin'. It was to the pilot and navigator, Flying Officer Garland and Sergeant Gray, in one of these aircraft that King George VI awarded the first two Victoria Crosses of the war, posthumously, after they had led five aircraft to the bridge at Maastricht to prevent the Germans crossing the Albert Canal, the only occasion on which two VCs have been awarded to the crew of a single aircraft for the same action. The aircraft's wireless operator/air gunner Sergeant Lawrence Reynolds was also killed but not honoured!

Bomber Command also carried out many attacks on high-profile targets such as the Dambusters raid on the Ruhr dams, the sinking of the battleship *Tirpitz*, the V-rocket sites at the Peenemunde Research Centre, the U-boat engine factories in eastern Germany and their bases on the French Atlantic coast. Indeed, the RAF sank more German U-boats during the war than did the Royal Navy. Early in the war, Blenheim crews carried out numerous highly dangerous, even by Bomber Command standards, daylight raids upon German shipping and ports, and helped to frustrate the Nazi's invasion plans of Britain. These raids were all low level and very costly in the lives of the crews. Mine-laying along the Baltic coast and amongst the German shipping lanes was another vital but dangerous role, as was the support of the D-Day landings. Moreover, bombers of the Middle East Air Force were also active overseas and in North Africa in particular throughout most of the war. It carried out attacks, often by day, upon the Afrika Corps and their Italian allies in the desert both before and after the Battle of El Alamein and against Axis shipping in the Mediterranean.

Bomber Command flew missions against the Germans on almost every day or night from 3rd September 1939 to May 1945, an incredible feat of courage, endurance and sustained effort by any standard. The chance of surviving a whole tour of operations, thirty missions, was just 1 in 4, worse than any other branch of the armed services. A further 10,000 aircrew were taken prisoner, lucky to have escaped from doomed aircraft, because the G-forces at work in an aeroplane out of control and spinning to earth trapped many airmen inside. Other aircraft, full of fuel, bombs and ammunition simply exploded when hit by flak or cannon fire. Some collided whilst in the bomber stream, others suffered mechanical failure, a few were hit by falling bombs from aircraft flying above them and inevitably some were lost to friendly fire and in training excersises.

Historian Professor Richard Overy has studied the bombing campaign at length and has proposed that, *"the critical question is not so much, 'What did bombing do to Germany?' but 'What could Germany have achieved if there had been no bombing?'"*

The bombing strategy may have been a blunt instrument by today's benchmarks, but at the time it took the war to Germany, and the 125,000 men and women of Bomber Command, with an average age of just twenty-two, made a larger and more sustained contribution to victory in Europe than any other part of Britain's armed services and in consequence paid a higher price in human life.

Albert Speer, Hitler's Armaments Minister knew only too well what the impact of the bombing campaign was on Germany when he said, *"It made every square metre of Germany a front. For us it was the greatest lost battle of the war."*

Perhaps then, the answer to Professor Overy's point is that Germany would have won the war, and the prevention of that is Bomber Command's greatest legacy to the free world. It is time that Britain properly honoured the courage and achievement of the men and women of Bomber Command. They did an outstanding job of work; nobody pretends that those young airmen enjoyed the carnage and destruction that their bombs wrought upon the German people, but to have allowed the Nazis to remain in power and to mount an invasion of Britain was not within civilised contemplation, and we owe the men and women of Bomber Command an enduring debt of gratitude which can only increase as the years pass.

"As great a warrior as these islands ever bred."
Sir Arthur Travers Harris, GCB, OBE, AFC, RAF

Kenneth JS Ballantyne   Laundry Cottage
LL.B[Hons], Solicitor   8th May 2010

Dawn Landings by Reg Payne. The moment of touchdown was always a great relief.

ANOTHER DAWN
ANOTHER DUSK

*The National Memorial at Alrewas in
Staffordshire from the north...*

*...and inside. The whole National Memorial Arboretum is
a beautiful setting of sixty acres of trees and open space.
Admission is free*

ANOTHER DAWN ANOTHER DUSK

CHAPTER ONE

"But to go to school in a summer morn, O! it drives all joy away; under a cruel eye outworn the little ones spend the day in sighing and dismay."
From The School-Boy by William Blake.

Dawn. The day had started bright and clear. The early morning sun was climbing into a cloudless blue sky, its gentle heat turning the dew into a thin mist which hung through the branches of the young trees like a calico cloak. A million diamonds scattered on the silver threads of gossamer spun during the night sparkled in the cool of the still air which held the rare promise of a flawless spring day. I had climbed the staircase of gleaming white steps up the earthen ramparts, reminiscent of an ancient burial mound, to the enclosed stone circle of the Armed Forces Memorial in the National Arboretum, and now stood at its centre, dwarfed by the Portland stone panels upon which were carved the names of over 16,000 men and women who have died in the service of this country since the end of the Second World War.

That had been my war, where I had made friends and then lost them in the blink of an eye. Like our fathers before us, our whole generation had gone to war, and like our fathers we had thought that we were doing it for peace and for a better life. For the first time in a thousand years we were fighting to protect these islands from an invader. Stretching out below me here at the Arboretum have been planted 50,000 trees, each one in memory of a person, an action or a ship. We had won that war: so why since then did all these young lives have to be lost? I was stunned by the seemingly endless list of names from over sixty years of purported peace and progress; whilst in stark contradiction to the horrors of war, the beauty and veneration of the memorial brought my own memories flooding back.

First wave leaving the coast [Reg Payne]. On our way out to another mission.

Coned [Reg Payne]. One of our squadron caught in the web of the searchlight beams.

We had been stood down. There would be no flying tonight and the unexpected idleness brought a certain relief with it. I sat in the quiet of the sergeants' mess reading that day's newspaper, but without much success. The news was all about the war, but I was living that war and didn't really want to read about it as well. I realised that I had turned several pages without having actually read anything and so I gave up the task, folded the paper neatly and, reaching across to the nearest table, put it with the other dailies which had been similarly discarded.

The fire in the grate was beginning to die down and I watched as Alf stirred from his seat beside the log basket and carefully placed three cut lengths of English ash onto the glowing embers. It was easy to see why Alf was such a good navigator; he was always so precise in everything that he did.

I watched for a few moments as the flames began to lick up around the wood, then got up and walked across to the window in the gable wall end of the room. It was late afternoon and even though it was the end of May, outside the dull light was already fading fast. Leaning on the window ledge, I looked out towards the trees and the airfield beyond and stared at the grey leaden sky, the reason for our enforced respite. The rain, driven by the easterly gale, was beating a hypnotic rhythm on the thin glass in front of me, each drop just for a moment caught motionless as it struck the pane, then dissolved to merge with all the others in the sheet of water that ran down the window and cascaded off the sill, disappearing briefly, only to be whipped up by the wind and forced to fly once more.

Fly. Some days I couldn't wait to fly and then there were others when I hoped that I would never have to fly again. As I stood there, gazing out into the failing light and watching the rain being driven horizontally across the airfield of RAF Station Skellingthorpe, deserted apart from the spectral outline of the closest Lancaster as it stood at its dispersal point, I heard the mess door open quietly and was conscious of someone coming noiselessly into the room. I didn't turn around to see who had come in. I didn't need to; I knew that it would be Stan Moston our steward. A moment later, there was a soft click as he switched on the wall lights which filled the room with a rather dim, but comfortingly familiar, warm yellow glow.

The light in the room darkened the scene outside and I

could no longer see the trees bending and waving their leaf-filled branches before the unseasonable gale as it blew with gathering force straight off the North Sea, across the flat open fields of the Lincolnshire countryside. For a moment, I watched Stan's reflection in the glass as he worked his way around the room drawing the blackout curtains. I turned my back on the window and walked away from it, glad to leave the wind and rain outside. It almost came as a surprise when he asked Alf and then me if we wanted anything bringing in from the bar in the next room. It was a bit early for a beer and with this storm set well in I knew that there would be plenty of time for a drink later on in the evening as the mess filled up.

I thanked him but declined the invitation and noticed for the umpteenth time that on his tunic first amongst his campaign medal ribbons from the Great War was the ribbon of the Military Medal, won at Passchendaele on the Western Front in 1917. It was not difficult to imagine this quiet, solid man leading his platoon through the mud and gunfire of that hell on earth to take out a German machine-gun position which had pinned down the advance in that sector for over an hour. He had been wounded several times by shrapnel but had said nothing until much later in the day when his officer noticed that the blood on Stan's uniform was still wet and sent him back to the field dressing station. Only there did the full extent of his injuries become apparent.

Standing there in the warmth of the mess, I tried to imagine the full horror of the Western Front, where for four years men had lived with the rats in the mud and filth of the endless network of trenches. Stan had been sent back to England to recover from his injuries, but after his recovery, he had volunteered for the Royal Flying Corps and returned to the Western Front. He became the observer in the two-seater bi-plane bomber, the de Havilland DH4, often referred to as the 'Flaming Coffin' because its huge fuel tank was located between the pilot and observer. However, after the Armistice on 11th November 1918, many of the newly formed RAF squadrons and stations were gradually disbanded and service personnel generally were demobbed. The majority of those who had fought so bravely in the Great War went on to face hardship during the Depression years of the late 1920s and early 1930s.

Ironically, it was Hitler's aggression which forced Britain to slowly re-arm and started the recovery from the Depression. The coalmines, the shipyards, the factories all started to roll again. Stan had been one of those who had been demobbed in 1919 but had taken the first opportunity to rejoin the service when war loomed once again. Although not able to fly with us now, he knew the dangers which we faced every time we took off and he did a splendid job of looking after us in the mess when we returned from operations; we valued him greatly.

Alf was still deeply engrossed reading John Buchan's classic novel, *The Thirty-nine Steps* and I did not want to disturb him; and in truth, I was glad of the peace and quiet for a little while longer. I sat and absently watched the flames flicking up around the ash logs which Alf had put onto the fire, but it was the image of a burning Lancaster bomber which stared back at me. I remembered how, from the cold, cramped seat in the rear gun turret of my own Lancaster, I had watched as the aircraft that had been flying slightly behind us was fatally hit, its burning shape suddenly springing out of the dark sky and all too quickly engulfed by the fire. I had seen three parachutes open before the aircraft plunged to the ground, and I could do nothing more than pray that they all got out. I had felt so helpless, and yet at the same time my nerves had suddenly been drawn even tighter: it must have been a night fighter which had shot down that bomber for we had run out of the flak; it would still be about and at any moment we could have been its next victim.

It could so easily have been us; we had been flying next to that Lancaster. I knew it was there, I could see the faint glow of its exhausts, not too close but there all the same, and then it was gone. That could have been me floating down on that parachute, floating down to the unknown, to captivity, to anything. I had seen so many aircraft shot down, so many streaming fire as they fell to earth, why this one troubled me so much, I do not know. Perhaps it was because it had been so close to us, perhaps because I was nearing the end of my second tour and I really did not want to be shot down for a second time.

This raid had been to Duisberg in the German industrial Ruhr, Happy Valley as we called it, on 21st May 1944 and had been particularly difficult. Some 510 Lancasters and 22 Mosquitoes from Nos. 1, 3, 5 and 8 Groups had attacked the city, which was covered by cloud, and the Pathfinders had used Oboe, a blind bombing marking device ideal in cloud where the ground was obscured, to mark the target. The bomber stream had also run into a lot of heavy flak over the target area and then Messerschmitt bf110 night fighters on the way back. Although we did not know much detail, we all knew that the invasion of Europe was not too far away, and so did the Germans. Their fighter interception tactics were as good as ever and that night we lost 29 Lancasters, 5.5 per cent of the force which had left these shores: 203 airmen who did not return home with us.

It was often several days before we knew the fate of crews lost on missions. Through the Red Cross, we would get word that they were prisoners of war, or that their bodies had been recovered. No news at all usually meant that they were dead but that no body had yet been found. Occasionally though, someone would evade capture and would be desperately trying to make their way home again, helped by the various resistance groups. A 'home run' either from a crash or a prison camp was always a matter for great celebration in any squadron.

The aircraft which I had seen go down in flames so quickly was Y Yorker, a Lancaster of No.625 Squadron from RAF Station Kelstern in No.1 Group, also in Lincolnshire, between Mablethorpe and Market Rasen, and just a few miles north-east of our own base at Skellingthorpe. At just nineteen years of age, Russell Margerison was the mid-upper gunner that night and on the way back from Duisberg he experienced the terror of a night fighter attack and an aircraft, full of fire and smoke, plunging to earth from 23,000 feet. Happily, Russ was on the end of one of those parachutes which I had seen, but he was floating down towards Meir in German-occupied Belgium. The pilot and flight engineer of Y Yorker did not escape the aircraft, but stayed at the controls and rode the Lancaster down to the crash point. They gave their lives in order to ensure that the other members of the crew had every possible chance to bale out. Russell recounts his story in his very good book, *Boys at War*, but I shall never forget the sight of Y Yorker going down, her port wing a mass of flames.

On this beautiful spring morning, the peaceful calm and dignity of the National Memorial echoed around its walls and my thoughts, left uninterrupted, drifted back further to my childhood in Shropshire and the years before the war had come.

I was born on 11th January 1914, a few months before the start of the First World War, in the little Shropshire village of Atcham. My mother had been visiting her sister who lived in the village when she went into labour and in the days before ambulances, that was that: it was probably the three miles my parents had walked that Sunday afternoon that had encouraged my arrival into this world. Atcham stands on the old A5 trunk road between London and Holyhead, which at that time was one of the country's priority trading routes. The first known bridge crossing the River Severn at Atcham was started in 1202 and completed twenty years later. In 1776 John Gwynn built a very fine stone bridge, which still stands today, but by the 1920s, the rise was found to be too steep for modern motor cars and a flatter bridge was built alongside it in 1929. Atcham is also the site of the imposing stately home of Attingham Hall, now owned by the National Trust, and a splendid parish church which stands next to the river.

The old road bridge at Atcham

Between the two bridges: I went fishing on this spot with my son Neville over fifty years later.

I was christened Trevor John and was the second son of a very ordinary family, living in our terraced house at 31 Crowmere Road Shrewsbury: it's still there today. The road was a pleasant open street with trees and fields, part of Crowmere Farm. Opposite our house and from my bedroom window, I could see across the Cavalry Training Ground to Monkmoor aerodrome, built during the Great War. The hangars were on one side of Monkmoor Road whilst the flying field was on the other. It was opened in 1918, not as an operational station but home to the Observers School of Reconnaissance and Aerial Photography. The RAF left it soon after the war, having trained only one course of twelve observers, but re-opened it for No.34 Maintenance Unit during the Second World War.

My father, Harry Lot Bowyer, worked for the Great Western Railway based in Shrewsbury and his middle name reflected the importance and influence of the church on ordinary people in Victorian England. He was a local lad who had gone to work on the railways straight from school at the age of twelve. My parents were not oppressively religious but they were regular church goers and attended services at Shrewsbury Abbey. I was baptised there in February 1914 and was also confirmed and took my first communion there in December 1926.

In the early part of the twentieth century, the railways played a pivotal role in the transportation of goods and people around Britain. The railway companies provided steady work with good prospects for those who wanted it: they were career employers and my father worked his way up to a cleaner/fireman, and then when I was about six he fulfilled every schoolboy's dream and became the driver of a steam engine. It was a sad day for him when he finally retired after a lifetime on the railways.

The Great Western Railway, or GWR, was affectionately known as God's Wonderful Railway because, in the days long before nationalisation, it was the train company whose tracks ran through some of the most beautiful countryside anywhere in England. Somewhat less flatteringly, its rivals called it the Great Way Round, since the topography of the area required the routes to meander alongside the picturesque rivers and valleys, rather than go in a straight line from A to B. The GWR's main London station was Paddington, where it had its headquarters, and from where the trains ran out to the West Country. In the 1920s and 1930s, probably the greatest period for the railways in Britain, the south coast of Devon and Cornwall was known as the English Riviera and the GWR travel posters portrayed it in all its summer allure. Pure Agatha Christie. The sun always shone, the palm trees swayed in the gentle sea breezes at Torquay and Penzance, and the Great Western Railway would take you there. However, it was not just the south-west that boasted fine scenery: God's Wonderful Railway also ran through the Welsh marches up to Shrewsbury and then Crewe.

My mother was born Ethel Harriet Marston to unmarried parents in about 1890, at Withington near Wellington, a market town since the Royal Charter of 1244, in the days when not only was there a social stigma attached to such an event but there were legal implications too, particularly surrounding inheritance. It was not until the Inheritance [Provision for Family and Dependants] Act of 1975 that that distinction was done away with. She was adopted by the Maddox family in Shrewsbury and, happily for me, the circumstances and timing of my mother's conception were not an issue with my father and he and my mother were married at the Abbey Church, Shrewsbury on Thursday, 9th December 1909.

Pretty as any picture: my mother, Ethel [NB collection]

Rather than go into service or work as a milkmaid, my mother developed her skills as a dressmaker and, since she was very good at it, she secured a position with Grocotts in Shrewsbury. Indeed, she still made clothes for the family until she was in her eighties when it was only her failing eyesight that forced her to give up. Grocotts' shop was at the corner of The Square and High Street, close to the mediaeval Guildhall amongst Shrewsbury's many superb black-and-white half-timbered buildings. The shop has gone and the Britannia Building Society has the corner frontage now; the old place has lost its charm and character at street level, with the anonymous wide plate-glass windows, so much a feature of today's town centres. However, if the bystander takes the trouble and time to step back and look up to the first floor, an impression of the building's former glory can be seen: a practice which can be employed when looking at most old buildings in the towns of Britain today.

My early education was here at the National School. The railway bridge with Shrewsbury Abbey behind it can be seen to the left of the picture

My early schooling was at the National School, in a building which had been built in 1708 and then enlarged nearly 200 years later in 1896. It stood almost under the railway bridge at the end of Abbey Foregate, close to the River Severn. Each time one of the great heavy steam locomotives thundered over the bridge, the whole structure shook and vibrated and the lesson had, for a few moments at least, to be brought to an abrupt halt, as even the formidable Mr Entwhistle couldn't compete with the Great Western Railway. There was many an occasion during my years there that I slipped up a prayer of thanks for the 10.29 to Cardiff, as it slowly and noisily rumbled overhead, belching out great billowed clouds of smoke and steam, granting me thinking time on some question of mental arithmetic. Those few moments of thunderous interruption gave me grace, and thus ensured that I avoided the cane, on that occasion at least.

The wall plaque commemorating the school's building and enlargement

My school days were not particularly enjoyable; in the 1920s, they were not intended to be. The object of the exercise at a National School was to educate the children to the best standard that each child could attain, within the limited resources available: a few books, a few pencils and a cane. For those who excelled, the Priory Boys' School was the next step; otherwise it was later education, an apprenticeship if you were practical, or night school for an office-based job, for those who wanted to get on. In each case, it was a matter for someone else to take on once we had left the National School.

I must have shown some promise, though, because at

ten, I did go to the Priory Boys' School, which was on the other side of Shrewsbury, close to the river and the Welsh Bridge. Here I gained a good academic education under a regime which by today's standards would be considered unacceptably draconian. Yet to us it was normal and, far from doing us any demonstrable harm, prepared us for the hardship, deprivation and tragedies of the war which unbeknown to us at the time, lay just a few short years ahead.

It was not that any of our teachers, in either school, were particularly harsh or cruel to us; they weren't, they were simply typical of their time and were products of their own Victorian upbringing. If we transgressed, we received a given amount of caning, the amount and severity of which correlated directly with the severity of the transgression. If we achieved, we were similarly proportionately rewarded. It was as straightforward as that and everyone knew the rules. Unlike today, 'no' meant 'no', and nothing else: disobedience brought swift punishment. As in all schools, some teachers were stricter than others, whilst, by the same token, some pupils were more badly behaved than others. Nevertheless, for the most part we all rubbed along for the nine years that my friends and I were at these two schools, and I learned the three 'Rs' and a great deal more besides. Two of the attributes which I did learn at school and which have always helped me in life were to be meticulous and to be neat. Both qualities spared me the cane, but more importantly, they were to shape my future in a way I could never have imagined at the time.

My childhood, as opposed to my school days, was a very happy one, and despite being my parents' second son, I grew up as an only child since my elder brother had died very young. I do not really remember anything about him, just a vague recollection of there being someone else in my life for a time; and then he was gone.

*With my mother in Cardingmill Valley at Church Stretton
at about 8 years old [Neville Bowyer collection]*

Shrewsbury, the county town of Shropshire, was a fine
and busy town in the 1920s, although much smaller
then than it is now. Sentinel–Cammell, later Rolls Royce,
had the Sentinel Works at Harlescott and was the jewel
in the town's manufacturing crown. Many young men
from Shrewsbury and far beyond longed to serve their
apprenticeship at the Sentinel–Cammell works, which
at that time made steam engines. One very reluctant
apprentice there in the 1930s, though, was Kenneth More,
who happily left the Sentinel works and, after wartime
service as a lieutenant in the Royal Navy, went on to
become one of our best-loved and quintessentially English
actors. In addition to his stage, radio and television
performances, most notably in *The Forsyte Saga* [1976]
and Terence Rattigan's *The Deep Blue Sea* [1954], he is

best remembered for the countless films he made over a long and distinguished career, including *Genevieve, A Night to Remember, The Thirty-Nine Steps, Reach for the Sky, The Battle of Britain, North West Frontier, The Man in the Moon, Sink the Bismarck,* and many, many more. I don't think that his autobiography, *More or Less* is still in print, but it is well worth the effort to trace a copy.

The town had been established in the Middle Ages upon the site of a much earlier settlement on the tabletop hill which forms the inside of a large natural oxbow bend in the River Severn. Close to the border with Wales, then a wild and troublesome land, it was an easy and ideal place upon which to build a castle to command the navigable river below and its two primary crossing points. To this day, the two main bridges which cross the river are on opposite sides of the town, and are known as the English Bridge, on the English side of the town and the Welsh Bridge, on the Welsh side.

By the time I was born, a thousand years later, the troublesome land of the day lay in the heart of Europe: the First World War, or The Great War as it was known at the time, was just about to start. The carnage of the Western Front was beyond anyone's comprehension and the existing hospital facilities in Britain were soon overwhelmed by the volume and severity of the casualties which were pouring back from the front line. In 1916, the Royal Shrewsbury Infirmary (RSI) was built in a prime location on the top edge of the hillside overlooking the River Severn and the Gay Meadow, the home of Shrewsbury Town Football Club until its move to a new site at Otley Road on the outskirts of Shrewsbury in 2007.

I was too young to remember the construction work, but I could look up to see this colossal structure perched on the side of the valley every time I went in and out of the National School building, sandwiched between the English Bridge and the railway bridge which spanned the old medieval road into the town. If nothing else, the war had given Shrewsbury a state-of-the-art infirmary which it would not otherwise have had, and it remained in service until the late 1970s when it was closed down and all the wards were moved to a new, bland, utilitarian box of a building at Copthorne. Nevertheless, the RSI survived and became a listed building. Today, it boasts a rather exclusive shopping complex and a number of residential apartments.

There were several factors about the 1914–18 war which set it apart from any war that had gone before or since. It was the first truly global conflict; the scale of death and destruction on the battlefield was without precedent; the Battle of Jutland was the last occasion on which the Grand Fleets of two great seafaring nations stood off and fought out a full-scale engagement; and aerial combat was born. In the overall history of Europe, there was just the merest glimpse of a window of opportunity for that war to have occurred; the Kaiser seized upon it and thirteen million people died. Fifteen years earlier, and neither side could have managed the logistical operation of keeping so many men supplied with food and munitions for four years along several hundred miles of trenches. Fifteen years later, and the technology for *Blitzkrieg* had made trench warfare a tactic of the past.

In February 1913, No.2 Squadron of the newly formed Royal Flying Corps was sent to Montrose in the north-east of Scotland to set up the very first operational air station in Britain. RAF Station Montrose was closed in 1919, but re-opened again in 1936 when war with Germany once more loomed.

The museum at Montrose Air Station is a fascinating place and amongst its treasurers are the oldest aircraft hangars in the world, the silk scarf worn by Major James McCudden, VC, and a piece of the tail from the Fokker tri-plane of Baron von Richthofen, the Red Baron. It is also the home of the ghost of Lieutenant Desmond Arthur, who was killed at the Station in a flying accident in 1913.

The Great War also brought its horrors to the civilian population for the first time in nearly nine hundred years. Not since the Norman invasion of England in 1066 had the general civilian population been directly fired upon by the enemy and the bombs which were dropped on London from Zeppelins in 1915 and then from heavy bomber aircraft in 1917 were a strong portent of what was to come some twenty years later. Warfare had developed a third element and would never be the same again. Indeed, it was the attack on London in 1917 that was directly responsible for the formation of the Royal Air Force. At that time, the Royal Flying Corps was a branch of the Army, but on 1st April 1918 the Royal Air Force, under the guiding hand of the man who became known as the Father of the RAF, Lord Trenchard, was formed from the RFC and the Royal Naval Air Service. The vital and pivotal role of the bomber in future wars was born.

With the ending of the war in 1918, many pilots leaving the Royal Air Force turned to stunt work to earn a living. The aircraft then were nearly all slow but very manoeuvrable bi-planes which were ideal for that kind of work. In truth, many of these chaps were happy to see the war come again because it gave them employment and the opportunity to fly the new breed of aircraft that I too was to fly in, but it was to be a very different kind of war.

One legacy of the Great War was to put aeroplanes into the sky and as a child I would spend hours gazing up into the azure blue above Shrewsbury watching those wonderful new machines wheeling and spinning and diving through the air. I looked forward to the long summer days because it was then that the planes from the nearby airfield at Monkmoor would fly over. I would wait to hear the splutter and chug of their engines as they flew nearer and I would rush out into the street to watch them go over and wave to the pilots: bi-planes, so modern and new they were then. I remember the feeling of excitement I got from watching them doing their aerobatics over the fields and chasing each other in mock battles. What fun that must be, to be free to fly wherever the wish took you.

At the age of fourteen, I walked through the door of the Priory Boys' School for the last time. Together with my friends, I leant on the railings at the edge of the wharf in the warmth of the late afternoon summer sunshine and for a few moments watched the lads from Shrewsbury School sculling gently along the smooth water of the River Severn. As we leant there, taking in the tranquil scene which unfolded below us, we were blissfully unaware of what the future held for us little more than ten years later; we were just happy to be finished with school and on the verge of the world of work. It was Friday, 25th May 1928.

In my Sunday best sailor suit at about 12 years old
[Neville Bowyer collection]

CHAPTER TWO

"Let not Ambition mock their useful toil, their homely joys, and destiny obscure; Nor Grandeur hear with disdainful smile the short and simple annals of the poor."

From **Elegy Written in a Country Churchyard** *by* **Thomas Gray.**

It is often said that what goes round, comes round; and how true that is. The Victorian era had left a lasting industrial legacy and in the years between the two world wars the three powerful engines of the economy, and therefore almost by definition of conflict, the mines, the docks and the railways, were still at the heart of Britain's manufacturing might. This trinity of industrial potency supplied the factories and kept the very wheels of production turning. They brought the raw materials to the factory gates, supplied the power for the great furnaces and machines, and then carried the finished products away to be shipped around the world: and amongst that trinity, the mines held sway.

In the days before oil, natural gas and nuclear power, coal was the raw material upon which the British Empire had been built and upon which it depended for almost everything. It was to the early twentieth century what oil has become today: the commodity without which little else functions. Coal powered the furnaces and the steam engines of our factories. It was shovelled by the ton into the boilers of railway engines and the ships of the Royal Navy and Merchant Service. Gas was extracted from it to supply Britain's buildings and streets with lighting and the by-product was the coke which kept fireplaces burning in a million homes and offices across the country. Coal was still seen as the bedrock of Britain's economy and thus the Empire: an essential industry, but one struggling to compete. The mine owners knew it and the mine workers knew it, and therein lay the seed of conflict and the road to the Rubicon.

After the end of the First World War, Britain's industrial

output began to decline. There was no government war machine to supply and international trade was slack as countries around the globe reduced spending in order to try to recover from the human and economic catastrophe of the conflict. Oil was beginning to replace coal in the boilers of such new ships as were being built, and the mine owners in Britain began to see their profits decline. The industry was still very heavily labour intensive and the easiest way of cutting costs was to cut wages, and in late 1925 the mine owners decided to do just that.

Stanley Baldwin's Conservative Government intervened and resolved to subsidise the miners' wages to bring them back to their previous level, and at the same time set up a Royal Commission under the chairmanship of Sir Herbert Samuel to investigate the problems within the mining industry. Sir Herbert reported in March 1926 and his Commission recognised that both mining practices and machinery were out-dated, many mines were nearing the end of their workable seams and the whole industry needed to be overhauled, but it stepped back from advocating nationalisation. However, its most damning recommendation was that the government subsidy should be ended and that miners' wages should be reduced. The subsidy ceased almost immediately and the mine owners cut wages further by between 10 and 25 per cent; anyone not accepting those wages would be locked out and effectively dismissed. There was little or no alternative work to turn to.

The Trades Union Congress met on the 1st May 1926 and declared a general strike "in defence of miners' wages and hours". Negotiations during the next forty-eight hours failed to bring about a solution, hardly surprising, since it subsequently transpired that the mine owners had used the six months of subsidised wages to stockpile reserves, and Winston Churchill later disclosed that the Government was deliberately set on a course to break the trade unions. The strike ended after ten days and all but the miners went back to work. They held out for several months but a combination of poverty, hardship and the coming winter forced a gradual return to work, having to accept even lower wages and longer hours. Many of the leaders were victimised and remained unemployed for several years. In 1927 the Government outlawed secondary strike action, required trade union members to 'contract in' to a political levy, and made mass picketing illegal.

In the early 1980s, Margaret Thatcher's Conservative Government went through an almost identical fight with the National Union of Mineworkers for pretty much the same reasons; to break the power of the trade unions. Her government outlawed secondary strike action, required trade union members to 'contract in' to a political levy, and made mass picketing illegal. Just one example from within my own lifetime that there is very little which is new in this world and what goes round does indeed come round!

Since my father was a railwayman he was on the front line of the General Strike and, whilst not a trade union leader, he came out on strike when called upon to do so. Although I was only twelve at the time, I clearly remember my mother worrying about how long it would all last and about making ends meet, and we were fairly well placed by comparison with many other families. I was an only child, and so there was just the three of us to feed, my mother was still working as a dressmaker at Grocotts, which was largely unaffected by the strike, and so we had some money coming in. But even so, there was not a lot of spare money in our house and they were both very pleased when the strike was over and the call came to return to work.

But that was two years ago, and now the sun was shining, it was Friday afternoon and my friends and I were standing on the riverside in Shrewsbury. We had looked forward to this day for so long, but now that it had arrived, I remember feeling a little awkward. Gone was the certainty of school days, of knowing what I was going to be doing each morning; now I stood on the brink of adulthood and I had to earn a living. There was no three years at university waiting for me, no 'gap year' to be had, no signing on and see what turned up; this was 1928 and I had to pay my way at home and the only way to do that was to find a job: not an easy task in Shrewsbury at that time.

From around 1880 for the next seventy years, railways played an important part in the life of the British people and Shrewsbury was an important railway town, standing as it does at the junction of the lines from the West Midlands, and therefore London, Wales and the north-west. Trains were the principal form of transport outside urban areas; they created the first commuters, opened up the countryside and gave birth to many of our coastal resorts. Farmers and fishermen could transport their animals, fresh fish and other produce to markets further afield and even to the great industrial cities across Britain, rather than simply to the nearest town. Trams, and later trolleybuses, were still the main form of public transport in the big towns and cities, but the railways linked Britain in a way that the canals had never done.

The years between the two world wars were the golden age of the railways in Britain. Indeed in many ways it was the golden age of travel – for those who could afford it anyway. The great ocean liners plied across the Atlantic between Europe and North America seeking the greatest prize of all, the Blue Riband.

One of the most famous and luxurious ocean-going liners of the day was the RMS *Queen Mary* and she was the last pre-war holder of the Blue Riband, taking it from the French liner *Normandie* in August 1938. When the war came, the transatlantic passenger service was suspended and the *Queen Mary* was to fulfil her role as a troopship. She was converted in the summer of 1940 and by and large had a fairly uneventful time, apart from the *Curacao* incident. The *Queen Mary* was only lightly armed and generally had no escort ship to accompany her; it was considered unnecessary because she was simply too fast for escorts and U-boats alike. At full speed, she required twelve miles of sea to stop. She had a service speed of twenty-nine knots and was easily capable of over thirty knots; she was, after all, the Blue Riband holder.

In point of fact the Admiralty refused to provide her with escorts after she sliced straight through the stern section of the cruiser HMS *Curacao* on 2nd October 1942. The *Curacao* was zig-zagging across the *Queen Mary*'s path as an anti-aircraft escort near the Mull of Kintyre, just off the river Clyde estuary on the west coast of Scotland. The great liner overtook her escort and they collided. Of the 430 Royal Navy sailors on board HMS *Curacao* only 101 survived the incident, which the Admiralty kept quiet for a long time. The *Queen Mary* suffered some damage but continued to sail to Glasgow with her eleven thousand troops on board, unable to stop and assist the crew of the stricken cruiser for fear of U-boat attack. By the end of the war she had sailed over 600,000 miles and carried nearly 800,000 troops.

The Blue Riband trophy, which is actually two trophies, one for westbound crossings and one for eastbound crossings, was given to the ship which made the fastest transatlantic crossing. The first ship to hold that honour was the *Sirius*, owned by the British and American Steam Navigation Company in 1838. In 1933, Geoffrey Hales commissioned and donated a trophy, the first holder of which, for three months, was the Italian ship the *Rex*. Between then and 1938 the *Normandie* and the *Queen Mary* each held it twice. Since 1952 it has been held by the American ship the *United States*.

As the 1920s drew to a close, civilian aircraft were throwing down the gauntlet with a glimpse of what was to come. Amongst the most comfortable of these were the Short Brothers' Sunderland flying boats, which were used by Imperial Airways and Empire Airways in the south Pacific. Mail and cargo were flown between the South Sea islands keeping that part of the British Empire supplied, whilst the passengers on these journeys enjoyed a level of comfort which would be the envy of any first-class ticket holder today. In 1939, some of RAF Coastal Command's squadrons, Nos. 201, 209 and 210 in particular, were equipped with the Sunderland, which proved to be an invaluable aircraft in the fight against the U-boats, before being gradually replaced by the American PBY Catalina from April 1941 onwards.

At the time, though, it was all another world to me and far beyond my horizon, which at that particular moment was no greater than to secure employment; but not just yet, not on this lovely early summer afternoon. These next few hours were to be my gap year.

That evening, when my dad came home from the railway, his overalls smelled as they always did of a mixture of steam, smoke, oil and coal. He had a wash, changed and we sat in the kitchen across the table from one another drinking a mug of hot, sweet tea whilst my mum busied about making the meal. Dad had been to Cardiff, driving the engine at the head of a passenger train. It wasn't the main express, but nor did it call at every station, only the larger ones, Ludlow, Leominster, Hereford, Abergavenny, Newport and Cardiff. Dad always liked this run and was cheery that night. He said that it went through some of the most beautiful countryside you could want, through the Welsh Marches and then into south Wales, the 'home of coal' he called it, because that was where the deep mines were which produced the coal for the steam engines.

Shrewsbury Station, classic GWR design

Mum and I always waited for Dad to come home before we ate a meal, unless his shift clashed too much. Tonight it was quite late when he got home, but not too late and so we had waited. I hadn't minded because it had meant that I had been able to stay out with my friends for longer, making the most of my 'gap year'. But now, as we sat at the kitchen table, with the smell of Mum's cooking filling the air, I knew that there was some serious talking to be done.

I grew up with railways; my father was an engine driver, my early schooling had been accompanied by the sound of trains passing by, if we went anywhere out of Shrewsbury, it was by train and in 1928 Britain had an enviable network of tracks and timetables which reached even the remotest parts of the land. Dr Beeching's decimation of our railways was still over thirty years away: an act of institutionalised criminality the folly of which should have been apparent to even the dimmest of our politicians. Nevertheless, much as I loved the railways, I did not really want to follow in my father's footsteps and become a railwayman.

I had continued to develop academically at school and retained my liking for neatness and detail; it just didn't seem to fit with a life on the railways. I was hoping for an administrative or clerical job, where I would come home at night clean and not smelling of oil and coal dust: but I wasn't sure how my dad would take it. I had talked to my mother about it and she had said that I would have to talk to Dad. Looking back, I think that she must have prepared him, although I don't think he needed much persuading. He knew how hard life was on the railways, even though being an engine driver was every schoolboy's dream.

"Well, Trevor, that's your school days over then," he said quietly with a finality which made any response unnecessary. "The world is waiting for you."
"Dad," I started, somewhat diffidently, "Dad, do you think I should get a job on the railways like you, or do something else?"

He chuckled almost to himself and said, "I think you should get a job wherever you can, my boy. There's not too many about. But you got your mother's brains and you've done well at school, you should look for something where you can use them and go somewhere. You don't want to spend your life around the coal depot if you can help it."

"Well, Mr Lanstern the English master said I should ask at the Post Office. He said it was a good job in the Post Office."

"Seems to me that Mr Lanstern knows what he's talking about and you should go up to Dogpole first thing on Monday morning."

So that was settled. First thing on Monday morning I would go up to the main Post Office buildings in St. Mary's Street to enquire about a job.

"What's Cardiff like, Dad? Is it like Shrewsbury?" I asked.

"Not a bit. It's noisy, dirty and full of coal dust, smoke and steam; at least the only parts of Cardiff that I ever get to see are. But the journey down there is so beautiful. You wouldn't believe how green the fields are and how lovely the wild flowers can be. A real picture it is, and that's the truth."

"Is it all like that?" I enthused.

"No, not it. There are parts that are as black as your hat from the coal mines and slag heaps everywhere. Why?"

"I just wondered, Dad."

"When you are a bit older, you will be able to travel all over the world if you want to. More and more I see these new aeroplanes flying about. You mark my words, Trevor, that's where the future is, not the railways." How right he was.

"Come on, you two," interrupted Mum, "that's enough talking for now. Your tea is ready." And with that she put three large bowls of delicious-smelling stew and a loaf of fresh home-made bread on the table.

Nobody spoke during the meal. My parents always took

the view that mealtimes were for eating; we could talk afterwards. That night, we all stayed up talking for quite a long time, at least by my parents' standards. I think that subconsciously they accepted that I was no longer a child but about to go out into the world to earn my living. Eventually, though, I was chased off to bed with a reminder that it was Saturday tomorrow and I had an early start.

At five o'clock the next morning I was up and about. Mum made me a mug of tea and, finishing off my doorstep of bread and jam, I rushed out of the house to walk across town to the little dairy in Frankwell owned by Mr Kynnerston, where each Saturday and in the holidays I helped Mr Davies with the milk round. It was pocket money, but meant the world to me. It was my own money and allowed me to save up for things which I would never have otherwise had.

When I got there, Mr Davies was leading Gentle, the black Welsh Cob out of her stable, ready for the day's round. As he backed the aptly-named horse in between the shafts of the cart, I filled her nosebag with feed and tucked it under the wooden seat upon which Mr Davies would spend most of the day and, if I was lucky, I would spend a little of it. The milk was ready, waiting in the aluminium churns as Gentle pulled alongside the raised platform of the dairy. We loaded them onto the cart and, with a "Walk on, Gentle" from Mr Davies, we started the round.

Shrewsbury was a much smaller town then than it is now and it was surrounded by many farms, most of which had milking cows producing an abundance of milk for the inhabitants of Shropshire's county town. We turned left out of the yard and, since the dairy was on the river bank, we inevitably had to climb up one of the three hill roads which led out of Frankwell on the Welsh side of the town. Our round was up Porthill Road to Roman Road, and then to Copthorne and back to the dairy. It was a fair old slog up that hill first thing in the morning with a full load on the cart, and poor old Gentle must have had to strain hard between the shafts to get up to the

43

top each day. I know that in the winter, Mr Davies and I would walk up the hill beside her to help ease the load on a frosty morning.

My job was to run to the back doors of the big houses and collect the jugs from the kitchen maids. Mr Davies would measure out the milk and fill the jugs before I took them back again without spilling a drop. Although I didn't think too much about it at the time, upon reflection it was quite interesting to see the different attitudes within these houses. At some, the kitchen staff were really friendly and the maid would come out with me to the cart, to save us time. These were usually the houses where we would be given a hot drink on a cold winter's morning and a tip at Christmas. At other houses, the reception was as cold as charity. Mr Davies said you always knew they would be bad payers at the end of the month; and he was usually right too.

Milk churns in the snow awaiting collection from the farm

and the ladle we used to measure out the milk

Snow always made the round more difficult and slower. One morning in the previous winter, just before Christmas, I went to the back door of a house which was built quite a bit lower than the level of the road. The young kitchen maid, barely a couple of years older than I was, came out to the cart with me as she usually did, and after the jug was filled to the brim with fresh milk, she set off very carefully down the sloping snow-covered path towards the back door, barely putting one foot in front of the other.

"You mind you don't go and fall now," Mr Davies called to her and then turned to me and said, "Well, don't just stand there, Trev, help the poor girl."

As I reached her I took her arm, just as her feet went from under her. She grabbed hold of me to try to stay up but it was no good, we both fell over and slid all the way down the path to the kitchen door on our backsides. All at the same time, the maid screamed, I yelled and Mr Davies shouted. The cook came rushing out of the house to be greeted by our arrival at her feet but was quick enough to take hold of the jug of milk which the maid had hung onto for all her worth and not a drop was spilt.

Just then the lady of the house appeared to see what all the fuss was about. When Mr Davies, who by now had also joined us at the back door, told her she laughed until the tears ran down her cheeks, whilst at the same time helping the maid up to make sure she wasn't hurt. We were asked into the kitchen and had a very welcome hot drink. We were lucky that it had happened at this house because the lady there was always so pleasant to us and to her staff. Very different from some of the other houses we called at.

As we made our way on the round, I told Mr Davies that I was going to get a job at the Post Office and that if I did I wouldn't be able to help him with the milk any more. He told me not to worry and that to see how I got on next week. I had the enthusiasm and naivety of youth; he had the wisdom of age to know that jobs didn't fall off trees.

Nevertheless, first thing on the following Monday morning I presented myself at the Head Post Office in St Mary's Street to seek employment of any sort. After informing several people of the purpose of my presence there, I was eventually confronted by a rather tall, officious-looking man, with the body of a rake and the complexion of rice pudding. He had a long, thin nose down which he barely noticed me, lips which were too thick for the size of his mouth, no chin and a very protruding Adam's apple, which moved up and down in the cavernous space between his shirt collar and his throat. He announced to a point about two feet above my head, that the appointed time for interviewing 'boys' was ten o'clock the following morning. I should bring with me my last school report and my birth certificate and I would be seen, with the others. Others? What others? Nobody had said anything to me about others. Slowly, the realisation dawned on me that I just might not get a job, and I thought back to Mr Davies' wry, knowing smile on Saturday morning.

At a quarter to ten the next day, 29th May, Oak Apple Day, clutching my school report and birth certificate, I again stood in that cold draughty corridor inside the Head Post Office building; but this time I was in the middle of a line of about a dozen lads all talking in whispers and all with the same purpose: to get a job.

The rake with the rice pudding complexion emerged from an office at the end of the corridor and quiet fell on us like a cold hand. He told us that we would be called into the room behind him in turn, that we were to remove our caps, call the appropriately named Mr Stamp, the Senior Supervisor who would be interviewing us, 'Sir', hand our report and birth certificate to him and answer any questions he asked of us quickly and smartly, because he was a very busy man and had much better things to do than spend his Tuesday morning with us. With those few warm words of greeting, he allowed himself a sickly half-smile of self-satisfaction and, in one seamless, oily movement turned, disappeared back into the office and closed the door silently, save for an almost inaudible click of the catch. Nobody spoke; nobody dared. Through the

46

silence, the heartbeat of noise, the lifeblood of the building, softly floated over us, just a hum at first, then seemingly getting louder and louder until I thought it would deafen me. Then in an instant it was gone: the rake stood in the doorway.

One by one he called us into the office with a hissed, "Next." In turn, each young lad entered the room and was then lost to our gaze behind the door which bore the word 'office' in bold letters across the smoked glass panel which formed its top half. Interviews were of indeterminate duration, depending upon the responses, or lack thereof, which were forthcoming to whatever questions were being asked. All too soon, I found myself standing next to the hissing rake.

"Next." The sound came from somewhere deep inside him, like the last breath of a dying man. I entered the room, removed my cap and handed my papers to the imposing figure sitting behind the mahogany desk in front of me. Mr Stamp, who actually turned out to be a decent sort of chap and was always willing to help those who wanted to learn and get on in the Post Office, wore a dark suit with a striped waistcoat, a high starched white collar and black tie. He seemed larger than life, had a ruddy complexion and sported a fresh flower in his buttonhole.

"What's your name, my lad?" he asked, already knowing the answer as he scanned my school report.
"Trevor John Bowyer, sir," I replied.
"Well, Trevor, you have a very good school report. Neat, tidy and punctual. That's what we like. Why do you want to work for the Post Office?"

I had thought about being asked this question but I couldn't tell him that I liked the idea because it was cleaner than the railways, so I told him that I enjoyed writing and figures and wanted to work my way up to an office job where I could use them.

"That sounds promising, Trevor," he replied. "We have a temporary vacancy for a boy messenger to cover for a lad that's away ill. Be here at eight o'clock tomorrow morning and we'll see how you get on. Mr Polling there will tell you what to do."

I turned round to see the rake peering at me, but I was so pleased that even he didn't dampen my spirits. "Thank you very much, sir. That's wonderful, sir, thank you." "All right, Trevor, on you go and we'll see you tomorrow," he said in a kindly tone, returning my papers to me.

The corridor outside Mr Stamp's office was already empty, the rake having dismissed the remaining boys even before I had made it out through the door. "Be here sharp at eight tomorrow, and don't be late," he exhaled as he once more turned and glided away as if on oil.

Unlikely though it was that Mr Stamp should work for the Post Office, he was by no means alone in following a calling so closely associated with his name. One memorable example was connected to the railways. Euston Station was the headquarters of the London and North Western Railway, which until 1923 was the largest company in the world and the arch rival of the Great Western Railway, whose head offices were at Paddington. However, by the 1930s the LNWR had become part of the London, Midland and Scottish group, whilst over at Paddington the GWR appointed a new station master, George William Reynold Lines: GWR Lines. Absolutely true.

That night I lay in bed looking up at the darkened ceiling, my head spinning with a mixture of excitement and trepidation at the prospect of starting work properly. A real job. In my wildest dreams I could not have imagined what would happen to me over the next twenty years; what I would do, where I would go and what I would see; and it is probably just as well that I couldn't, too.

So it was that at eight o'clock on Wednesday, 30th May 1928 I entered the world of work as a part-time boy messenger with the General Post Office, registered number SN/R/A/1777. At five o'clock that same day I was gleefully informed by the insipid rake that my services were no longer required as the lad I was covering for had recovered from illness and would return the next day. I was devastated. Still, at least I had the milk round to fall back on and I could work with Mr Davies every day.

Three weeks later, on Friday afternoon the 22nd June, I had just finished cleaning out Gentle's stable and was getting her feed ready, when I heard the familiar voice of one of the other boy messengers from the Post Office. "Eh, Trev. Trev Bowyer. You in 'ere?"

I looked out through the top of the open stable door and saw Eric Chaffner walking up the yard, the hobnails of his black boots striking on the cobbled surface. His flat cap, tilted slightly back on his head and at an angle, sat incongruously with his GPO-regulation starched white collar and black tie – but that was Eric.

"Hello, Eric. What brings you down here on a Friday afternoon? They haven't finished you too, have they?"

I came out of the stable and closed the door behind me. I didn't want Eric stumbling about in there and upsetting Gentle now that she was ready for her feed.

"Nar, not they. I've a message for ye from Mr Stamp. 'e says you're to report to 'is office at eight o'clock on Monday morning." And then he added with a grin, "Looks as if you're in again, Trev."

He slapped me on the back, turned and walked back down the yard with something of a swagger. As he got to the road he scooped a bottle of milk out of the crate which stood at the dairy entrance, flipped the top, took a drink and called back to me, "See you on Monday, Trev. Tarah."

Eric wasn't stealing: the dairy put any unsold milk from that day, which was surplus to requirements and would otherwise have been thrown away, into crates at the side of the road in Frankwell, for people to help themselves. For some it was the only fresh milk that they would have. A simple example of how the community tried to look after itself.

The medieval setting of the dairy in Frankwell.

Although he was a couple of years older than me, I had known Eric throughout my school days; he had been at the Post Office since he had left in 1926. He had three younger sisters and he was the main breadwinner in the family. Life was not easy for us but it was a great deal harder for Eric's family, yet despite this he was always a cheerful lad. His father had been killed in Flanders on the Western Front on 24th September 1918. He had served in the 1st Battalion of the King's Shropshire Light Infantry, which had spent the entire war in France and Flanders. The KSLI had been formed in 1881 by the amalgamation of 53rd (Shropshire) Regiment of Foot, founded in 1755 and the 85th Regiment of Foot, founded in 1793. In 1959 it became part of the Light Infantry Brigade and in 1968 it formed the 3rd Battalion of the Light Infantry.

The KSLI has several events of note and interest in its history. It is one of the oldest infantry regiments in the British army; the very first soldier to die in action during the Second World War was Corporal Priday of the 1st Battalion; it has ten Victoria Crosses in all: six in India, one in the First World War in Palestine and two in the Second World War. The remaining VC came in Africa at the famous siege of Rorke's Drift, the subject of the film Zulu, and was awarded to Acting Assistant Commissary James Langley Dalton, who at the time was aged forty-six and whose experience was undoubtedly valued by the commanding officer, Lieutenant Chard. Indeed it was largely due to Dalton's experience that Chard was able to build the mission station's defences so effectively.

There were eleven VCs awarded for the Rorke's Drift action on 22nd/23rd January 1879, the most ever awarded for a single incident and all but two of the recipients had the same fates: they died relatively young and within a few years of the battle. Lieutenants Chard and Bromhead were both promoted to the rank of major, but Bromhead died of typhoid in India in 1892 and Chard, by then a full colonel, of cancer in 1897. Most of the others died of a variety of respiratory illnesses from tuberculosis to pneumonia; only Surgeon James Henry Reynolds and Private John Williams lived into retirement. Reynolds retired from the army as Brigade Surgeon Lieutenant Colonel and died at the Empire Nursing Home in London aged eighty-eight on 4th March 1932. John Williams, whose real name was John Fielding stayed in the army and served in the South Wales Borderers throughout the First World War. He outlived Reynolds by a mere eight months although thirteen years his junior, but in so doing became the last survivor of the Rorke's Drift Victoria Cross holders. He died aged seventy-five on 25th November 1932 at Cwmbran, South Wales.

Colour Sergeant Frank Edward Bourne, who was awarded the Distinguished Conduct Medal for his actions at Rorke's Drift, outlived everybody. Like John Williams, he remained in the army, was commissioned in 1890 and retired with the rank of Lieutenant-Colonel. He was appointed OBE in 1918. In 1936 he made a radio broadcast about the action at Rorke's Drift. He died at the age of ninety-one on 8th May 1945 – VE day, and is buried at Beckenham in Kent in the same cemetery as the cricketer WG Grace, the car designer Frederick Wolsley, the inventor of the lavatory Thomas Crapper, and VC holder George Evans, who was awarded his medal in 1916.

Although I didn't think about it at the time, as I grew older it fascinated me to think that my life had overlapped with the survivors of that action in the Zulu wars. It had happened in the 1800s in what seemed like another world, so remote; and in truth it was. To think that night after night, I had sat behind my four Browning .303 machine guns in the rear turret of a Lancaster bomber and flown over Frank Bourne as he relaxed in his armchair at his house in Beckenham and listened to Alvar Lidell reading the evening news: a man who had actually fought at Rorke's Drift, when a single-shot rifle was advanced technology. How much change in the world had he seen since then? On those two January days under the blazing African sun in 1879, at barely twenty-four years of age, he could never have imagined that he would live to see men fly over his house with weapons the destructive power of which could devastate a whole city, kill thousands of people or sink an immense iron ship with just one eleven-ton load of bombs.

The KSLI's last VC was awarded to Private James Stokes just nine weeks before the end of the war. His award was published on 13th April 1945 in the London Gazette, the newspaper in which all decorations and officers' promotions are announced.

James Stokes was a long way from home in the KSLI and ended up in the regiment thanks to a dance-hall thug. A Scot from Hutchesontown in Lanarkshire, he was living in the Gorbals area of Glasgow with a wife and young son when he got into a dance-hall fight over a local hard man's unwanted attentions towards his wife. The man ended up in the hospital, and Stokes ended up in prison, sentenced to five years' hard labour for inflicting grievous bodily harm; which seemed fairly harsh under the circumstances. His sentence was commuted by his agreement to go straight from prison into the 2nd Battalion of the KSLI.

On 1st March 1945, during an attack on Kerbenheim in Holland, he was a member of the leading section of a platoon pinned down by heavy fire from a farm building. The section found themselves faced by a seventy-yard gap swept by a lethal hail of enemy fire. Armed only with a rifle, he dashed forward through that hail of bullets and although he was wounded in the neck and on his own, he captured a small building and twelve prisoners. He was ordered back to a Regimental Aid Post, but refused to go. The platoon continued to advance, but again came under heavy enemy fire, this time from a house. Once more he rushed forward, receiving more wounds, but again silencing the enemy fire and returning with five more prisoners. Still refusing to leave his comrades, severely wounded and suffering from loss of blood, James advanced again with the platoon under further intense enemy fire. Twenty yards from the objective he was swept by a hail of bullets and fatally wounded. He lay on the ground still firing his rifle and as his comrades ran past him to overrun the German position, he raised his arm to them and shouted, "Goodbye". It was found that he had been wounded eight times in the upper part of the body. There is no doubt that his sacrifice saved his platoon and company many heavy casualties. He had turned thirty three weeks earlier. He is buried in the Reichswald Forest War Cemetery in Germany.

James Stokes' Victoria Cross

Eric's message was great news for me and cheered me up no end. I had enjoyed my one day at the Post Office and was just glad of whatever circumstances had arisen to give me another chance. On that Monday morning I was taken on as a boy messenger, was only paid for the days that I actually worked and had no holiday money until I was eighteen, at which time my service became reckonable for a pension: a wonderful innovation in the days when a welfare state was no more than the political dream of a few and was still nearly twenty years and a war away in the future. Eight weeks before my nineteenth birthday, on the 13th November 1932, I was made a permanent member of the staff, or became 'established' as it was known.

I was growing up and wanted to move on. There was more to life than the Shrewsbury sorting office and so I transferred to Crewe, one of the great railway towns of the day, and the opportunities which it would offer to me.

CHAPTER THREE

"This is the Night Mail crossing the border, bringing the cheque and the postal order, letters for the rich, letters for the poor, the shop at the corner, the girl next door. Pulling up Beattock, a steady climb; the gradient's against her but she's on time."

From Night Mail *by WH Auden*

I didn't know it at the time, but my move to Crewe would shape the course of my life for the best part of the next fourteen years. It might be difficult to understand now, but in 1933, in the days before universal car ownership, before motorways and cheap air flights, when Britain's wealth came from its manufacturing industries rather than financial and other services, Crewe was a hugely important town. The railways were the very lifeblood of the country's transportation system. There was a small embryonic road haulage industry, but it was mainly for local goods and deliveries: the great majority of freight, commuters and long-distance travellers were moved around the country by the railways.

In 1922, there were 120 different railway companies operating in Britain and it had become a hopeless task trying to co-ordinate them all into an efficient national network; some of them even ran to a different time, so that five o'clock in Penzance was not necessarily five o'clock in Inverness or Manchester. The government of the day passed legislation to amalgamate them all into four main railway companies: the Great Western Railway [GWR], the London, Midland & Scottish Railway [LMS], the London & North Eastern Railway [LNER] and the Southern Railway [SR]. Ten years later, as Britain slowly began to emerge from depression, people needed to travel, whether for business or pleasure and in the days before mass car ownership they did so by train and these four companies vied with each other for those passengers. They also carried on that great transport tradition which still pertains today – to be the fastest carrier in the business. On 6th June 1932 the Cheltenham Flyer express became the world's fastest train when the GWR engine *Tregenna*

Castle pulled it the 77.3 miles from Swindon to Paddington in fifty-six minutes and forty-seven seconds; a journey time scheduled to take sixty-five minutes.

Crewe was at the centre of this great industry. The railway station was not built to serve a town, as there wasn't one, but purely as a junction station to link England's four largest cities. The land was purchased from the Earl of Crewe and on 4th July 1837 Crewe station was opened. As rail traffic increased, a larger workforce was needed and so the town was built as a new town [what goes round comes round] by the Grand Junction Railway Company, although little of the original town is left today. It gradually expanded as its geographical importance grew, and included a major engine-building facility. By the time I arrived in 1933 it was in its heyday and was the headquarters of the LMS engineering operation. The company's chief mechanical engineer was William Arthur Stanier, who had joined it from the GWR on 1st January the year before. He went on to design some of the most famous pre-war steam engines including the Princess and Duchess class locomotives as well as the universal workhorses, the Black Fives. Stanier was knighted in 1943 and upon his retirement the following year, was elected a Fellow of the Royal Society, the only railway engineer other than George Stephenson to receive the honour.

Growing up in a railway family, it was inevitably in my blood and I am sure that that is part of what drew me to Crewe. But it wasn't just to be working in a railway town, it was that the famous North Western Travelling Post Office, the TPO, called at Crewe on its way from London to Glasgow. I wanted to work on that TPO and working in the Crewe sorting office was an important step on the way.

I was young, free and single and, like thousands before and after me, I was drawn to the opportunities which London offered. Fortunately, I had relatives who lived in Islington at number 25 Granville Square, and so a year later I transferred to the Mount Pleasant sorting office in

Farringdon Road, the largest sorting office in Britain at that time, and perhaps it still is. This would allow me to apply to join the TPO team and since only existing sorting office staff could apply, London was where I needed to be. My aunt and uncle's house in Granville Square was just off King's Cross Road, which ran into Farringdon Road and was only about five minutes' walk from the Mount Pleasant sorting office. They were happy for me to take up lodgings with them and I expect that the money helped them out a bit too.

25 Granville Square, Islington

In due course I made an application to join the North Western TPO team and was successful. The team was based at Euston Station which was only about a ten-minute walk from Granville Square. I would leave the house at half past six in the evening, cut through into King's Cross Road, along Acton Street and then walk a short distance along Gray's Inn Road to come out at the busy junction of Euston Road, York Way, Caledonian

Road and Pentonville Road opposite King's Cross Station and probably the most beautiful of all Britain's railway stations, St Pancras. Two minutes later I would walk through the Eversholt Street side entrance of Euston Station. Sometimes, just for the sheer pleasure of it, I would go round to the front of the station and walk through the grandeur of Euston's main entrance, the majestic Doric Arch. I am very glad now that I did that whilst I had the chance because the Euston Arch was demolished in the 1960s amid a public outcry, to make way for the redevelopment of the station, the final approval for its demolition being given by the then Prime Minister, Harold MacMillan. The actual site of the arch in the new station is somewhat ignominiously located at the end of platforms nine and ten, without even a mention.

The Travelling Post Office was a uniquely British innovation. The essence of it was that mail posted in one part of the country could be sorted during the train journey, dropped off along the way at numerous automated collection points as the train sped through without stopping, and be ready for delivery the next morning. If only it was that efficient today. The TPO system, which basically ran north–south, was so reliable and successful that the poet WH Auden wrote his evocative poem *Night Mail* in celebration of the service.

The Romans had introduced a very efficient postal system but, as was the case with so much that the Romans did for Britain, when they left around AD 450, the postal system fell apart. The Dark Ages were well named. The country remained largely without any sort of postal service for the next twelve hundred years, and even by the reign of Elizabeth I it took a stage coach an average of thirty-five hours, plus stoppage time to change horses and rest, to travel from London to Holyhead; and that was on one of the best roads in the land – a road which, incidentally, the Romans had built.

Although the General Post Office, the GPO, was formed in 1657 the delivery of mail and indeed travel generally had deteriorated even further. In that year it took six days to travel from London to Chester in uncomfortable stage coaches, on unmade roads and at the mercy of highway robbers. The exchange of domestic post remained an unreliable form of communication. All that changed with the coming of the railways.

In 1830, the Manchester & Liverpool Railway opened and for the first time mail started to be carried on a regular basis between the two growing industrial cities. Then on 4th July 1837 the Grand Junction Railway opened between Birmingham and Warrington and, apart from establishing Crewe at its hub, the railway opened up London to mail deliveries from the rapidly expanding industrial power house of the north of England. The GPO started negotiations with the railway companies in earnest and in 1838 the first TPO ran from London to Bletchley.

As always, speed was important and Nathanial Worsdell developed the early version of the line-side exchange equipment. Ultimately, though, it was a design by a Post Office inspector named Dicker which was introduced in 1852, after Worsdell's patent had expired. The Dicker-designed equipment remained in operation for over a hundred years and was a familiar sight beside railway lines all over Britain, and later even featured as part of Hornby model railway train sets.

There were several Travelling Post Offices all working at the same time and on the same principle between various cities up and down Britain. Mail would be collected during the day from, in our case, London, and loaded onto the train at Euston Station. Whilst the train steamed steadily through the night towards Glasgow, and the fireman shovelled Welsh coal into the firebox of the powerful engine, we would sort the mail as we went along, deftly slipping letters and small packages into the pigeon holes in front of us. However, since not all the post on the train was necessarily destined for Glasgow, Dicker's line-side exchange equipment enabled us to drop mail off along the way and pick up fresh mail ready to be sorted.

Simplistically, the equipment worked by hanging a leather pouch, into which the mail had been packed, onto a pole at the side of the track. As the mail train thundered past in the dark, a net extended from the side of the mail coach would catch the pouch and take it inside, where the mail from that location was sorted by the on-board staff, people like me. Mail which had already been sorted and was due for delivery to that particular area was delivered by the same principle but in reverse. The pouches could hold up to sixty pounds in weight of post and in this way mail was being continuously collected, sorted and delivered along the route. Quick, simple, and efficient: all one class of post, at least two collections and deliveries a day, and three in some cities; there was even a late posting box on the train for receipt of post from the public when it was in a station and the extra 1d stamp guaranteed next-day delivery at the other end of the country.

Where did the post office lose its way, I wonder? Perhaps when it abandoned the TPOs under the tenuous pretext that they were a Victorian solution to a Victorian problem, preferring instead to greatly increase its carbon footprint and air pollution by using a fleet of lorries and aircraft to move the mail around the country, often unnecessarily. The very last time that the line-side exchange equipment was used was at Penrith on the night of 3rd/4th October 1971 and the last TPOs ran on the night of 9th/10th January 2004. The end of an era.

In the 1930s the service was in its heyday and the North Western TPO was the most prestigious of them all. Each train was made up of six sorting coaches and seven ordinary coach brake vans for parcel traffic. It was staffed by an assistant superintendent, thirty-five sorters and two porters: the only railway employees on the train were the driver and the fireman in the engine cab, and the guard in his van at the back.

I soon settled in to the routine of starting work at Euston Station in the early evening. At seven o'clock the empty mail train would be shunted into No.2 platform and we would start sorting the mail as the post vans brought the collections in from all over London and the south-east. At ten to eleven, with the sorting well under way, we would feel the train start to move and pull out of the station on its long journey north to Glasgow. Sometimes I would be having a break just at this time and would lean out of the window to watch us leave, a fascination with steam and smoke and noise and power which was with me from my childhood and which I never grew out of.

The peep of a whistle would blow from somewhere near the back of the train and the platform superintendent would wave his green flag towards the driver's cab. Steam hissed and poured out across the platform from the valves of the powerful engine in a deafening crescendo. Its own whistle blew and split the air as the great driving wheels began to turn and eased us forwards: we were off. Smoke and soot belched from the funnel and settled on the station staff and any late travellers who were nearby, alike. With another roar from the engine we slowly slipped past the platform, clouds of billowing soot huffing from the funnel. As I continued to hang out of the window, breathing in that wonderfully evocative smell of steam and smoke mingled together, the smell of steam engines, I felt the train slowly gain a little speed and then heard the wheels start to chatter excitedly as they crossed over the many points which led out from the platforms and which gradually drew all the tracks into the one artery leading to the north. Then, quite suddenly, the station and the platforms were gone, enveloped by the steam.

"C'mon Trev," Charlie called, "when you've finished gazing out of the window, Auntie Mabel's birthday card is waiting for you to sort it."
"I'm coming, Charlie," and I smiled to myself. He was our assistant superintendent and was a good sort. He had created a happy team and we all worked well together.

By now the train had gathered some real speed and was moving out towards Watford Gap. The gentle swaying of the carriages was a pleasant motion and after a while not something which we really noticed. I suppose it must be the same for sailors with the motion of a ship. I stood in front of the rows upon rows of pigeon holes, each one with the name of a town on it, not in alphabetical order but in geographical order. The sorting frames were built to different dimensions to take letters, packets, registered letters and newspapers.

The route of the North Western TPO was roughly what has today become the West Coast main line from Euston, through Tamworth, Crewe, Wigan, Preston, Lancaster, Penrith, Carlisle, Motherwell and Glasgow. However, the TPO did not stop at Lancaster or Penrith to take on and unload mail, instead it collected and delivered via the line-side equipment.

None of the crews on this TPO worked the whole route: some would go as far as Crewe and then return to London the same night on the Up train and the rest of us would go as far as Carlisle where another crew would take over, since the mail would not only go to Glasgow, but also to Edinburgh, Perth and Aberdeen.

The main concern of the GPO was that there shouldn't be an accident which would interfere with the delivery of the mail. Safety on the tracks was the responsibility of the railway companies, but safety inside the train was left to the GPO and consequently we always had very good lighting. This came from a row of lights down the length of each coach and was entirely in the interests of the GPO, since removing the gloom from the workplace greatly helped to avoid address-reading mistakes and reduced tripping hazards to a minimum.

It wasn't just the crews who enjoyed this good lighting, though; it warmed the very soul of those who saw us passing by. There was a friendliness, a comfort, a security in this sight, a reassurance that all was well. The glow of the lamps lit up the small windows of the coaches as the train raced its way through the towns and countryside late at night, each window casting a pale yellow brush of light to be flicked back and forth from a myriad of shapes and surfaces along the way. A thin trail of smoke streamed back over the coaches from the engine stack whilst the glowing embers from the firebox dropped out underneath and danced along the sleepers, shining like the tiny candles of a distant procession. On occasion, if the onlooker was lucky, just as the train passed by, the fireman would open the door to the firebox in order to shovel in more coal and a shaft of bright orange light would strike up into the night sky, silhouetting the crew in the open cab like a flickering apparition; then we were gone, swallowed by the darkness, with only the fading tap-tap, tap-tap, tap-tap of the last coach passing over the joints in the rails to record that we had ever been there.

On a personal level, all crews had to be physically fit as the work was very tiring. Apart from our break periods, we were on our feet the whole time, moving up and down the coach to the various pigeon holes as we sorted the letters, working quickly and concentrating hard to make sure the letters went to the correct destination. We had to know all the towns in Britain and which counties they were in; it wasn't as easy as just making sure that a letter for Manchester went to Lancashire, there are sixteen different Prestons in Britain, as far apart as the Scottish Borders and Devon, and we knew them all. Inevitably, especially in winter, there were delays due to snow and fog, and the heating system, which was fairly hit and miss at the best of times, always seemed to break down in the coldest of weather. Consequently we were all required to be fairly slim, of a robust constitution, even tempered, nimble on our feet and quick with both our eyes and our reactions – they were just the skills I was going to need to stay alive when I became an air gunner four years later.

The rhythm of the wheels striking the joints in the rails with that familiar and not a little hypnotic tittli-tat, tittli-tat, tittli-tat, accompanied the bundles of letters into each steadily filling docket, marking off the progress of our journey north. From time to time someone would come along and empty the dockets and start to tie them up into the leather pouch, getting it ready for dispatch at the next collection/drop-off point. In the summer months it was quite a welcome relief from the stale humid heat in the coach when the side door opened and a rush of cool air came in as the pouch was hung out ready for the drop and catch, but in the winter months it was an arctic blast which came in, especially as we climbed Shap Fell on the way to Penrith, sitting as it does between the Pennines to the east and the Cumberland mountains of the Lake District to the west.

The line over Shap Fell was, and still is, the highest main line railway in England and getting over the top was not always a foregone conclusion in the winter months when the snow drifted across the tracks from the surrounding hills. On some occasions we had to wait in Lancaster for the snowplough train to clear the line ahead of us before we could get through. For the most part, though, the train had no difficulty with the weather but the gradient was always a challenge. Depending on the power of the engine pulling us, a banker, a tank engine used at the back to push, would sometimes join us at Tebay just north of Oxenholme near Kendal, but once clear of the top of Shap, it was downhill all the way to Carlisle.

If all had gone well, by this time our work was nearly finished but we could rarely relax and had to keep sorting right up to the end, though that didn't stop us looking forward to the meal and the beds that awaited us at our lodgings. Not for us the stately Station Hotel, now known as the Lakes Court Hotel, which had been built in 1852, however, the rooms which the Post Office arranged for us were more than adequate. Each landlady took great pride in looking after 'her' lads and a real bond grew up between the crews and these stalwart women, who thought nothing of preparing a hot meal for us at some unearthly hour on a winter's morning when we were tired, hungry and often very cold too.

The TPO ran to a very strict timetable in order to co-ordinate the collections and also so that the supervisor knew exactly where we were on the route. We were due at Carlisle Citadel Station at seventeen minutes past five and would gather up our jackets, bags, sandwich boxes, tea mugs, and other assorted bits and pieces and hand over to the crew from Glasgow. Carlisle was always a busy station and was one of Britain's foremost railway junctions located at the meeting point of main line routes coming in from Scotland, the west, the north-east, and the south. Even at this time of the morning, there were several trains standing at the platforms of the Citadel: indeed, in the early 1920s, only London had more railway companies running out of it than did Carlisle.

Carlisle Citadel station

As we left the shelter of the train, on all but the balmiest of nights the wind which blew through the station was always cold and in winter would cut you in half, so we wasted little time in climbing the steps of the iron bridge which spanned the tracks and heading for our respective lodgings. Before we had made it through the station doors, the TPO whistle had blown and the new train crew were easing her out and on her way for the final part of the run through to Glasgow; for us, though, a hot breakfast, a cup of tea and a bed were all we really wanted. Another shift completed, but what a great job.

After a few hours' sleep we would be up around mid-day, have lunch and then generally we would each go off, either on our own or maybe with one or two others. What we actually did tended to depend upon the weather, the time of year and the day of the week. In the summer time when the weather was good, we might get on a bus and go out into the surrounding area. The Eden Valley is still lovely, but at that time there were miles of unspoilt countryside just a few minutes' bus ride away, waiting to be enjoyed.

I suppose that having grown up in Shropshire, the fresh air and the smell of the wild flowers in the hedgerows was the one thing that I missed the most after I moved to London. Cars were a fairly unusual sight outside Carlisle city and it was easy to see that there was nothing like as much money in the local economy as there was in the south. Life was a lot harder up here, especially in the 1930s, and it showed on the faces of the people.

If it was wet, which it very often was, and particularly in the winter, we would sometimes go to the local cinema to see whatever films were doing the rounds, but afterwards or perhaps instead of, we inevitably ended up in a pub somewhere to have a couple of beers before starting work at seven o'clock again, ready for the train to leave Citadel Station at eleven o'clock. Over the years that I was on the North Western TPO, I got to know most, if not all, the pubs in and around Carlisle. The local dialect took a bit of getting used to at first. Being a country lad, it wasn't too bad for me, but some of the others on the crew who were born-and-bred Londoners really struggled to understand it at first; but I expect it cut both ways!

At the time, few of us realised that 1936 was a watershed year. Empire Day is, or was then, celebrated on the 24th May each year, although in 1936 it fell on a Sunday, so the celebrations were held on Saturday the 23rd, a great disappointment to the millions of school children who usually got out of school early to dress up and join the afternoon's fun and events. A whole day away from school was not devoted to an annual event. The origins of Empire Day go back to Queen Victoria and a celebration of the achievements of the greatest empire the world has ever seen and upon which the sun never set. Ironically, it did not start to be celebrated until after Victoria's death, the earliest recorded event taking place in New Zealand in 1910.

Nevertheless, by 1936 it was well established and the country was in holiday mood for the day. I was due a treble rest, that is a long weekend from Friday morning until Monday night, and as I had not visited my parents since moving to London, I thought that it would be a good opportunity. So on the morning of Friday, 22nd May 1936, after my duty on the return TPO from Carlisle, I got back on a train and travelled up to Shrewsbury.

The Prince Albert, my local just around the corner from Granville Square

CHAPTER FOUR

"Where Napoleon failed, I shall succeed. I shall land upon the shores of Britain."
Adolf Hitler, Nuremburg Rally

It is interesting now to look back at the events of the mid 1930s which led up to the war. With the benefit of hindsight, it is easy to criticise the nation's leaders. Although I have no doubt that a certain amount of criticism is justified, nevertheless, the events in Europe need to be seen in the perspective and context of the times. As 1936 dawned, the Great War had ended less than twenty years earlier. There were only a handful of families in the whole of Britain who had not been touched by the conflict, which had cost Britain alone 3,049,972 casualties, of whom 886,342 (CWGC report 2007/08) had been killed, and to put the country on a war footing once more without irrefutable evidence of need and cause, so soon after the greatest conflagration the world had ever seen, was unthinkable for most politicians. Winston Churchill, exiled from government, stood above the rest and recognised the threat that Hitler and Nazi Germany posed to the peace of Europe. At this time, though, he was a voice in the wilderness and not many people wanted to listen to him.

Like most ordinary people of the day, I was largely unaware of the implications and enormity of what was beginning to unfold in Germany. Those who had been through the Great War didn't want to think about another one and preferred to focus on their more immediate needs. Unemployment was still desperately high and October 1936 saw two hundred men from the Jarrow shipyards march the three hundred miles to 10 Downing Street to protest at an unemployment rate of 75 per cent in their town, only to find that Prime Minister Stanley Baldwin would not meet them.

I was glad to have a job, and work on the TPO carried on as normal with a regular pattern of duty. London provided the enjoyable social life for a young single man just as much then as it does now. There was no shortage of dances to go to, girls to go out with and films to see. Inevitably it was more expensive to live in London than it was in Shrewsbury or Crewe but the wages were higher and duty on the TPO paid well, and with the extra allowances, I enjoyed a good standard of living. Once I had paid my auntie for lodgings, the rest of my income was mine to spend. However, I had been used to working for my money and saving whenever the chance arose, even back in the days of the milk round with Mr Davies, and so I put money aside in a savings account. I also sent money home to Mum and Dad every week to try to help them out a bit, as I was conscious that even though I had now left home, they were having to work hard to make ends meet and they were not getting any younger.

The year of 1936 was an interesting one which, domestically at least, started badly and seemingly ended badly, although history has shown that fate had perhaps dealt a much better hand to our nation than might at first have appeared. On 20th January King George V died and the Prince of Wales acceded to the throne as Edward VIII. The trouble was that Edward VIII of Great Britain, Ireland and the British Dominions beyond the seas, King and Emperor of India he may have been, but he was now in love with a married woman, the American Wallis Simpson. Marriage to Mrs Simpson following her divorce was not a constitutional event that was within serious contemplation in 1936 and the King had to choose between the woman he loved and country he was born to serve, and no doubt loved too. Mrs Simpson won the day and Edward abdicated, to be succeeded by his brother Albert, who became George VI, the father of our present queen.

In the days before universal television ownership people read the news in the papers, listened to the BBC on the wireless or watched the Pathé newsreel pictures at the cinema. As the events in the royal household developed, the country was gripped by the drama and many queues outside cinemas were as much about seeing the most recent developments as about seeing whatever film was showing.

It wasn't all depressing news, though; on 24th July, at the third stroke, the GPO introduced that great British institution, the speaking clock. Jane Cain, who was a London telephonist, won a prize of ten guineas and became the first voice of the speaking clock. She remained so until 1963 when she was succeeded by Pat Simmons, who was a telephone exchange supervisor, also in London. It was Pat's voice on the clock until 1984. Both Jane (who was also sometimes called Ethel, though I have no idea why) and Pat are now dead, but they lived to be 87 and 85, respectively. In 1984 the voice of Brian Cobby took over: his is also the voice on the 5-4-3-2-1...Thunderbirds-are-go theme tune for the Gerry Anderson television series. Sara Mendes da Costa has been the voice of the clock since 2007.

At first, the speaking clock was only available in London, but even so it received around thirteen million calls in its first year. The service was extended to the whole country in 1942 and today receives about one hundred million calls per year. One of the main reasons why the GPO introduced this service was that until then people simply rang their local operator and asked her what the time was by the clock on the exchange wall!

In a strangely ironic juxtaposition of events, on 5th March the iconic Supermarine Spitfire had its maiden flight, and with its graceful lines, speed and manoeuvrability, was to symbolise both the future and our fight for survival in the aerial combats of the Battle of Britain in the skies over southern England. On 6th July, the German airship *Hindenburg*, which symbolised past German imperialistic ambitions, crossed the Atlantic in forty-six hours, but ten months later to the day on 6th May 1937 the *Hindenburg* exploded whilst docking in New Jersey, killing around thirty passengers and crew. The days of the airship were over: the aeroplane had arrived.

The year 1937 also saw Neville Chamberlain take over as Prime Minister, Oxford win the boat race after thirteen years of consecutive victories by Cambridge, the coronation of King George VI, the opening of the world's longest bridge, the Golden Gate in San Francisco and the death of JM Barrie the author of *Peter Pan*, the future royalties from which he bequeathed to the Great Ormond Street Children's Hospital in London. In 1987 his copyright in the book was about to expire but Parliament came to the rescue and embodied his bequest in the Copyright, Designs and Patents Act 1988, the only time Parliament has ever done this, ensuring that sick children continue to be the beneficiaries of Peter Pan, the perpetual child.

The news from across Europe became more serious by the month; Hitler's Nazis were now in complete control in Germany and on 13th March 1938 invaded Austria. As the balmy summer days of that year rolled into a September of mists and mellow fruitfulness, it became clear that the storm clouds of war were once again gathering across the Channel. The Royal Navy was mobilised and, thanks to the wisdom and foresight of Air Chief Marshal HCT Dowding, the Spitfire and Hurricane fighter planes were introduced to the RAF as a matter of priority. To this day, Lord Beaverbrook's factory at Castle Bromwich in the West Midlands celebrates its proud association with the Spitfire production years.

At the end of September amid real fears that Britain and France were to be invaded by Germany, the two governments made one last effort to avoid another pan-European war and on the 29th, Neville Chamberlain travelled to the international conference in Munich. The outcome was that Britain and France would agree to accept Hitler's annexation of Austria and the Sudetenland in Czechoslovakia, providing that that was the end of his territorial claims in Europe. When he returned to Heston airport a few days later, Chamberlain gave his now famous press conference in which he claimed that his deal with Hitler meant 'peace in our time'. However, there were many people in and around the government who felt that war was now inevitable and a military build up in Britain and France began. If Chamberlain had done nothing else at Munich, he had at least secured a vital period of time, eleven months in the event, during which Britain could seriously prepare for war.

Probably because I was living and working in London, I became much more aware of the build up to the war than was apparent in some other parts of the country, although the team that came down from Glasgow to relieve us at Carlisle were fairly well clued up too: they were seeing the warships gathering along the quays and docksides of the River Clyde waiting for their crews.

It was in the early summer of 1938 that I decided I would go to Paris whilst I still could do so in peace. I had wanted to go for a long time but had never really got around to it. I had been to the Odeon cinema in Leicester Square one night with a girl I knew to see Katherine Hepburn and Cary Grant in the film *Holiday*. As was the custom in the days before everyone had a television at home, the main feature film was preceded by twenty minutes or so of Pathé newsreels. Although these were not quite as up to the minute as today's twenty-four-hour news coverage, they were topical and gave film goers a valuable visual take on world affairs and current events which we didn't get from newspapers and the wireless. It was one of the Pathé News items that featured Paris and some of the contrasts between the fear of war with the Germans who were just across the border and the easy-going café culture of the city which made up my mind. I had a long weekend due to me and since the girl I was with did not seem to think that her father would agree to her spending a weekend in Paris with me, I resolved to go on my own anyway.

I mentioned my plans to Peter, the other single chap on the TPO team, and he thought that going to Paris before the Germans got there to spoil it all would be a really good idea, and so the next day we went into the Thomas Cook office at Victoria and booked our trains, passage across the Channel and a modest hotel in Paris. Well, we were like a couple of children in a sweetie shop: two twenty-four-year-old single lads in the romantic capital of Europe in the summer time. The beer was awful but the wine was smooth and the women were fun. Little did I know, as we sat at a small table beside the river Seine watching the people going about their daily business, that six years later I would be back, this time in a Lancaster bomber. April in Paris would not be the same in 1944 as it was in 1938; but I could never have guessed how different.

On the TPO we talked of little else but the coming war, when we had time to talk, that was. There was a steady but noticeable build up of post across the country and in particular those little brown On His Majesty's Service official envelopes. On 27th April 1939 the call-up started: all twenty and twenty-one-year-old fit and able-bodied men were being drafted into the forces and the TPO was carrying the news to thousands of households across Britain.

On Friday, 1st September the Germans invaded Poland, with whom Britain and France had made a defence treaty. Even before war was declared, many children were being evacuated from London, and they had become a familiar sight in the stations over the preceding few weeks. However, the news that day turned a steady flow into a flood and created what seemed to be a great exodus. When I went into work at Euston Station late that afternoon, the platforms were filled to overflowing with hundreds of young children, many of them crying, most of them afraid and all of them wearing a tell-tale brown parcel label tied to their jacket or coat, if they had one.

The headline boards of the newspaper vendors standing on the street corners selling the London evening papers told the story: the Evening News, 'HITLER INVADES POLAND', the Evening Standard, I WILL GIVE POLES A LESSON – HITLER' and The Star, 'POLAND INVADED – OFFICIAL'. This was in the days before twenty-four-hour news coverage, satellite broadcasting and the internet: it took time for news to travel across Europe, and although the invasion had started at first light that day, it was only as the day progressed that real confirmation of what was happening began to filter through.

We were a very busy but very sombre crew that night as we worked our way through to Carlisle. Our scheduled journeys had been increasingly delayed and interrupted since late July, as more and more troop movements occurred on the railways, and although we were, as a mail train, a priority, we were no longer the top priority on the system. It was all these little signs as much as or more than what we were being told officially, that when added together made it clear that the war was coming. It was a very uncomfortable feeling but by now I don't think that anybody doubted the inevitability of the impending conflict.

By chance, 1st September was also the day that the BBC launched its new wireless programme, the Home Service, now rather anonymously and uninspiringly known as Radio 4. The first news was read by Alvar Lidell, who, as the war years progressed, became a familiar and strangely comforting voice on the airwaves: "Here is the ten o'clock news and this is Alvar Lidell reading it." And so it was Alvar Lidell who, at a quarter past eleven on Sunday, 3rd September 1939 drew the whole nation into expectant silence gathered around their wireless sets, as he introduced Neville Chamberlain. I sat with my aunt and uncle in their little front room at 25 Granville Square in Islington and listened to those fateful words of the Prime Minister.

> *"I am speaking to you from the Cabinet Room of 10 Downing Street. This morning the British Ambassador in Berlin, handed the German Government a final note, stating that unless we heard from them by 11 o'clock that they were prepared at once to withdraw their troops from Poland, a state of war would exist between us. I have to tell you now that no such undertaking has been received and that consequently, this country is at war with Germany."*

We all knew that it was coming, but that didn't lessen the impact of Chamberlain's words and the three of us sat in stunned silence for a few moments. At length, my uncle got up and went across to the Marconi wireless standing on the polished table in the corner and turned it off.

"Well, that's that then, Trev. It's started. You'll be called up soon enough, my lad."

He was right of course, but I was twenty-five and knew that I would have a little while to wait yet.

The Government put into action its contingency plans and that very day started to issue gas masks, with instructions that they had to be carried everywhere and at all times. Gas had been a real weapon on the Western Front in the Great War, and people were quite rightly very fearful of it. The perceived official wisdom at this time was that this would be a war similar to 1914–18 but that the bomber would be the weapon to carry the war to the enemy. It was considered that whatever else happened on the way, the bomber would always get through. This concept of front-line fighting and the myth about the bomber were both very quickly dispelled when a few months later the Germans swept across France with their Blitzkrieg tactics. They had tested them in the Spanish Civil War and had perfected them in Poland. Our lads suffered badly because our military leadership had not kept up to date and learnt from what was before their very eyes.

Before then, though, we had the phoney war. There were a few scares when the air-raid sirens went and everyone ran into the underground stations and other shelters; but the Luftwaffe didn't come and the gas didn't come and the weather was very pleasant and everybody not in uniform became all rather relaxed about it. The first real shock of the war for the public came on 14th October 1939 with news that in the early hours of that day the German submarine U-47, commanded by Kapitänleutnant Gunther Prien, had crept past the supposedly impenetrable defences at Scapa Flow in Orkney and had torpedoed the World War I veteran battleship HMS *Royal Oak*. The country was stunned by this audacious attack and it was a reminder to us all that we were at war. Prien and his crew made it safely back out to sea and returned to Germany to a heroes' welcome. They were flown to Berlin where Hitler awarded Prien the coveted Knight's Cross.

Part of the 'Churchill Barriers'; sunken ships to protect the entrances to Scapa Flow, Orkney Islands [Lynn Forsyth]

Today, the Royal Oak still lies on the seabed at Scapa Flow and is off limits to divers: the wreck is a war grave as the bodies of most of the 833 sailors and civilian workers who died on her that night are still in her. Neither Gunther Prien nor U-47 survived the war. They were sunk on the night of 7th/8th March 1941 whilst attacking convoy OB-293.

The bridge nameplate from HMS Royal Oak, illegally taken from the wreck but now in the Orkney museum [Lynn Forsyth]

The TPO still ran up and down to Carlisle and whilst in some ways life carried on as normal, there were clear signs that we were at war. Although as a Royal Mail train we had a certain degree of priority, our progress was increasingly delayed by the large numbers of troops now being moved all over the country and the stations were bristling with uniforms, much more so than even just a few weeks earlier. Soldiers, sailors and airmen; some were coming home on leave and being greeted with smiles and laughter, others were leaving and being seen off with tears and silent prayers.

The other big impact upon the stations were all the children who were being evacuated from the towns and cities to the relative safety of the countryside and, no matter what time of day or night we stopped at a major station, they were all around the platforms. They sat or stood, their brown labels tied to their coats, some had tear stains on their cheeks, some simply had mucky faces either from life in the city or soot from the steam engines – it was difficult to tell which – but they all had the same blank expression, not really understanding why they were being taken away from home.

The winter of 1939–40 was one of the severest of the twentieth century and we very often struggled to get over Shap Fell. The carriage heating systems broke down, the line-side exchange equipment froze up and wouldn't work, despite the efforts of the station staff along the way, and the wind cut through us like a stiletto knife whenever we opened the door to load the bag to the catcher arm. It wasn't much better at the Citadel Station as the wind came straight off the frozen hills of the Scottish southern uplands.

As that bitterly cold winter drew to a close across Europe, so did the phoney war. On 9th April 1940 the Germans invaded Norway and Denmark. The British campaign in Norway was plagued by bad planning and bad luck, and was a complete disaster, which led to Chamberlain's resignation as Prime Minister.

I had met a rather pretty girl about a month earlier at a

dance in the church hall not far from Granville Square. Apart from going out for a beer with my friends, I hadn't really been out very much during the winter. This was partly because it was so desperately cold everywhere and partly because working nights on the TPO was inevitably a fairly unsociable routine. It did have some compensations, though, and long weekends were among them. It was late afternoon and the weather was fine and dry; it was starting to turn into that beautiful summer of 1940. We were walking though Gordon Square, one of the smaller parks near Russell Square, between Euston Road and Tottenham Court Road, and although the sun was still shining, the shadows were beginning to lengthen and there was a chill feeling to the air. Lydia shivered and clutched her cardigan around her shoulders a little tighter. I held her other hand as we left the park and crossed the road towards Goodge Street underground station on the Northern Line, to catch a train to Leicester Square for the cinema. There at the station entrance was the Evening Standard newspaper headline board announcing in bold letters that Churchill was now the Prime Minister. It was Friday, 10th May.

The British Expeditionary Force, the BEF, had been steadily building up in France since before war had been declared and by 10th May, when the Battle for France really began, there were 394,165 men over there, of whom 237,319 were assigned to front-line duty. The same day as Churchill entered No.10 Downing Street, the Germans started their Blitzkrieg into the Low Countries and France. In just six weeks the BEF had been forced back to the English Channel, evacuated from Dunkirk and the French army had surrendered: an unprecedented military achievement by the Germans.

At the beginning of May, No.12 Squadron was based at Amifontaine, part of the Advanced Air Striking Force and found itself in the front line. It was equipped with Fairey Battles, an obsolescent slow-moving light bomber armed with 250lb bombs, one wing-mounted forward-facing machine gun and a 1914-18 Lewis machine gun in the rear part of the cockpit. It carried a crew of three and was woefully inadequate for the job which the crews were asked to carry out in it. The Battles were shot down in vast numbers and too many airmen lost their lives. Nevertheless, despite the shortcomings of this aircraft, it was the rear gunner in a Battle which, on the 20th September 1939, shot down an Me109 fighter, the first German aircraft loss of the war.

No. 12 Squadron's own first loss came on the 10th May when the Flight Commander's aircraft was shot down. Flight Lieutenant Simpson was pulled from the wreckage by his gunner and navigator, but was so badly burned that when the Germans later found him in a French hospital they repatriated him to England.

Two days later, on Sunday, 12th May 1940 the squadron experienced very mixed fortunes when it was awarded the first two Victoria Crosses of the war. On that bright sunny morning five aircraft took off from their base at Amifontaine in northern France with orders to destroy, at all costs, the bridge over the Albert Canal at Maastricht, over which the Germans were pouring men and equipment into Belgium.

Flying Officer Donald Garland was the pilot and courageous formation leader of the five aircraft; his navigator was Sergeant Thomas Gray. The area around the bridge was very heavily defended, but nevertheless Sgt Gray coolly and resourcefully navigated the formation through to the bridge, whereupon they came under vicious and sustained artillery and cannon fire. Despite the curtain of fire which the German forces put up against them, all five aircraft successfully attacked the bridge by dive-bombing it from very low level, dropping their bombs on target. As they pulled away from the canal they were attacked by a large number of Messerschmitt 109 fighters, firing 20mm cannon shells at the poorly armed Battles. Only one of the five aircraft which had taken off returned to its base. Their orders had been to attack the bridge at all costs: for twelve of those fifteen young men at all costs required the ultimate sacrifice. Flying Officer Garland and Sergeant Gray were awarded posthumous VCs and together with their rear gunner Sgt Lawrence Reynolds, are buried in Haverlee War Cemetery, Belgium. It remains the only occasion on which two airmen in the same crew have been awarded the Victoria Cross for the same action.

War does not discriminate and has no respect for anyone or anything. Flying Officer Garland was the son of Mr Patrick Garland, himself the recipient of the Conspicuous Gallantry Medal from the Great War. Mr and Mrs Garland had three other sons, Flight Lieutenant Patrick Garland, Flight Lieutenant John Garland and Pilot Officer Desmond Garland: they were all killed on active service during the war.

Across the Channel, in Fighter Command Headquarters, its Commander-in-Chief Air Chief Marshal Dowding realised the hopelessness of the situation in France and, more importantly, recognised the folly of sending further scarce fighter aircraft to the continent in a vain attempt to stem the inexorable German advance upon a French army on the verge of surrender. He recognised, correctly, as history has shown, that only the RAF could prevent an invasion and that it was therefore essential to keep every aircraft and fighter pilot in Britain at that stage. So convinced was he of this proposition that he wrote his now-famous memorandum to the Permanent Secretary of State for Air, and was duly summoned to the Permanent Secretary's office to explain it:

To the Permanent Secretary of State for Air,
Sir, I have the honour to refer to the very serious calls which have recently been made upon Fighter Command in an attempt to stem the German invasion of the continent. I hope and believe that our armies may yet be victorious in France and Belgium, but we have to face the possibility that they may be defeated. In this case, I presume that there is no-one who would deny that England should fight on even though the remainder of the continent of Europe is dominated by the Germans.

I must therefore request that not one more fighter

*be sent across the Channel. If the Home defence
is drained away in desperate attempts to remedy
the situation in France, defeat in France will involve
the final, complete and irremediable defeat of this
country.*

*I have the honour to be, Sir,
Your obedient Servant,
HCT Dowding
Air Chief Marshal, Air Officer Commanding-in-Chief,
Fighter Command, Royal Air Force*

"You do realise, Dowding, that Churchill will have to see this?" whined the Permanent Secretary.
"That's why I wrote it," replied Dowding laconically.

No further aircraft were sent across to France and as many as possible of those that were already there were withdrawn back to Britain. Even so, it was more than a month before they were all back in Britain: Dowding had lost 20 per cent of his experienced pilots and almost 50 per cent of the fighters that had been sent across the Channel in a fruitless effort to save France.

For the most part, what remained of the BEF was trapped around Dunkirk, and the story of their remarkable rescue has been told and documented elsewhere. Less well known is that several thousand men made their way south into Vichy France and to the ports of St Nazaire, Brest, St Malo, Cherbourg and La Havre. Some fifty British ships of the Royal and Merchant Navy were waiting to take the troops off and of these, nineteen had been detailed to pick up those waiting at the port of St Nazaire; among these ships was the HMT *Lancastria*.

She had been built on the River Clyde at the William Beardmore yard as a medium-size luxury liner for Cunard's trans-Atlantic and Baltic routes. Launched on 31st May 1920 and originally named the *Tyrrhenia*, her name had been changed to the RMS *Lancastria* in 1924. She was requisitioned as a troopship in April 1940 and was part of the evacuation fleet from Norway.

Some years ago I came to know Robert, a former army officer who was taken off the docks at St Nazaire and ferried out to the *Lancastria*: this is what he told me. On the early morning of 17th June, the *Lancastria* was anchored five miles off St Nazaire in 72 fathoms of water and from then until late afternoon she took on board something over six thousand troops, together with as many as three thousand civilian men, women and children, all fleeing from the advancing German army. All this time, the Luftwaffe, using a combination of Junkers Ju87 Stuka dive bombers, Me109 fighters and Ju88 bombers, attacked the town and strafed the waiting troops and civilians on the docks. There was very little cover from the RAF, a result of over-stretched resources, fuel and aircraft shortages and Churchill's instruction at the request of Air Chief Marshal Dowding, that no further aircraft were to be sent across the channel to defend France. Dowding could see what the summer would bring.

Although various Luftwaffe aircraft flew over the *Lancastria*, none turned in to attack her until at four o'clock on that fateful afternoon, a single Ju88 flew over the ship and dropped four bombs, one of which ruptured the fuel tank and another fell straight down her funnel and into the engine room, where it exploded. With hundreds of gallons of fuel oil spilling into the sea, the *Lancastria* soon rolled onto her side and sank within twenty minutes, trapping thousands of people. Those who could, jumped over the side and into the water, hoping to be rescued by the ships and boats nearby, but for some rescue came too late as the German pilot, now joined by several Me109s, turned his aircraft back over the scene of devastation and his crew machine-gunned those in the water as they floundered helplessly amongst the bodies, the oil and the debris. Only 2,447 survivors were pulled from the water: what the real death toll was that day no-one knows but it is estimated to be well over four thousand.

There is no doubt in Robert's mind that the Germans had deliberately waited until the *Lancastria* was ready to sail before they attacked her and thus maximised the loss of life: in the space of just a few moments the lives of over four thousand people were ended that afternoon. Virtually unarmed, the *Lancastria* stood little or no chance. Robert had been very lucky: he had been blown off the deck of the ship by the explosion and then, disorientated in the water, he had been attacked by an Me109, but its cannon shells had entered the sea just in front and to the side of him. He was eventually pulled to safety by French fishermen, just two of many who had taken to their boats to try to rescue the survivors, and transferred to a Royal Navy ship by which he returned to England the next day.

The loss of the *Lancastria* and the circumstances of it were so appalling that the Prime Minister Winston Churchill put a D Notice on it, and the press were forbidden to report it. It was hidden from the British pubic until fairly recently and remains Britain's worst maritime disaster of all time, accounting for a much greater loss of life than the *Titanic* and the *Lusitania* added together.

The following day Churchill made his famous 'This was their finest hour' speech in the House of Commons: I don't doubt that it was, but it didn't feel very much like it to Robert as he walked down the gangplank of the destroyer at Plymouth docks that day, not knowing whether any of his men had survived with him.

RMS Lancastria *in better days*

RMS Lancastria *in her last moments. Note the people still clinging to her and in the water*

CHAPTER FIVE

"Let us therefore brace ourselves to our duty; so bear ourselves that if the British Empire and its Commonwealth lasts for a thousand years, men will still say, 'This, was their finest hour.'"
Winston Spencer Churchill, British Prime Minister, 18th June 1940.

The summer of 1940 belonged to the RAF. Day after day, the young men of Fighter Command took on the full might of the Luftwaffe over the fields of southern England and along the east coast. It was not a glamorous few days of dog fights, but a gruelling grind of sorties, day after day taking off any time from first light until darkness fell.

The job of the Luftwaffe was to gain command of the skies over southern England so that the German invasion of Britain, Operation Sea Lion, could get underway. There had been a steady and substantial build up of German troops along the Channel ports, together with landing craft, barges and escort vessels since May: the first invasion fleet against these islands since the Spanish Armada was ready to set sail. Reichsmarschall Hermann Goering had promised Hitler that he would sweep the RAF aside in a matter of days.

Goering's plan was to attack the convoys in the English Channel and draw the RAF fighters up, whereupon his own Messerschmitt bf109 and bf110 aircraft would shoot them down in large numbers. Without fighters in the air, the invasion fleet could sail across the Channel and land reasonably unmolested as the Royal Navy would be kept busy by attacking German aircraft and surface vessels. Although the evacuation of Dunkirk and the ports of western France had secured the rescue of over 350,000 men from the BEF, they had left nearly all their weapons and equipment behind as they steadily retreated to the sea. Only the Royal Air Force stood between freedom and conquest, between hope and the total domination of Western Europe by the Nazis. Britain was alone and virtually defenceless, but at the time most of us simply did not realise that our future hung by such a slim thread.

Air Chief Marshal Dowding had put it characteristically succinctly when in early July he told the Secretary of State for Air Sir Archibald Sinclair, "The essential arithmetic is that our young men will have to shoot down their young men at the rate of four to one if we are to keep pace at all." The stark fact facing him which led to that observation was that in May 1940 the RAF had 650 fighters against 2,500 Luftwaffe aircraft.

In poor weather, the Luftwaffe started attacking convoys in the English Channel, and although this had no great impact on the shipping it did have a significant effect on the pilots of Fighter Command. The attrition caused by the daily stress of flying several sorties a day, and the personal tragedies of seeing friends killed before their eyes began to weigh heavily upon the young pilots of the front-line squadrons. Nevertheless, the Germans were suffering disproportionate losses, consistently losing more aircraft and crews each day than was the RAF, but, as Dowding had observed, they could afford to, never sending more than half their bomber force at a time. In addition to attacking the convoys along the south coast, the Luftwaffe was carrying out night-time bombing raids across England and up into Scotland as well and the strain was beginning to tell on their crews too. On 10th July even the little fishing port of Tobermory on the Scottish west coast island of Mull was bombed. I can only think that they were aiming for Oban and Kerrera Sound, where No.210 Squadron of Coastal Command had just arrived with their Sunderland flying boats from Pembroke Dock in South Wales, exchanging stations with No.209 Squadron.

Whilst Fighter Command engaged the enemy over our convoys and coastal towns, Bomber Command had been authorised to carry the war to the German heartland and every night, weather permitting, a variety of bombers including the Hampden and Wellington squadrons would fly out across the Channel to targets in Germany. It was also directed to carry out daylight raids on the invasion barges which were lined up in the Channel ports and on 18th July a formation of Bristol Blenheim light bombers carried out a successful raid on these barges in Boulogne harbour.

Indeed, at the time these raids caused the enemy some considerable concern as was evidenced by an intelligence report on 26th July:

> *It is reliably reported that the RAF's night bombing of Germany is most effective and is worrying the German High Command. It is also reported from another source that the RAF raids are causing serious damage. The Germans are stated to be considerably worried by these raids and our delayed action bombs are particularly unpopular.*

After nearly six weeks of almost unrelenting attacks on our convoys in the English Channel, the Thames Estuary and the Western Approaches, RAF fighter pilots were suffering battle fatigue and exhaustion. The individuals needed some time to relax, but the squadrons were at constant action stations during daylight hours and their ground crews were tired and stretched to the limit trying to re-arm and re-fuel aircraft between raids and then service and repair damaged fighters at night. Each day, at nine o'clock in the morning, the Air Ministry reported the number of fighter aircraft which were serviceable.

Then, on 12th August Goering, realising that he was not going to win by aerial combat alone, sent his bombers, mainly Heinkel He 111s, Junkers Ju88s and Dornier Do 17s, to bomb the fighter aerodromes of Manston, Hawkinge and Lympne in southern England. Simultaneously, his Junkers Ju87 Stuka dive-bombers attacked the radar stations at Ventnor on the Isle of Wight and at Poling. This change of tactic was a response to the combined efforts of Fighter and Bomber Commands: 13th August was the day which Hitler had declared as 'Adler Tag', Eagle Day, the day on which the RAF was to be obliterated, clearing the way for the invasion of Britain to begin, and yet the

Luftwaffe was nowhere near in control of the skies over the English Channel. The RAF needed to be defeated if the Germans were not to put back their invasion plans; the Battle of Britain was still finely balanced, but it was just about to tilt very slightly in our favour.

The weather was generally settled during that summer and as a result the enemy were able to launch repeated waves of aircraft to attack the aerodromes of southern England. However, this did not come without a high cost in German fighter pilots and bomber crews, and by late August those losses had mounted to significant levels. The front-line RAF fighter squadrons had also learned from their earlier mistakes and had changed their tactics by being more flexible, adopting the German method of attacking in pairs, a method still used today, and also using the 'Big Wing' tactic devised by Douglas Bader and promoted by Air Vice-Marshal Leigh-Mallory, where, with the advance warning given by the radar stations, several squadrons would come together and then attack the invading bombers in large numbers. Not only did this increase the numbers of bombers being shot down, it provided enough cover to deal with the fighter escort.

RAF recruitment poster - Battle of Britain

The aerodromes, though, were taking a terrible pounding: Manston, Hawkinge, Biggin Hill, Kenley, Tangmere, Dover, Hartlepool and Abbotsinch were all too often unserviceable by night and many squadrons were being moved out from their normal bases and dispersed around small country flying clubs – a move which generally did not warm the hearts of pilots and ground crew alike. The RAF also had a shortage of pilots and on one occasion Dowding was heard to reflect, "Must have more pilots or we lose." It wasn't only pilots and aircrew who were being killed, many ground crew were lost or wounded as the Luftwaffe attacked the airfields. In particular, the maintenance crews and armourers were often caught in the open by the attacking Me109s when working on aircraft in the open dispersal area.

Whilst all this was going on during the day, Britain's cities, with the exception of London, were being repeatedly bombed and the civilian casualties were beginning to mount. Up and down the route of the TPO we could see the evidence for ourselves. We didn't understand why London had escaped, not knowing that Hitler had forbidden the bombing of London, but plenty of other towns and cities were being attacked on a regular basis. There were many nights that we would be held up by an air raid and have to stop, especially when going through the Midlands and the north-west. These were still the days of steam engines and when the fireman opened the firebox to shovel on more coal, a great shaft of bright orange light shot out skywards; just the sort of invitation to attack us and the main railway line that we did not want to give to a passing bomber group, so we had to heave-to and wait until the raid was over.

These stops were a mixed blessing in a way because although they made us late arriving at Carlisle's Citadel Station, on some occasions even after breakfast, it gave us more time to sort the mail, which had increased enormously with all the people now away from home and anxious to keep in touch and reassure those left behind. It was not just the men who were away from home, many women had taken the opportunity to join up, particularly the Women's Auxiliary Air Force, the WAAFs, which had been formed in 1939 and at its peak in 1943 had a strength of over 180,000.

I knew that my call-up would not be too far away and that I would have to leave the TPO and go to war. I was no more or less keen on the idea than the next person; it was simply something that had to be done, something that involved everybody in one way or another if we were to defeat Germany and remain a free country. There was talk amongst the lads that the TPO was going to be stopped anyway as it was too dangerous to have priority trains running up and down the country showing the Luftwaffe the position of vital rail links. I had been weighing the relative merits of the army, the navy and the air force for some time, usually whilst languishing in some quiet siding waiting for the all-clear to sound. The army was not at all attractive to me since I was not particularly keen to spend the war marching up and down a parade ground for hours at a time being shouted at by some manic drill sergeant, living in a tent and eating bully beef out of a mess tin waiting to die in the mud of some far-off battlefield. I did not want to become forever part of that distant corner of England in some foreign field. It was just a little ironic that I was later posted abroad and lived in a tent in the desert for some considerable time, eating God knows what out of a mess tin.

The navy held even less attraction for me: bobbing about on the sea was not my idea of fun at the best of times. I had no desire to live in a sardine can for months at a time: a sardine can that was either being buffeted by the unforgiving sea or at risk of being blown up by an unseen enemy. It was no contest really; I wanted to fly. Flying was an unfulfilled wish for me and the war would give me the chance to live that dream – it was rather a pity, though, that every time I was to live the dream, someone would be trying to kill me. Nevertheless, I just wanted to fly, to be up there in the blue sky looking down at the earth beneath me. How different, I thought, it must all look from somewhere up there. The patchwork of fields, the ribbons of country roads, the villages, the towns, the cities, and the coastline with its thin string of surf as the waves pitched up onto the shore or crashed into the rocks off some craggy point.

So the RAF it would be. I was happy with this conclusion as I remembered the fascination I had had as a child for the bi-planes flying over our home in Shrewsbury.

I was twenty-six and could expect to be called up any time in the next six months. I was also conscious that most people I passed in the street were in uniform and it was beginning to trouble me that I wasn't doing as much as I could. I was no great athlete but I was young and very fit; working on the TPO made sure of that. I knew that if I volunteered, I would be able to choose which service I joined rather than simply being sent off to the one that was in the greatest need of manpower at that particular time. I talked to Lydia about the idea of volunteering for aircrew and asked her what she thought.

"We wouldn't see very much of each other, Trevor," she said.
"I know, but it won't be for a while yet. I just wanted to know what you thought about the idea."
"Well, I've been thinking of joining the WAAFs too, I wasn't sure how to tell you. I'm fed up working in that office, but let's leave it a little while yet though before we decide, shall we?"

Saturday, 7th September 1940 changed all that. The Luftwaffe bombed London. It wasn't so much that there was anything special or sacrosanct about London, it wasn't even my home town, but it was where I lived and worked. During the bombing that September, in the centenary year of the 1d postage, twenty-three London post offices were destroyed and every London railway station was put out of service. The war had now become very personal to me; I was under attack. The raid during that day was a little way down the road in east London, around the docks, but then as darkness fell, the air-raid sirens sounded once more and the Greater London area was bombed for about six hours.

On the following two nights, Sunday the 8th and Monday the 9th September, the Blitz started in earnest for the City of London area and the East End. On Sunday night there were major fires in Great Arthur Street and King William Street, and extensive damage was caused to property near 'The Old Lady of Threadneedle Street', the Bank of England, and Mansion House. At St Pancras Station the line was blocked, in the Strand the law courts and at Knightsbridge the Barracks were both hit. To the east at Shoreditch the railway lines were damaged and a public air-raid shelter was destroyed, and in Stepney several serious fires along the docks provided a navigation beacon for later waves of bombers. The main telephone exchange was hit and roads all over the city were strewn with masonry. At Battersea a series of delayed action bombs put all the railway lines between Queenstown Road and Clapham junction out of action. The next morning, commuters coming in from the south had a tortuous journey to get to work before the lines re-opened, but that was something which they had to get used to very quickly. It was a steep learning curve for us all and brought it home to us that this was going to be a war in which we were all involved, not just the armed services on the front line.

At twenty past five that Sunday evening, the air-raid sirens sounded: we knew that this was not a practice; they had stopped those a long time ago. I helped my aunt and uncle along Acton Street towards the safety of King's Cross underground station but not before the bombs started to drop. It was a terrifying experience and one which haunted me in the years to come when as a member of a Lancaster crew over Germany I knew exactly what the people below were experiencing. For now, though, I needed to get the three of us to safety. We were not yet used to these bombing raids but at least it was still full daylight and we could see where we were going. As the aeroplanes headed across the city to the West End, our part of Islington caught the first bombs, which caused major damage to roads, cables, sewers and the gas and water mains.

It is difficult now to describe the deafening noise and destruction of that evening. The heavy drone of the aircraft overhead, the fear as another stick of bombs whistled down followed by a series of 'crumps' as they exploded one after another across several streets. One bomb fell on a building in Acton Street just after we had turned into Gray's Inn Road and although we were shielded from the blast, bricks and glass and wood and everything else rained down upon us. I pulled my two elderly relatives into a doorway to shield them from the raining debris, but several other people in the street were not so lucky. I was just glad that it was not a weekday as all this would be happening during the rush hour. Little did I know then what the following day would bring.

Somewhat shaken but otherwise unharmed, we got to the shelter of the underground station; it was the first of many such nights for my aunt and uncle.

I had arranged to meet Lydia that evening and I was worried about how she and her family had fared, but for the time being I was stuck in the underground. After about an hour the all-clear sounded and we struggled back up the stairs to the fading daylight of that September evening. All around us there were the signs of bomb damage and fires were burning in every direction. People were starting to move about and pick their way over the debris towards their homes in and around the King's Cross area. I made sure that my aunt and uncle were safe inside and then walked across to Lydia's home in Torrens Street, a small row of terraced houses running back off City Road just behind the Angel underground station in upper Islington. I knew that they would all have gone into the underground when the air-raid siren sounded. Although at the beginning of the Blitz it was not the general haven it was later, people very quickly realised the safety of the underground and it wasn't long before whole families simply adopted the routine of moving in for the night as soon as the commuters had gone.

I saw Lydia coming towards me as I made my way along Pentonville Road between the fallen masonry, broken glass and general confusion. As she came closer, she simply stopped and stared at me; I had left my uncle's house without looking in the mirror and hadn't given a thought to my appearance. I was covered in dust from the bomb in Acton Street and my clothes looked as if I had slept in them for a week. We laughed as the young do at such things and then, not really knowing what to do, we started to wander somewhat aimlessly down Farringdon Road, past the sorting office and towards the Thames. I don't think that it occurred to either of us that the Luftwaffe might return and that the night's bombing had only just started. Why should we? We hadn't experienced anything like this before.

The closer to the river that we got, the greater and the more widespread the destruction seemed to be. Fire tenders were everywhere and it looked as if every other building was ablaze. By now it was dark and as we turned the corner into Ludgate Hill we saw the great dome of St Paul's Cathedral outlined against the fires and the smoke. As we stood mesmerised by the scene in front of us, the air-raid sirens sounded again and the searchlights came on, reaching far into the night sky to strike at the belly of an enemy bomber: how I came to hate searchlights.

For a few minutes we stood transfixed at the sight of those shafts of light criss-crossing the orange sky behind St Paul's, whilst all around the Cathedral a thousand fires raged. I think that it was in that moment, as I felt the anger well up inside me as for the second time that day I witnessed what the Nazis were doing to my country, that I finally resolved to join the RAF and volunteer for Bomber Command aircrew. I was jerked back to the more immediate danger when Lydia started coughing and choking in the smoke-filled air which was swirling around us; it pulled us to our senses and we ran down Blackfriars Lane and into the underground once more as the first bombs started to fall on the docks a short way to the east.

St Paul's cathedral in the Blitz

Two weeks later, at five minutes past nine on the morning of Saturday, 21st September 1940, having told Lydia, my Mum and Dad and the wonderfully named Egbert Ramsbottom, the head supervisor of the TPO, I presented myself at the Royal Air Force recruitment office in Islington intent on becoming a bomber pilot.

Generally, in the 1930s pilots were drawn from a particular background and schooling and the applicants for pilot training would be called to RAF Headquarters at Adastral House in London's Kingsway and interviewed by First World War veterans from the same background and schools: consequently most pilots were officers. By today's egalitarian standards, it must seem all very privileged, but that's how it was then and the system worked because everybody had a place in society and knew where that place was. The war changed all that, along with a lot of other things – not always for the better.

Those who passed the interview at Adastral House became

civilian pupil pilots and learnt to fly Tiger Moths. Once having got the hang of the rudimentary rules of flying, those who made it through the meticulous and exacting training would go on to the RAF flying school and hold the rank of Acting Pilot Officer, but on probation: civilians in RAF uniform where the training regime was even stricter. There were some Sergeant pilots though; at the beginning of the war these were the men who had made the Service their career and had won their wings either in the last war or by graduating since. Usually they were the instructors and they were exceptionally good at what they did.

The Battle of Britain quickly demonstrated that the officer ranks alone could not provide all the pilots and that it was a man's ability which determined whether he had a chance to become a pilot, not the school he had attended. In the air we were all equal: before God and before the enemy.

I had longed to be a pilot as I stood and watched those biplanes twisting and turning over our house, perhaps now I would have the chance.

I entered the church hall in Merlin Street, a wonderful omen for a future Lancaster crew member, with a mixture of destiny and expectation: I was going to join the RAF and I knew that the decision which I had already made and which I would today act upon would shape the rest of my life, and might just cut it very short.

I sat in one of the seats that lined the wall and waited my turn to go forward. When it came, I got up and approached the desk behind which sat a grey-haired Flight Sergeant with a row of First World War medals and a face to tell a thousand stories. I looked at the medals carefully and I could see the pride in his eyes and the pleasure that I had given to him simply by taking notice of what this man had done even before I could talk. He had a kindly manner about him and indicated to me to sit down upon the chair which faced his table. Much later in life when watching Dad's Army on television, the smooth infectious charm of actor John le Messurier reminded me of this man in so many ways: it was easy to see why he was in recruitment and not in training.

"Now then, lad," he said in a soft north of England accent, adjusting the crisp blank form which lay in front of him, "what's your name?"

"Trevor John Bowyer," I said and for a moment I was that fourteen-year-old boy again, standing in front of Mr Stamp in the Shrewsbury GPO.

"What's your address, Trevor?" he asked, still writing my name. I told him. "You're a bit older than most of t'lads that come in 'ere; how old are you?"

"I'm twenty-six."

"Got your birth certificate?"

"Yes, here."

"Occupation?"

"I'm a sorter with the GPO. I work on the Travelling Post Office," I told him with pride.

"Try and call me Flight Sergeant, Trevor. You'll need to get used to it where you're going."

He smiled at me with that genial smile that older people have when they know what awaits the young, as it waited for them too, and then added, "That's an unusual job. I don't think I have had anyone else from the Travelling Post Office."

"Probably not, Flight Sergeant, it's not that easy to get into."

"Nor is the RAF, lad," he rejoined. I felt suitably rebuffed.

The faint glimmer of a smile creased the corners of his eyes and we carried on through the formalities. Finally he turned the form over and looked straight at me, "Which part of the RAF are you volunteering for, Trevor?" he asked.

"Ideally I would like to be a pilot, but I don't mind just so long as I can be part of a bomber crew."

He handed me a slip of paper with a number on it. "Good lad. Wait over there until the doctor calls your number, then go through the door at the end of the hall."

"Yes, Flight Sergeant. Thank you."

As the minutes ticked by I was gradually joined by three

other young men, each one holding a ticket with a number on it. It wasn't an automatic progression; war or no war selection for aircrew was a demanding and rigorous process. The Flight Sergeant was the first stage in a sifting process which went on for weeks and saw many lads being considered unsuitable for aircrew for a variety of reasons – although air sickness was not one of them. If it had been there would have been precious few aircrew, since most of us suffered from it at some time or other.

After about forty minutes the four of us were called in to the second stage of the sifting process, the doctor. I was not at all worried because I had to have an annual medical in order to stay on the TPO and I knew that I was physically very fit, as was duly confirmed by the doctor. The medical was the usual fairly cursory examination for enlistment during wartime: he listened to my heart and lungs, told me to take deep breathes, cough, drop my trousers, cough again, pull up my trousers, sit down, cross my legs, then he tapped my knees with a rubber hammer for reflexes and turned over the form which the Flight Sergeant had meticulously filled in with his careful handwriting.

"Oh, you're volunteering for aircrew. Wait a moment."

The other three lads were each given a green slip of paper and told to hand it back to the Flight Sergeant on their way out.

"Right, let's see what your eyesight is like." It was clearly a rhetorical remark which was addressed to anyone who happened to be in the room at the time, rather than to me in particular, and there followed a fairly rigorous eye test at the end of which he told me that I had excellent eyesight, gave me a pink slip and directed me back to the Flight Sergeant.

I handed the slip over to the veteran behind the desk.

"Well done, Trevor, you're on your way. You will hear more in a few weeks." Then he smiled and said quietly,

"Good luck, lad."

"Thank you, Flight Sergeant."

The church hall in Merlin Street stood next to the little school which served the area and as I walked out of the hall and stood on the footpath for a few moments, I had time to take in the scale of the destruction, damage and debris inflicted upon us by the previous night's bombing raids. Fires were still burning in what was left of the houses opposite the school: smoke and a strangely acrid smell seemed to fill the morning air. London has never smelt sweet, but this was different, a toxic combination which I later came to recognise as the smell of death. In that moment a warm feeling of satisfaction washed over me as I realised that, God willing, I was going to be part of a bomber crew and get my chance to take the fight back to the Germans.

Vickers Wellington bomber

CHAPTER SIX

"Never in the field of human conflict was so much owed by so many to so few. All our hearts go out to the fighter pilots whose brilliant actions we see with our own eyes day after day. I hope, indeed I pray, that we shall not be found unworthy of our victory if after toil and tribulation it is granted to us. For the rest we have to gain victory. That is our task."
Winston Churchill, 20th August 1940.

The 15th September was the day when Fighter Command inflicted unprecedented losses upon the Luftwaffe in the skies over south-east England. It was the day which settled the outcome of the Battle of Britain. The Royal Air Force had won the contest and the threat of immediate invasion was removed, although we were very far from being safe: Britain and the empire still stood alone.

Bomber Command had made a number of successful raids upon the barges and support vessels tied up in the Channel ports along the French coast, but inevitably at a terrible cost in the lives of the young men who carried them out. Nevertheless, the loss of significant numbers of vessels, and Fighter Command's superiority in the air combined with the approaching autumn and a break in the good weather, doomed the German invasion plan.

Hermann Goering was furious that his numerically superior Luftwaffe had been unable to break the RAF and take control of the skies over the English Channel. Without this victory, he had to report to Hitler that he could not guarantee the safety of the invasion fleet as it crossed the Channel. Operation Sea Lion was postponed and ultimately cancelled.

The daytime raids over London decreased significantly from the 15th onwards, although the night time was an altogether different story, and the next few weeks were a difficult and frustrating time for me as I waited for my call-up. At around the same time that I applied to the

RAF, Lydia resigned from her job as a secretary in the offices of WS Jamieson in Northumberland Avenue, just off Trafalgar Square, and joined the WAAFs at the end of October. I think we both knew when we went dancing in the West End the night before she left to start her training, that it would be our last date. Neither of us mentioned anything about it until we started to walk home but it had hung in the air between us all evening, not spoiling our enjoyment, simply being there waiting to be addressed.

"I will write to you, you know, Trevor, and tell you how I'm getting along."
"I don't suppose you will have time. You know what they say about training being all work and no play," I joked.
"I wonder where I shall get posted to."
"Well, wherever it is, I hope you enjoy it and that you keep safe."
"Thank you, Trevor. I hope that your application comes through soon. You never know, we might even end up on the same station. That would be fun."
"It certainly would, but the entertainment opportunities will be very different from London, of that I am sure."

We laughed quietly. At the top of Tottenham Court Road we turned down Euston Road and could see the sky towards the east lit up with dozens of fires, the deadly crump, crump of the exploding bombs drifting towards us on the wind.

"It looks like the East End and the docks again tonight," I said as we each pulled our coats tighter around our necks against the cold blast of chill air which rushed at us between the buildings.

We had deliberately walked home the long way, but when we eventually stood outside Lydia's house she turned and smiled at me in the same captivating way which had attracted me to her the first time that we had met the previous April standing in the rain outside the church hall waiting for the dance to start. "Thank you for a wonderful evening, Trevor. I have had a lovely time: tonight and over the last few months." In the light of the orange glow

101

from the sky, I could see that she was crying. I held her closely and whispered, "Me too, Lydia."

We kissed goodnight, tenderly and slowly, both thinking about our happier evenings together. Eventually we stopped, knowing that this time she had to go inside on her own. Tomorrow she would leave London to start her training in the WAAFs.

"Good luck, Lydia and don't forget to write."
"I won't, and thank you for everything."

I watched her go up the steps and in through the front door of the little terraced house. I never did see Lydia again and she must have forgotten to write after all; but that's war. I've often thought about her over the years and wondered what became of her, and what might have been. I hope that she made out all right.

On Monday 4th November I received my call to report to the Air Crew Recruiting Centre in St John's Wood. There would be a selection board interview to assess my suitability as a pilot, followed by a most stringent medical. Two days later, having been granted leave of absence from the previous night's TPO run to Carlisle, and dressed in my best suit, I presented myself to the reception at the Recruiting Centre and then went through to the waiting room; it was full of other hopeful young men, all of them clearly four or five years my junior. After what seemed an eternity in the waiting room we were all called through to a much larger room where an examination awaited us. There were several papers each covering separate topics and each was strictly timed; English, mathematics, geography and general knowledge I particularly recall.

I managed very well in the geography as my time on the TPO stood me in good stead, whilst I had always been quite good at English in school and general knowledge was taught in those days as a separate school subject, but the mathematics paper was much harder than I had anticipated and as it had been twelve years since I had left school, I definitely felt somewhat rusty. I was more than a little apprehensive as I handed my papers in to the presiding officer and went outside for some fresh air. Nevertheless, I passed all the papers: it was all or nothing then and failure meant only one thing, rejection. The next stage was the interview by three First World War officer pilots. They asked me many questions including why I had volunteered for the RAF and particularly why I wanted to join Bomber Command as aircrew.

The Group Captain, sitting in the centre of the three officers, then went on to explain to me what the odds were against my survival: they were not great. If I survived my training, I was more than likely to be shot down within my first ten missions. One ray of hope was that the more missions I returned from, the greater my chances of survival: until the last few. The losses in Bomber Command were very high at this stage of the war and they continued to worsen for some years to come. Indeed, during the course of the war, Bomber Command lost more aircrew as a percentage of total personnel than any other part of the entire Allied Armed Services. By the end of hostilities over 55,000 aircrew had been killed.

I remember replying to the Group Captain, "If any of us sat down and thought too much about the odds of survival, we would not go to war at all. I want to join the RAF and do what I can whilst we still have a country to call our own, sir."

I was sure that my age would probably help me but I think that reply must have swung it because I was recommended for pilot training [RAF authorisation number 13 ACSBF 2171, 27.11.40], handed another slip of pink paper and told to report to the office across the corridor. Clutching my precious slip, I knocked on the door and entered upon the command. The LAC WAAF clerk who greeted me took the pink slip from my hand and read it, which was more than I had done.

"I see that you are recommended for pilot training and that you are to start straight away."
"Am I?" was all I could say.

"Well, not this afternoon." She smiled pleasantly and added, "Wait a moment please, and I'll prepare your travel warrant. You are to report to RAF Cardington in Bedfordshire on Saturday. That is the day your service will commence, and then you will go on to Bridgnorth in Shropshire. Do you know where Bridgnorth is?" she asked conversationally as she busily typed my travel warrant.

"I do, actually. It's about twenty miles from my home town of Shrewsbury. It's a pretty little town. It has an old stone bridge over the River Severn, you know."

"Yes, I suppose it would have, with a name like Bridgnorth." She smiled mischievously and handed me the warrant. "Good luck with your training."

"Thank you very much. Goodbye," I replied.

"Goodbye."

Nice girl, I thought. Everyone in the RAF seemed so pleasant and civilised. I was soon to find out that such a description did not apply to the training corporals and sergeants at RAF Cardington, Bridgnorth, or anywhere else for that matter.

I went straight to Euston Station to see Egbert Ramsbottom and told him that I was now at His Majesty's command and that I was on my way.

"We shall miss you, Trevor," he said. "You've been a good member of the TPO team and I know that you will fit in well with your new comrades. When all this lot is over I hope that you will come back to us. There will still be a job for you. Good luck, Trevor, and God go with you." He shook my hand and told me to go up to the pay office where my outstanding wages had already been put up for me.

That evening, after I had had my tea, I returned to Euston Station to say goodbye to my TPO colleagues before the train pulled out for Carlisle Citadel Station, this time without me on board. I had been with the team for four of the best years of my life; it had been a wonderful time. We were a close bunch and had endured unsociable hours, heat, cold, hard work but most of all, a sense of belonging and looking out for each other; all the facets and assets which I would experience as part of an operational crew in Bomber Command.

As the hands of the grand clock in the station moved towards ten to nine, the LMS engine *Duchess of Sutherland*, leaving two hours early to allow for delays, was steamed up and ready to go. In her wartime dress with covered lights and matt paint she was still a wonderful sight. Designed by Sir William Stanier, no-one quite knew just how fast the Duchess of Sutherland would really go, because they simply could not shovel the coal in quickly enough. I stood on the platform as the superintendent blew his whistle, and with an enormous gush of steam and smoke the great driving wheels started to slowly turn. Harry, the driver that night, leaned out of the cab, waved, called goodbye and gave me a short blast on the Duchess's whistle. I felt a real sense of loss and sadness as I stood there. I knew that whatever happened to me in this war, my golden TPO days were over. Suddenly 1936 seemed a long time ago, in a different age and I wished I was back there again.

I watched the train pull out of the station and over the jumble of points as the engine searched for the set of rails which would take it up the west-coast route and ultimately to Glasgow by dawn the next morning. When I could no longer see the last carriage, I slowly turned and walked back down the platform towards that dramatic archway and out onto Euston Road.

I was in no great rush to go back to Granville Square and pack up my case for the next day, so I called into the Green Man in Percy Circus off King's Cross Road for a few beers. It was a really good night, but inevitably it was brought to a fairly sudden end by the sound of the air-raid sirens. In due course the all-clear was sounded and I stumbled back home and fell into bed.

Over the past few months I had rather naturally spent most of my off-duty days with Lydia, and as a result it had been some time since I had been home to see Mum and Dad. So I thought that it would be an ideal opportunity to stay with them for a couple of days before travelling to Cardington to start my initial training. Travel on the railways at this time was very uncertain as delays were caused by all sorts of things. Domestic civilian travel was at the bottom of the priority list for use of the lines and it took nearly eight hours to travel from Euston to Shrewsbury.

Mum and Dad were really pleased to see me, although Mum was understandably worried about her only son now that the moment of my going into the RAF had come. On Friday morning I went round to Eric Chaffner's house to see what had become of my school and Post Office friend. The door was answered by Dorothy, one of Eric's sisters and I went inside. Mrs Chaffner was out working but Dorothy told me that Eric had joined the Army when the war came and had gone across to France with the BEF. He had been wounded and captured by the Germans just before the Dunkirk withdrawal. At least he was alive; I don't know what Mrs Chaffner would have done if she had lost Eric as well as her husband. After the war when I returned to Shrewsbury, I caught up with Eric and he told me about the terrible time that he had had as a prisoner of war: they were still fighting the Germans, just in a different way. It is often forgotten that these prison camps tied up thousands of German troops who would otherwise have been released for front-line duty.

There was another war going at this time too, it was the war for our very survival in commodities, from sugar to petrol, in the raw materials for machinery and munitions, and it was being fought by the men of the Merchant Navy Service every day out on the cold empty expanses of the Atlantic Ocean. I suppose that living in London, I hadn't altogether appreciated how hard things were becoming. The TPO was a priority service and we were somewhat wrapped up in it: I hadn't realised how hard it had become for Mum and Dad. Everything that we did not grow, mine or produce from our own raw materials had to be brought in by ships sailing across seas which were patrolled by

U-boats. Violent disaster awaited them throughout every treacherous mile of their journeys into and out of our ports.

Blake Turner, Second Radio Officer, SS Calabria *outside Aston House Farm [Turner family collection]*

At the start of the war, many young men joined the Merchant Navy to help to keep Britain's lifeline open: Blake Turner was one of them. Born onto the family farm at Aston near Wellington, Blake was the eldest of the three Turner boys. Unusually for the 1930s, he owned a car which he had bought with a little windfall money which had come his way. He was very fond of that car, but nevertheless, when the war came in 1939, he and his brother Dick volunteered for active service. He put his car into one of the farm buildings, threw an old blanket over it to keep it clean until his return and closed the heavy barn door, without knowing that he would never see that little sports car again.

Blake had always wanted to go to sea and so joined the Merchant Navy as a Radio Officer, and November 1940 found him in Freetown, on the west coast of Africa. It was here one night, when chatting to a pal, that he learnt that there was a vacancy for a Radio Officer on the SS *Calabria* which was bound for Glasgow in the next few days. If he joined the ship, he would be home for Christmas and able to share a few precious days with his family. A couple of days before that ill-fated conversation, Blake had been fairly sure that wherever he was for Christmas it wouldn't be in Aston, and so he decided to send his parents a present from Sierra Leone. Knowing that luxuries were in short supply in Britain, he bought them a box of glacé fruits and posted it off to Aston House Farm.

Two days later, with thoughts of being home in Shropshire for Christmas and enjoying a family reunion around the dinner table tumbling through his head, Blake cheerfully joined the SS *Calabria* as Second Radio Officer and set sail for Britain on Tuesday, 19th November, part of convoy SLS-56.

Many of the ships in that convoy were also heading home, as they had been built in the Glasgow shipyards, which at that time lined the banks of the River Clyde. Yards which had a proud history and had built so many of the famous ships of the day including the *Queen Mary* and, probably the most famous British warship of modern times, HMS *Hood*, both ships having been built by John Brown & Company Ltd. HMS *Hood* had been launched on the afternoon of Thursday, 22nd August 1918, by The Honourable Lady Hood, whose husband Sir Horace had been killed at the Battle of Jutland just two years earlier.

The *Calabria*, a single-funnelled, coal-fired former passenger ship, flying convoy pennant number 42, had taken her place in the three lines of ships which made up SLS-56 as they slowly steamed out of Freetown Bay. She had been built by AG Weser in Bremen in 1922, for the German Norddeutscher Lloyd Company's Far East service and named the SS *Werra*. Ironically, this was the same yard which in 1939 built the U-boat that was to sink her. In 1935 she had been sold to the Italia Line for its East Africa and Asia service, and was renamed SS *Calabria*. On 10th June 1940, she was in dry dock in Calcutta, where she was seized by the British authorities and transferred to the British India Steam Navigation Company. She was due to be renamed the SS *Empire Inventor* when she reached Britain.

SLS-56 was a slow-moving convoy of twenty heavily laden ships which were joined two days later by forty-two faster-moving vessels, including their single escort vessel, HMS *Bulolo*. Their route would take them up the west coast of Africa, past Gibraltar and the entrance to the Mediterranean, keeping wide of the Bay of Biscay and the German U-boat bases there, and then up the west coast of Ireland where the ships would make for their respective destinations of Belfast, Liverpool and Glasgow.

As he watched Freetown and the coastline of West Africa slip away behind him in the tropical heat of that late afternoon, Blake's anticipation of soon being home was tempered by the knowledge of just how dangerous this voyage was going to be. A few weeks earlier, on 7th September 1940, as the Battle of Britain was reaching its climax in the skies over southern England, the Battle of the Atlantic was just beginning.

It was on that day that the German U-boats had started hunting in packs when four submarines, including U-47 commanded by the German hero Gunther Prien, who a year earlier had penetrated the defences at Scapa Flow in the Orkney Islands and sunk the battleship HMS *Royal Oak*, had attacked convoy SC-2. Blake knew that their convoy was going to be crossing the U-boat lanes, in and out of their bases at Brest, Lorient, La Pallice, St Nazaire and Bordeaux. The fall of France in the summer of 1940 had serious and often disastrous consequences for the men of the Merchant Navy Service.

As the convoy headed north away from the tropics and the heat of the sun, the weather worsened and on the morning of the 5th December the ships ran into an Atlantic winter storm which was to last for six days. Blake looked through the porthole of the radio cabin where he had been on duty since four in the morning.

Sunday, 8ᵗʰ December dawned grey and dismal. It was difficult for the lookouts to decide where the sky met the sea: there was not even a watery sun trying to break through the clouds to give them a clue.

The *Calabria* had a crew of 150 officers and men, and in addition, on this trip carried a gunner, 230 Indian seamen, who were to be crews for other ships, and 411 Lascar seamen. With an original passenger capacity for 154 people and weighing 9,515 tons, conditions on board were cramped and uncomfortable from the start and made worse by the storm. Most of the fixtures and fittings from the ship's passenger service days had been stripped out by the Italians, who had latterly used her as a troop ship: but this was wartime not cruise time and there was no room for anything but the barest essentials.

The bad weather had brought other problems with it too. The *Calabria* was heavily laden with 4,000 tons of iron, 3,050 tons of tea and 1,870 tons of oilcake and with her engines labouring under the combined strain of cargo and weather, she began to fall behind the main body of the convoy, making her an easy target for a U-boat, and U-103 had already found the convoy and was shadowing the stragglers.

The torpedo struck the *Calabria* at two minutes to nine on that cold, soulless night when she was 295 miles west of the Irish mainland at Slyne Head. The explosion ripped a great hole in her side and the icy waters of the north Atlantic rushed in, engulfing the Lascar and Indian seamen on the lower decks.

In the confusion of the dark, the storm and the already listing ship beneath him, Blake did what he was trained to do; he sent out his last vital message: that message, which pinpointed their position, saved the lives of twenty-one sailors, but he was not to be one of them. The heavily laden ship had little chance of staying afloat for long as 4,000 tons of iron in her cargo hold pulled her down: the *Calabria* took her crew with her.

Three days later, on 11ᵗʰ December, Hitler awarded the U-boat captain Victor Schutze, the Knight's Cross. He was to go on to sink thirty-five ships, totalling over 180,000 tons.

A few days later in Aston, the postman reluctantly pushed his bicycle across the farmyard, the telegram in his hand, dreading the task that lay before him. "I'm so sorry, Mrs Turner," was all he could say. Blake's mother took the brown envelope from him with trembling hands; which of her two sons would it be? The weak winter sun offered her no warmth as she watched the retreating postman, without really seeing him. The envelope remained unopened on the table until her husband came in from the farm.

It was three days later when the postman once more cycled into the yard of Aston House Farm. This time, amongst the letters there was a parcel wrapped in brown paper and tied with string: the address was hand written and it had been posted in Sierra Leone. Blake's Christmas present, sent with love and youthful cheer, broke his mother's heart.

It was the quiet bravery and determination not to be beaten of the men of the Merchant Navy Service, like Blake Turner which kept Britain supplied with food and materials through the dark days of the Battle of the Atlantic. When put into the context of the sacrifice made by these sailors, it is easy to see why theft of or malicious damage to such war materials carried the death penalty under the Defence Regulations. The Battle of the Atlantic, like Bomber Command's battle over Europe, lasted for the entire duration of the war.

On St Andrew's Day, the 30ᵗʰ November 1940 I said goodbye to Mum and Dad and walked into town to catch the train to Cardington. Shrewsbury was a much busier railway junction in those days than it is today and the station was bustling with passengers and trains going to just about every part of the country. Most of the people on the platforms were in a uniform of one colour or another and I began to feel a little self-conscious that I was not, but that would change before the weekend was out.

There was a lot of noise in the station, with whistles blowing, guards shouting along the platforms and the powerful steam engines just arriving or just leaving with great clouds of smoke pouring from their chimney stacks and jets of steam hissing out of the piston valves. After about ten minutes two lads, who must have been no more than eighteen or nineteen, came and stood next to me.

"Are you going to RAF Cardington?" asked one of them, looking at my battered old suitcase.
"I am, yes," I replied. "You both too?"
"Yes. Do you mind if we travel along with you, please?"
"Not at all, I shall be glad of the company." Dear God, they looked so young to be going to war, it made me feel old. When I eventually became part of a bomber crew I was one of the oldest on the squadron: I was to find out that twenty-eight was old for aircrew.

We chatted for a few more minutes and then our train came in. It was a bit of a scramble to get a compartment with three seats, but having each put our cases up onto the rack, I decided to hang out of the window for no particular reason other than to watch us pull out of the station. In that moment I saw the strain etched across the faces of so many people who had come to wave goodbye to their loved ones on this and other trains. A whistle blew from somewhere along the platform and with a deafening crescendo of steam and smoke seemingly pouring forth from every part of the engine we began to move slowly out of the station. As the smoke and soot filled the air, it settled on the waving crowd; the silent tears of mothers, sisters and girlfriends leaving pink watery tracks through the film of coal dust on their cheeks.

A few hours later we arrived at Cardington railway station and were hustled into a waiting 15cwt truck to be taken to the camp to start our initial training. The next day we were all issued with our uniforms and kit and then sworn in: I was Aircraftman 2nd class [AC2], number 1382405

Trevor John Bowyer in His Majesty's Royal Air Force, feeling anything other than a trainee pilot. I suppose the memory of Cardington which stays with me the most is that we were accommodated not in huts but in Bell tents, which was a bit of a shock to the system since we were going into the winter.

However, for me there was a little ray of sunshine in my training because within the first week, together with the two lads I had met at Shrewsbury railway station, I was sent from Cardington to do the rest my initial training at RAF Bridgnorth, just as the WAAF orderly had promised. Initial training is never fun, but at least it was close to home.

Our travel warrants sent us back up the line we had travelled a few days earlier to Shrewsbury, where we caught a connection to Bridgnorth. It was something that you could do in those days following the valley of the River Severn to Cressage and Buildwas where you would change trains in the split level station for Much Wenlock, the home of the modern Olympic Games thanks to Dr William Penny Brookes, not Pierre de Coubertin as is so often quoted, especially by the International Olympic Movement.

By the time we arrived at Bridgnorth station it was pitch dark in the blackout and the three of us slowly stepped down from the chocolate-and-cream coloured coach of the local mixed-traffic GWR train into the swirling steam from the little tank engine. We stood silently together on the platform for a few moments trying to let our eyes get accustomed to the darkness on that cold and foggy December night. Two short blasts on a whistle split the air and the train casually chuffed its way out of the station, southwards down the Severn valley towards Kidderminster. The remnants of the steam gently drifted away to become part of the fog around us, leaving us to peer into the blackness. Each carrying our suitcases, we walked towards the gateway and, showing our travel warrants to the elderly ticket collector, asked the way to the camp.

He examined the warrants in the dim light of his covered torch and then without answering us he carefully removed his spectacles, pulled a clean handkerchief from his trouser pocket and knowingly began to slowly polish them, with an air of deliberate expectancy: our answer was not long coming.

"What the 'ell are you lot waiting for? Get over 'ere at the double," came a voice out of the darkness.

The ticket collector gave us a thin smile and, with a hint of resignation and pity in his voice, said, "The camp's that way," and jerked his head towards the formless voice from the darkened station forecourt.

We walked through the gateway, past our kindly informant and clambered into the 15cwt truck. We were very lucky to have a lift up to the camp; normally recruits arrived on troop trains and were then marched the two miles from the station, through Low Town, over the bridge, up the Hermitage Bank and along the Stanmore Road to the camp.

We bounced and rocked along the narrow road to the bridge and then on up the hill to the camp. At the guardroom, we jumped down from the back of the truck and were officially booked in by the duty sergeant. Our chauffeur had disappeared and was replaced by a much older and no doubt wiser man, who wore the medal ribbons of the Great War and introduced himself as Corporal Entringham. He called us to attention and explained that he would be our training instructor for most things during our six weeks at Stanmore. He informed us that the NAAFI was open and that we would be billeted in hut 29. He briefly explained the way to go and then dismissed us.

The training there was the same as in all recruit centres, but one big improvement was that we lived in wooden huts instead of tents. Having been kitted out at Cardington we now learnt how to march, square bashing as it was universally known, how to salute, how to recognise the RAF rank insignia, especially that of senior NCOs and officers, how to keep the hut clean and tidy, how to make up our beds each day, how to enjoy cross-country runs and football to get fit, and so on and so forth. For the most part it was tedious but essential and simply had to be done and got through before moving on. Since Christmas and the New Year fell in the time that I was at Bridgnorth we had a decent Christmas lunch in the mess hall and a good time in the NAAFI on New Year's Eve, but otherwise the routine remained the same.

Towards the end of our training we did get a couple of twenty-four-hour passes. For most of the lads it was not long enough for them to get to their homes, but for me it was fairly easy to walk the two miles to the other side of Bridgnorth and hitchhike a lift on the A458 road to Shrewsbury. Getting a lift, especially when wearing a uniform, was never a problem in those days, usually in a lorry as there were not nearly so many cars on the roads as there are now.

Bridgnorth is a very old bridging settlement along the River Severn and the town has two parts, High Town and Low Town. High Town is the original fortified area built onto the Old Red Sandstone buttress which stands above the river. Low Town is the area around the bridge and the old quayside built in the days when the river was navigable from Bristol to Shrewsbury. Charles II said that the view across the valley from the Castle Walk was amongst the finest in his kingdom, which, although a wholly justified observation, was a little ironic since his father's argument with Oliver Cromwell all but caused its destruction along with the castle during the civil war. Cromwell's men built an earth rampart just outside the town for their guns to stand upon and from which to bombard the castle. The rampart remains today and is known locally as Pam Pudding Hill. Fortunately the Northgate and many of the medieval buildings survived the civil war and are still there to this day.

RAF Station Bridgnorth was built about a mile to the east outside the town at Stanmore. RAF Stanmore Park already existed in Middlesex and so this station was officially known as RAF Bridgnorth No.4 Recruit Centre, although referred to as Stanmore by locals and recruits alike. It opened on 6th January 1939 and remained a training camp until it closed on 8th February 1963. A few weeks after I had finished my training there, Princess Elizabeth visited the station and then in April that year it became No.1 Women's Auxiliary Air Force Depot, training WAAF recruits until September 1942 when it reverted to training men.

Surprise hut inspections were always a threat to any rest period in the day and anyone who caused the hut to fail also caused the whole hut to be put on fatigues, known as jankers. In the end we decided that every hut in the camp sooner or later failed an inspection, irrespective of how hard we all tried to keep them spick and span, so that all the dirty and tiresome jobs around the place could be counted upon to be done.

My training period was unremarkable and the same as the training for thousands of other recruits during the war. I have no particular memories of Stanmore; it was simply something that had to be got through.

One remarkable story that does attach to the Stanmore camp happened several years after the war when it was used for training National Servicemen, and was told to me by one of the people involved. A few years ago I fell into conversation with a fellow patient at the Royal Shrewsbury Hospital. He was a priest and lived in a small Shropshire village in the south of the county. It soon became clear that we both knew the local bobby who still lived in the village even though he had long since retired.

"What a coincidence," I said.
He smiled and replied, "Let me tell you about coincidence."
This was his story.

He had been born in Shropshire in 1936 and the Second World War had dominated his childhood. His father was in the Royal Artillery and had gone off to war as part of the BEF in the spring of 1940. However, by 1955 and

116

long before joining the priesthood, he was old enough for National Service and was called up into the RAF. He was stationed at RAF Bridgnorth where, during his two years' service, he developed a friendship with the camp's handyman, a German former prisoner of war called Klaus.

Klaus had been an ordinary soldier, had been captured by the British shortly after the D-Day invasion and had finished the war as a POW. He had remained in Britain after the war, married a local girl and secured the handyman job at the camp. It seemed that Klaus had had a fairly ordinary upbringing in Germany, had been drafted into the Army in early 1938 and had been part of the German Blitzkrieg across Western Europe in 1939, culminating in the capture of Dunkirk following the British evacuation.

As their friendship developed, Klaus related more and more of his wartime experiences and my companion, in his turn, recounted those stories which his own father had told him. On one particular winter's evening, as they sat chatting in the warmth of the camp's boiler house, sheltered from the cold wind outside and enjoying a mug of tea, Klaus was particularly anxious to talk about the days his Division moved into Dunkirk, even as the British Army was being plucked from the beaches by the armada of boats which had come across the Channel to save them.

My companion explained to Klaus that his own father had been taken prisoner at Dunkirk and that he had not seen him again until late 1945. As they talked and compared details, it was obvious that his father and Klaus had been enemies at the same place at the same time. They had fought in the very same streets of the town and had inevitably tried to kill each other.

After some reflection, Klaus suddenly said, "I know your mother's name and the day she and your father were married." My companion had sat astounded as Klaus recited the details and then said, "Wait." He went to his jacket which was hanging on its usual nail behind the boiler house door and, looking very embarrassed, handed to the young National Serviceman a silver cigarette case, saying, "Go on, open it." He did so, and for the first time he read the loving words which his mother had had engraved inside the case for her husband on their wedding day in 1934.

Klaus was overcome that the man he had taken prisoner all those years earlier and whose son had befriended him, now lived just a few miles away. He asked my companion to return the cigarette case to his father and to ask forgiveness for having taken it from him on that violent day in the streets of Dunkirk in May 1940.

In due course the two former enemies met, shook hands and embraced. They had both killed to avoid being killed; they had both thought they were fighting with God on their side and they had both survived the prison camp. They became, and remained, close friends until their deaths a few years ago.

RAF Bridgnorth memorial

CHAPTER SEVEN

"The whole fury and might of the enemy must very soon be turned on us. Hitler knows that he will have to break us in this island or lose the war."
Winston Churchill, 18th June 1940.

After completing my initial training at Bridgnorth, I had a week's leave before my next posting. I spent the weekend with my parents in Shrewsbury and then used my travel warrant to go down to London and have the rest of the week with my friends, staying once more with my aunt and uncle at Granville Square, which I had given as my home address when I volunteered. On the morning of Friday, 24th January 1941 I set out from St Pancras Station on my way to RAF Station Cranwell, the Royal Air Force College, to begin my training as a pilot.

RAF Cranwell was commissioned on 1st April 1916 as the training establishment for the Royal Naval Air Service. Two years later to the day it passed to the Royal Air Force and on 5th February 1920 it became the first Military Air Academy in the world, under the command of Air Commodore CAH Longcroft. It is said that the site for Cranwell was chosen by sending a young RNAS pilot to fly around Lincolnshire until he saw a suitable site which was large enough and flat enough for a training airfield. He must have been spoilt for choice because Lincolnshire is not known as Bomber County for nothing: during the war aerodromes were located every few miles across the county and even today it has more operational airfields than any other county in Britain.

Originally a collection of wooden huts built in the Lincolnshire countryside, the present stone buildings in the style of Sir Christopher Wren were completed in September 1933 at a cost of £321,000.

My pilot training continued happily enough and after the theory work in the classroom we got the chance to start flying those early bi-planes that I had seen doing

119

aerobatics over our house in Shrewsbury all those years ago. I had great fun and really enjoyed what I was doing although the work was very hard. It was not just the physical effort of learning to fly which was hard, but the evening 'homework' and preparation which we had to do.

The Tiger Moth is a wonderfully forgiving aircraft, which is why it was used to start pilots off at the very beginning, unlike the Harvard which had a terrible reputation and killed many experienced pilots, never mind countless trainees. Sitting in the front of the vibrating Tiger Moth, I listened to my instructor telling me about the take-off procedure again; we had been through it a dozen times in the classroom, but it seemed so different now, sitting here in the cockpit.

I did learn to fly, just, but I was not destined to be a pilot and did not gain my Flying Badge, my wings. It was with no little disappointment that I was told that my eyesight, although generally very good, was not sufficiently so to be a pilot. I was slightly colour blind. Nevertheless, I was at least passed fit for other aircrew duties and so could remain in the RAF. I had no desire to be a navigator, wireless operator, bomb aimer or flight engineer and left Cranwell destined to be an air gunner even though I had never owned or fired a gun in my life before, nor for that matter did I ever do so again after the war.

I was subsequently posted to various training establishments during 1941, including Blackpool, where the opportunities for a good social life in our off-duty hours were certainly better than at Cranwell, until on the 11th October I arrived at No.8 Air Gunnery School, RAF Evanton on the banks of the Cromarty Firth in the north-east of Scotland, near to Invergordon. Two days later I was promoted to the rank of Leading Aircraftsman.

At AGS we learned how to shoot, first on the ground and then in the air. We also learned how the .303 machine gun worked, all four of them. We had to take them apart and then put them back together again. We did this over and over again until we had it down to a fine art, and when we had mastered that little trick, we had to do it blindfolded so that we could find, diagnose and fix a stoppage at night under pressure, should the guns jam whilst we were being attacked. It wasn't just the guns that we had to master, though, but the control and hydraulics of the Fraser Nash turret with its sighting, deflection and so on. It was a fairly complex piece of equipment and as the Gunnery Leader reminded us time and time again, just because we were not the pilot, it did not mean that we did not hold the fate of the aircraft in our hands every time we met the enemy.

At last, on the 30th October we started to fly and just before Christmas I qualified as an air gunner and was promoted to Sergeant. We used Botha and Whitley aircraft which had a mid-upper turret and we would fire at drogues which were pulled across the sky by a variety of aircraft including the Fairey Battle, which by this time had been recognised by senior officers and the Air Ministry alike as being wholly unsuitable for combat service, although as a training aircraft it was good enough. However, the pilots of these aircraft were very definitely at high risk every time they took off because we were firing at the drogues with live ammunition and near misses on the towing aircraft were not uncommon.

We also had simulated attacks from fighters to train us in both taking evasive action and firing at a fast-moving target. For this purpose, though, we did not use live ammunition and our guns were fitted with an early form of synchronised camera which would record our shooting efforts – it was much safer than giving us live ammunition and allowed us to review our results, or lack of them, afterwards. At the start of this stage of training most of us suffered from dreadful air sickness, made worse by the stench of fuel oil and the failure of the turret's previous occupant to keep his breakfast down. The last unfortunate soul who was still in the turret when we landed had the unenviable task of cleaning it out. However, anyone not up to it, and few of us were, could purchase the services of the ground crew for a few shillings, which was a lot of money, and because early on this was a daily event we pooled our resources. As the course progressed, the air sickness wore off and we were better off at the end of the week.

At nine o'clock on the morning of Thursday, 4th December we took off in a Blackburn Botha for our usual hour-and-a-half shooting practice. We had barely climbed to one thousand feet when the starboard engine spluttered, stuttered and burst into flames. From my position in the mid-upper turret I had an altogether first-class view of a scene which I would rather not have witnessed, especially at such a low height. Our Polish pilot, Sgt Brachmanski, activated the fire extinguisher in the engine and called up the control tower at Tain airfield on the R/T to say we needed to make an emergency landing and that we were on fire. Still in the turret, I could see the airfield getting closer although I could also see that the fire had gone out, the extinguisher having done its job. At the last minute Sgt Brachmanski told us to take up crash landing positions, which for me simply meant sitting on the floor with my back against the main spar and facing the rear, having first removed my helmet and intercom lead before leaving the turret.

I had remained connected to the intercom just long enough to hear the pilot tell us that the undercarriage had failed to lock down and that the landing would be a little bumpy! The aircraft was losing what little height it had very quickly and as I sat on the floor I looked up through the Perspex of the mid-upper turret at a beautifully clear blue sky and wondered whether my war was going to end before it had even begun on this lovely day.

The next thing I heard was a terrible grinding and whooshing sound as Sgt Brachmanski crash-landed the Botha at Tain airfield. The aircraft skidded along the ground with a sickening rending of metal for what seemed an eternity as the fire tenders and ambulance waited for us at the anticipated stop point. As we slowly slewed to a stop, the crew got out faster than we had ever done before as the risk of explosion was very real. Fortunately, because this was to have been a short training flight, we were not carrying a lot of fuel which no doubt helped reduce the risk of fire. I had survived my first crash landing, and although I did not know it then, it was not to be my last.

The whole trip, from take-off to crash-landing, had taken only fifteen minutes. There were no injuries to anyone and at eleven-thirty, after a cup of tea, we were back into another Botha, this time piloted by the Commanding Officer of Evanton, Wing Commander Williams, and flown back to base. Undeterred by the whole incident, at one o'clock that afternoon, Sgt Brachmanski and the rest of us clambered back into this aircraft and proceeded to carry out an hour-and-a-half of gunnery practice: this was no place for the faint hearted.

The course lasted for ten weeks and I had spent 22 hours and 20 minutes training in the air, which actually wasn't very long when faulty guns, failed drogues and a crash landing are all taken into account. At the end of the year, we sat our final examinations. As long as I passed these with good enough marks I would have made aircrew and could move on to operational training, the final stage before going to war.

Christmas 1941 at Tain was a lot more enjoyable than it had been the previous year at Bridgnorth, but because we were in Scotland, New Year was even better. Because we were not an operational station, there was a more relaxed atmosphere for a couple of days and this coincided with some particularly bad weather which caused a cessation in all flying training: probably just as well!

My end-of-course report said that I needed more experience, but that didn't trouble me because I knew that where I was going that would very quickly be remedied; the enemy would see to that. We were all given some leave and once more, because my home address was registered at Granville Square, my travel warrant took me to London, where I spent a few days, before going up to Shrewsbury to see Mum and Dad.

My next posting was to No.21 Operational Training Unit at Moreton-in-Marsh, Gloucestershire, a very pretty Cotswold village where the houses are built of honey-coloured stone with red pantile roofs. I arrived there on 24th February 1942 in a bitterly cold snow storm. The RAF posted its aircrew individually and so once having been issued with my travel warrant, it was up to me to get from where I was to where I needed to be by the appointed time. Needless to say, the combination of wartime disruption on the railways and the bad weather made it a fairly tortuous trip and I was very pleased that I had left plenty of time for the journey.

In the very early days of the war crews were allocated by the RAF but fairly soon it was recognised, as Squadron Leader Tony Iveson said, there is nothing closer than a bomber crew and you depended on each other. The lives of the whole crew rested in the hands of each one of us. If the pilot was not at one with the crew, the aircraft would sooner or later crash; if the navigator was not at one with the crew, the aircraft would sooner or later get lost, run out of fuel and crash; if the air gunner was not at one with the crew, the aircraft would sooner or later get shot down and crash, and so on through the whole crew. Consequently it was vital that all the crew members gelled together; there was little room for big egos in a bomber crew and part of the time at OTU was to give crews time to get to know each other and to learn to work together. Those who could not do so were weeded out at the Operational Training Unit stage. By the time I got to OTU the RAF had settled upon the practice of letting crews find themselves.

On my first morning, I stood on the parade ground with around a hundred other novice aircrew members. There were pilots, observer/navigators, air gunners, and wireless operators. The officer in charge called us all to attention and then told us that we would be training on Wellingtons and that we were to form up into five-man crews made up of a pilot, a second pilot, a navigator, a wireless operator, and a gunner. We were then left alone for the rest of the morning to do so, but rather carelessly at the end of the process we seemed to be short of a main pilot. Inevitably the other crews had plenty to say about this, along the lines that we had already frightened all the pilots away and that no-one would risk their lives flying with us. After a while it became a badge of honour and we maintained that the only reason that we didn't have a pilot was that the RAF hadn't yet found one good enough to fly with us.

The next two weeks were spent familiarising ourselves with the Wellington bomber, or Wimpy as we knew it, its capabilities, range, bomb load, armaments, construction, and so on. The Wellington design team had included Barnes Wallis, who went on to design the Dambusters bouncing bomb and after the war, the world's first swing-wing aircraft. He was a very gifted designer and there were many Wellington crews, me included, who would slip up a prayer of thanks to Barnes Wallis for the brilliance of his geodetic design which gave the aircraft its enormous strength to withstand a frightening degree of battle damage and yet still return home, and of course to the people at Vickers who built them.

At precisely two o'clock on the afternoon of 12th March 1942 I squeezed into the rear turret of Wellington R1242 and began the practical part of my operational training. Our pilot that day was Flight Lieutenant Hamlin, DFC and it was a great comfort to know that we had such an experienced man at the helm as he put us through our paces over the English countryside for the next two hours.

Five weeks later we started night-flying exercises. This was a real test for us all, especially the pilot and the navigator as we took off in the pitch dark to fly to the north of Scotland and then back again. Today this might not seem to be a particularly difficult task, but at the time it certainly was. We were at war and so there were no lights on the ground anywhere to give us a clue as to our position. Even in 1942, navigational equipment was still fairly primitive and we were inexperienced. Happily we all returned safely, but many crews did come to grief. Throughout the war about 15 per cent of Bomber

Command fatalities were as a result of accidents in training; 8,195 airmen lost.

One of the tactics which we practised here was how to evade an attacking fighter. It was a manoeuvre called corkscrewing. It involved the pilot putting the aircraft into a dive to port, then climbing to starboard, then diving to port and climbing to starboard and so on. When looked at from above it had the alignment of a corkscrew, hence its name. The flight of the aircraft through the air in this fashion made it very difficult for a fighter to line it up in the gun sights and it was the most effective tactic an individual bomber could take against attack. A lot of aircrew suffered from air sickness at some time or other, and the corkscrew manoeuvre certainly turned even the strongest stomachs, although later when we had to use it to save our lives in combat, no-one had time to think about being air sick.

By the end of April we had attracted our own pilot and for the most part Sgt Phillips flew us uneventfully through the rest of our training at Moreton-in-Marsh. Well, almost uneventfully.

At the end of May we were right at the top of our training programme at Moreton and ready for our posting to an operational squadron. We became aware of a definite tension in the air. All flying had been cancelled for several days and there was a lot of activity going on around the aircraft. The ground crews had been particularly busy but could only tell us that a thorough overhaul of all aircraft had been ordered and no-one was permitted to leave the base. In the morning of 30th May we were told to air test our Wellington, and then in the afternoon all selected crews were called into the main briefing room where an expectant buzz filled the air. There were rumours that we were to be involved in some sort of operational role and as if to confirm those rumours we had passed RAF policemen at the door to the room.

Our Commanding Officer, Wing Commander Claydon, entered the room and we all stood up. "Sit down please, gentlemen," he said, words that I was to become very familiar with during the next three years. He stood on the small raised staging area from where our instructors usually tried to instil some knowledge of tactics into us. Behind him was a large board which generally held an uncovered map, but this evening the map was hidden behind a large cloth.

The Wing Commander began by telling us that we had done very well in our training and that as a result he was satisfied that we were able to fulfil a vital role that night. With that he removed the cloth from the map and said, "Operation Millennium, gentlemen. Your target for tonight will be Cologne, Germany's third-largest city." The map showed a piece of red tape stretching from our airfield, across the North Sea then dog legging down to Cologne. We were to be attached to Bomber Command and take part in the largest airborne attack that the world had ever seen. It was the first ever thousand-bomber raid. We couldn't believe our ears; what a raid to cut our teeth on.

After the hubbub had died down he explained that this was the idea of our Commander-in-Chief, Air Chief Marshal Arthur Harris and was a demonstration of the size of Britain's bomber fleet. It was also the first test of a new tactic for Bomber Command that would create a bomber stream and allow one thousand bombers to pass over the target area within a ninety-minute period. The tactic was devised to ensure that all the bombers which were aiming for a particular target were heading in the same direction at the same time and following the same course in pre-arranged time and height slots. The idea was to reduce the time that our aircraft would be exposed to the enemy's night fighter and radar boxes along the route, thereby reducing casualties and the risk of collision, which was always a very real and present risk with so many aircraft flying close together in the dark.

Up to this time individual bomber squadrons had tended to make their own way across Europe to the target, thus spreading out the attack period and helping the defending forces by not overstretching them at any given moment.

Even this was an improvement upon the very early days of the war, when individual crews would take off whenever they felt the time was right without any sort of co-ordination. Guy Gibson and his crew often went to the cinema after the briefing and then went on the raid.

In early 1942 the morale and success rate of Bomber Command was probably at its lowest point since the beginning of the war. Less than 10 per cent of bombs were falling within five miles of any notable target and a consistent 5 per cent of all aircraft taking part in the raid were being lost.

The bomber stream tactic began to change all that. With so many aircraft approaching and bombing the target area in such a short space of time, the plan was that the enemy defences would be overwhelmed and with the advances in night fighter technology, it was important not to expose the bombers to these fighters for any longer than was absolutely necessary.

The original target for the operation was to have been Hamburg and in particular the shipbuilding yards which were launching one hundred U-boats each year, but the weather conditions in northern Germany were too poor and so it was Cologne that took the full force of the first one-thousand-bomber raid in history.

In order for Operation Millennium to happen maximum effort was required and every possible squadron had to be ready to fly out, including those second-line aircraft such as our own from training squadrons. In the event 1,047 aircraft from 52 airfields took off that night to attack Cologne.

Each Section Leader went through a briefing for his particular area of responsibility; navigation, wireless operators' signals, bombing, gunnery, meteorology and finally the intelligence reports to let us know the worst about the searchlights, flak and fighters.

At the end of the briefing, the CO summed up, reminding us how important it was to stay with the bomber stream and of the likely consequences of not doing so; we would become fighter fodder. He then read the following message sent to all bomber crews by our Commander in Chief, Arthur Harris:

"The force of which you form a part tonight is at least twice the size and has more than four times the carrying capacity of the largest air force ever before concentrated on one objective. You have an opportunity, therefore, to strike a blow at the enemy which will resound, not only throughout Germany, but throughout the world. In your hands lie the means of destroying a major part of the resources by which the enemy's war effort is maintained. It depends, however, upon each individual crew whether full concentration is achieved.

Press home your attack to your precise objective with the utmost determination and resolution in the foreknowledge that, if you individually succeed, the most shattering and devastating blow will have been delivered against the very vitals of the enemy. Let him have it – right on the chin."

We walked back to our quarters full of expectation and no little trepidation at what lay ahead of us that night. At around nine o'clock, it was time to get ready and we went to the crew room to put on our flying kit. I can still remember how I felt as I slowly dressed, trying to sound confident as we chatted without any conviction. Gradually the talk dwindled away and we finished dressing in silence; we all knew that this was what we had spent all those months training for. We also knew that as novice crews the chances of survival were stacked heavily against us, although we did have some small comfort in the knowledge that our pilot Bob Phillips had been on a raid a few nights earlier without us. He had flown as second dickey [second pilot] with an experienced pilot and crew in order to give him some valuable experience of what to expect. Whilst he had shared this all with us, it was still impossible to imagine the emotions and tension which I was now beginning to feel.

In the event, the operational training crews fared somewhat better on the night than did the regular bomber crews, with 3.3 per cent losses as opposed to 4.1 per cent, and those aircraft with pupil pilots suffered fewer losses than those with instructor pilots. I think that one of the main reasons was simply that the operational training crews largely went in on the third wave, by which time the defences had become progressively overwhelmed with the sheer volume of bombing and the build up of smoke from the fires.

Presently, all kitted up, we left the locker room behind and went outside to the waiting bus which would take the crews to their aircraft at the various dispersal points around the airfield. As each crew struggled out of the bus with parachutes, flasks of hot coffee and escape kit, we all wished each other good luck. Leaving my kit on the ground outside the aircraft, I quickly moved into the Wellington's rear turret and tested the hydraulics, having checked that the bullet channels were full of ammunition. That done I went back outside and as each crew member concluded his checks, he joined me on the grass until we were all there. Our skipper tried to keep us occupied but we were anxious to get on with the job now that the time had come.

My crew and Wellington. I'm on the far right [NB collection]

At last it was time to go. The ground crew fired up the Bristol Hercules engines and I settled into my turret, feeling a little better now that I could concentrate on the take-off, and plugged my intercom lead into my helmet. We joined the line of aircraft slowly moving along the perimeter track towards the take-off point and at ten to eleven that night Wellington DY598, straining at the brakes, was released and started down the runway. I was surprised to see the ground staff standing by the Controller's van and waving us off but was to come to understand that this always happened and was part of the bond between aircrew, ground staff and the aircraft: it was a team effort and this was how they showed us that they were with us too. I waved back and a moment later we were off the ground and climbing into the lighter sky of southern England.

I looked out through the Perspex from the isolation of my rear turret and as the minutes ticked by and we gained height, the light from the west brightened the sky for a few minutes and all I could see around me were hundreds of aeroplanes all flying in the same direction. The sky was black with aircraft: it was a wonderfully reassuring sight for me but would have been terrifying for an enemy to look up and see. However, forty-five minutes later we were very pleased to see the landing lights of the airfield switch on beneath us as our skipper nursed DY598, by now with only one engine running on full power, back down to the ground, complete with our bomb load of incendiaries. I had narrowly missed another crash landing.

Afterwards, we all felt rather cheated and guilty that we had not managed to get across to Germany but at the same time pleased that the engine had packed up over England and not over the target area. We also congratulated our pilot for a great piece of flying and dwelt upon the fact that it had been worth taking all that ribbing at the beginning of our operational training and waiting for a good pilot. We had a quick debrief, a cup of tea and then waited for the returning aircraft. There was no point in going to bed; we had all taken our wakey-wakey pills. We were lucky, albeit disappointed, because we came home that night; forty-one aircraft did not return.

The Avro Manchester was not a bad aircraft, but its twin Rolls Royce Vulture engines were notoriously under-powered and owing to the type's unreliability record it had been kept as a second-line training machine. Indeed, the Manchester's engines were regarded as being so unreliable that not only were more lost to engine failure than to enemy action, but also the general view was that once one engine failed, the aircraft was doomed. However, there is always one which is different and fortunately for Flight Lieutenant 'Kipper' Herring and his crew, L7432 proved to be a cut above the rest when he flew her all the way back from Berlin on one engine. He was awarded an immediate Distinguished Flying Cross [DFC] for an extraordinary example of flying skill.

Not all Manchester crews were so fortunate. Every available aircraft had been scraped together for this raid and that included L7301 'D' Dog, the twenty-eighth Manchester to be built, and which was allocated to Flying Officer Leslie Manser of No.50 Squadron based at Skellingthorpe in Lincolnshire, part of No.5 Group.

Earlier in the day Leslie Manser had gone over to RAF Coningsby with another pilot to collect two Manchesters from No.106 Squadron and fly them to RAF Skellingthorpe ready for the raid that night. Although the rather grubby training aircraft passed its airworthiness test, it had no mid-upper turret and a permanently secured rear escape hatch. In today's language, L7301 was not fit for purpose. The lack of a mid-upper turret left Manser with a spare crew member, that of his wireless operator/air gunner. It was suggested that the aircraft should take two Vickers gas-operated machine guns and in the event of an attack the gunner was to make a hole in the fuselage of the aircraft and fire through it at the enemy. It is hard to believe now but not surprising for the time that this suggestion was actually taken up and so Leslie Manser, an experienced pilot and veteran of thirteen previous missions, took off for Cologne.

By one of those strange coincidences of life, he had taken off from Skellingthorpe at exactly the same time as we had taken off from our own airfield and within a short period of time he too experienced trouble with the aircraft's engines of his Manchester. Having been tested without a bomb load that afternoon, the aircraft had performed well enough, but with a full load of 1,260 4lb incendiaries in fourteen containers, together with enough fuel and ammunition for Cologne and back, L7301's engines just did not have the power to climb to the twelve thousand feet bombing level of the main stream.

This in itself would have justified his decision to turn back to Skellingthorpe had he wished to do so. However, Manser, though having just turned twenty less than three weeks earlier already had a reputation for coolness, competence and skill as the captain of an aircraft and had been promoted to Flying Officer on the 6th May. He decided to carry on and to make his bombing run at seven thousand feet, the maximum height he had been able to reach, much to the concern of his co-pilot, Leslie Baveystock.

He coaxed the labouring Manchester across the North Sea and an hour and a half later they approached Cologne, easily identified from a distance by the intense red glow in the sky from the raging fires which seemed to be consuming the whole city. As the pilot began his bombing run the aircraft was quickly picked out and coned by some ten searchlights and targeted by very heavy flak. Totally focused upon the job in hand and conscious of his aircraft's inadequacies, he did not take evasive action, but held her steady for the bomb aimer, Flying Officer 'Bang On' Barnes, who delivered another direct hit on the target.

As soon as the bombs were gone, Manser turned his aircraft away and almost at once was caught by a direct hit on the bomb bay doors. He dived down to eight hundred feet where he had to fly through a curtain of 20mm cannon fire to gain the relative safety of darkness. L7301 though had taken a number of hits and was full of fire and smoke and the rear gunner, Sgt Naylor had been wounded by shrapnel.

Knowing that things could have been a lot worse, Manser decided that he would try to get his aircraft and crew safely back to England, and so once more nursed the ailing Manchester up to two thousand feet. Soon afterwards, however, the port engine suddenly burst into flames, which spread along the wing and threatened to ignite the main 600 gallon fuel tanks. Having ordered his co-pilot to feather the propeller blades and activate the fire extinguisher, he coolly waited for ten minutes until the flames died away. The composure and quiet determination of this young pilot both astounded and inspired his crew at this critical time.

As the aircraft flew on, it became increasingly difficult to control with only one engine and despite the efforts of Flying Officer Barnes and the second wireless operator Sergeant King to cut away and jettison any surplus equipment to reduce the weight, there was nothing Manser could do to prevent their gradual descent as the remaining starboard engine continued to overheat. He ordered the crew to put on their parachutes and to prepare to bale out. Finally Manser recognised that he would not be able to control his aircraft for much longer and that its end was near. With the Manchester's airspeed now down to 110 knots and dangerously close to stalling, he gave the order to the crew to bale out. Sergeant Mills the front gunner released the forward escape hatch whilst Pilot Officer Horsley helped the injured Naylor to the fuselage door, clipped his parachute on and put the ripcord ring into his hand; he then pushed Naylor out of the doomed aircraft and quickly followed him through the doorway.

Manser knew that if he left the controls to save himself the aircraft would immediately stall and dive straight into the ground, now only a few hundred feet below, killing them all. He continued to battle with the Manchester to keep her level so that his crew could get out and have a chance of survival: thirty seconds would be enough and his whole being was focused on doing that for them. Baveystock went forward to help Manser at the controls and Flying Officer Barnes joined Sergeant Mills at the forward escape hatch through which they both left the aircraft in quick succession.

Baveystock attempted to clip a parachute onto the pilot's chest but Manser pushed him away and shouted his last words to him, "For God's sake get out, we're going down." As L7301 reached the point of stall violently vibrating and bucking, the co-pilot crawled to the front escape hatch, doubled up and dropped through it, not knowing that the Manchester was virtually at tree-top level as he did so. He did not have time to open his parachute before he hit the Belgian countryside, but he was not to die that night and incredibly landed in a dyke containing some five feet of water, which cushioned his fall.

A few seconds later he saw the Manchester crash into the wooded ground a hundred yards beyond the dyke and burst into flames, killing his pilot. Flying Officer Leslie Manser had done everything and more that any crew could have expected or wished for from their captain. With calm and calculated courage he had sacrificed himself so that his crew had a chance for survival. He knew that had he not remained at the controls, his crew would most certainly have died, but he also made a much earlier decision for his crew; by continuing to fly the stricken Manchester long after the point at which he could have got out of it alive he gave his crew the best possible chance of evading capture and returning home to continue the war.

L7301 crashed some three miles east of the Belgian village of Bree, not far from the Dutch border and ended the life of an immensely courageous young man. 'Bang On' Barnes was injured during his parachute descent and two days later was betrayed to the Germans by a Belgian peasant farmer. Baveystock, Horsley, Mills, King and the injured rear gunner Naylor all had better luck and evaded capture as Manser had hoped. They were hidden by the local resistance group and within forty-eight hours were on their way along the 'Comet' escape line to Liege, Brussels, Paris, St Jean de Luz, over the Pyrenees to St Sebastian and into Gibraltar. A week later they were flown back home to England and it was from the information which they all gave at their debriefing that the details and courage of their captain's actions came to light. He was immediately recommended for a posthumous Victoria Cross and on 23rd October 1942 the citation appeared in the London Gazette, as do the citations for all gallantry awards. Leslie Manser was needlessly killed in an aircraft that need not and should not have been sent out at all. He is buried in Haverlee Cemetery, Belgium, close to those other two VC holders, FO Garland and Sgt Gray.

Flying Officer Leslie Thomas Manser, VC [1922–1942], whose brother-in-law, Captain JN Randle was also awarded a posthumous VC in the Far East

On 20th September Flying Officer Barnes and Pilot Officer Horsley each received the DFC and Sergeants Baveystock, Mills, King and Naylor each received the Distinguished Flying Medal [DFM] for their own actions that night. They had all demonstrated the very highest commitment to each other in the face of grave danger. No-one was left behind other than their captain who gave life to them all.

They are the finest example of what Tony Iveson meant about a bomber crew being close and depending upon each other.

Leslie Baveystock returned to active duty and moved to Coastal Command with No.201 [Flying Boat] Squadron flying Sunderlands in which he sank two U-boats in fairly quick succession. Before the war ended he had been awarded the Distinguished Service Order and a Distinguished Flying Cross and bar, to add to his DFM. Fate or luck, whatever name it is given, plays a very large part in a person's survival in war. It was an incredible piece of luck that Leslie Baveystock landed in that dyke; had he left the aircraft a split second sooner he would have fallen short of it and a split second later and he would have over-shot it. If that was not enough, whilst on No.201 Squadron he was given a few days' compassionate leave following the death of his father. His Flight Commander Squadron Leader 'Babe' Ruth took over his crew for the next mission, from which they failed to return.

Upon the confirmation of Leslie Manser's Victoria Cross, Arthur Harris wrote to his parents; the letter contained the following paragraph, *"His shining example of unsurpassed courage and staunchness to death will remain an inspiration to his Service and to him an imperishable memorial."* How true.

Today there is, however, also a very visible memorial to Leslie Manser, close to the crash site. A few years ago whilst work to the dyke system was being undertaken, the contractors unearthed one of the propeller blades from his Manchester in remarkably good condition. That blade forms the central part of a very fitting memorial to the only crewman of a Manchester to win a Victoria Cross.

"Today we take our freedom for granted. At one time it was a different matter. Let us hope that it helps those who follow us to recognise the true price of national liberty, personal freedom and peace."

The memorial to Leslie Manser a few yards from the crash site

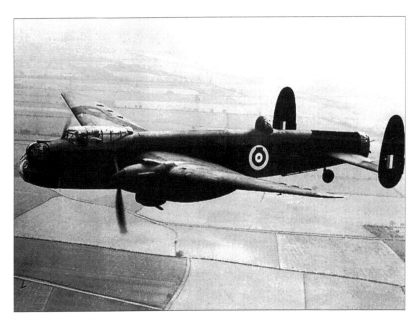

The AVRO Manchester

CHAPTER EIGHT

"There is nothing more close than a bomber crew. You had to have confidence in each other. Each one had to know his job thoroughly... ...you depended on each other. No matter what difference in rank, as a crew you were a unit and the closer you were the more confidence you had, the better you were."
Squadron Leader Tony Iveson, No.617 Squadron.

We were still attached to Bomber Command and the late afternoon of 1st June saw us once more gathered in the briefing room to prepare for the second thousand-force raid. This time the ribbon on the map stretched across to Essen in the German Ruhr, the industrial heartland and what became known to the crews as 'Happy Valley'.

Later that evening I pulled on my various layers of clothing and with the rest of the crew climbed aboard the bus to be taken out to Wellington P9240 standing at its dispersal area. With our pre-flight checks carried out, we once more gathered around the rear of the aircraft for a last cigarette before taking off. The skipper Bob Phillips, solid, calm and dependable as always, assured us that the ground crew had double checked this aircraft and she was definitely going to get us to Essen and more importantly she was going to get us back home again. We all gave a slightly nervous laugh and our second pilot Reg Smith said quietly with a smile, "I bloody well hope so." Reg was already a Flight Sergeant pilot but had a great sense of humour.

It wasn't long before from around the airfield the sound of heavy engines spluttering into life and then picking up with a deep roar, split the quiet of the evening still: it was time to go and I scrambled over the tail spar and settled behind the four Brownings of my Fraser Nash turret. The ground crew fired up our own engines and the aircraft began to vibrate, to come alive. I plugged in my intercom lead and oxygen tube and, maintaining strict radio silence, we joined the line of bombers slowly taxiing along the perimeter track to the head of the runway. As we slowly got closer to the take-off point I looked out of the turret into the darkness at the vague shape of the Wellington following us up the line. I hoped that we would both return tomorrow.

At twenty-five past eleven we turned onto the main runway and the skipper held the aircraft as the power mounted, straining at the brakes and waiting for the green light from the controller's van. Then I felt a jerk as the tail lifted my turret up into the air and a moment later the brakes came off and we started forward, gathering speed as we raced down the main strip. Standing in the gloom at the start of the runway the ground staff and those few crew not flying that night were there to wave us off. Even though I could barely see them in the dark, I waved back eagerly in what was to become a good luck ritual with me. The runway unfolded into the night in front of me until the noise of the wheels ceased and I knew that we were airborne.

We climbed steadily to the bomber stream meeting point and then set out for Essen, slowly gaining more height until we reached twelve thousand feet, our bombing height. We had taken off thirty-five minutes later than we had done two days earlier and the light had more or less faded away, even at this height and I strained my eyes all the time looking out for other aircraft in the stream which might stray too close to us for comfort as well as, in my inexperience, for German night fighters.

The minutes ticked by and all too soon we crossed the coast of occupied Europe. I swallowed my 'wakey-wakey' tablets, given to us to stop us falling asleep under the strain of the sortie, and winced at the bitterness of their taste on my tongue. Sitting behind my four .303 Browning machine guns I suddenly felt very exposed as I slowly swung the turret from side to side and up and down staring into the darkness for that slightly darker silhouette which would warn of an approaching fighter. I knew that we were towards the end of the stream, and if I stood up and leaned forwards and looked back towards the wings I could see the flak coming up at the aircraft ahead of us, although it seemed to be spread out over a very large area.

Presently the skipper banked the Wellington to starboard and I knew that we were on the last leg of the route in to the target. The cloud below us had thickened up and it was not possible to see the ground. Suddenly flak was slicing up at us through the clouds, bursting all around and I felt the Wellington buck as several shells exploded close by. The flak lit up the sky in great white flashes and I had to concentrate hard not to lose my night vision. I searched left and right, up and down. Just below us and off to one side I could see the silhouette of a Stirling making its bombing run. At the same time the skipper's voice came through my headset,

"Ok everyone, we're on our run. Quick as you can, Reg."

Amen to that, I thought.

"Left, left, right a bit, steady, s t e a d y, bombs gone." Thank God for that, I thought and felt the lift in the aircraft as our load of incendiaries dropped silently out of the bomb bay and cascaded earthwards.

Nose-down to gather speed, we banked away from the target area as Pilot Officer Tom Prothero, our navigator, gave the course for home to the skipper. We were far from safe but at least we were going in the right direction.

It was always a temptation to look down at the target area and become mesmerised by the boiling inferno below, but to do so meant taking my eyes off the sky and leaving us vulnerable to an unseen fighter attack. However, tempted though I was, the heavy cloud cover meant that I would have seen little anyway and it helped me to concentrate and resist the urge. All I could think about was that we had got to Essen safely, dropped our bombs and now we were on our way home and I kept willing the aircraft on, on towards England and safety and rest. The more I thought about getting home safely, the harder I looked out into the night sky around me, determined that we would get home. I knew that the Wellington was particularly vulnerable to attack from the side since it did not have a mid-upper turret and I kept straining forward in my seat to try to see as much of the wings as possible and as far sideways as the darkness would allow.

The cannon shells ripped through the fuselage just behind my turret and I swung the Brownings round, dragging the tracer onto the fighter as it dived away to port, at the same time shouting to the skipper to corkscrew. In an instant the pilot thrust the Wellington into a port dive, the G-force throwing me up in my seat, banging my head on the top of the turret. Then we started to climb to starboard and roll at the top before diving to port again in the next part of the evasion manoeuvre we had practised so often. I had lost sight of our attacker as he had dived away from us, even though for a few moments I glimpsed the glow from his exhausts before I had hit the top of the turret and now I searched the sky outside like never before, looking for his return. To the east, the first wisps of dawn were beginning to show, perfidious light which would let me see further, but which would betray us in an instant.

The skipper carried on the corkscrew for what seemed an age as I searched deep into the faint grey sky for a speck coming at us, for anything that might mean an attack, straining to give me that vital second or two of advantage to fire first. As the aircraft pitched and dived and rolled I could feel the vomit coming up into my throat and I had to concentrate and swallow hard to keep it down, but after a while, and in the rapidly growing light, there was no further sign of our attacker. Bob levelled the Wellington out and we headed for the North Sea and home. The skipper with his usual reassuring calm checked around the crew to make sure that we had all survived and gently guided us onto Tom's new heading.

From my vantage point in the rear turret I watched the dawn break on that Tuesday morning as we crossed the enemy coast and started to fly over the miles of sea back to our island home. The cloud which had covered the Ruhr last night had not spread this far and I had a good view all around. As it got lighter, I was surprised to see so many aircraft in the sky. I don't know why I should have been so surprised, after all 956 aircraft had taken off the previous evening and hopefully they were all now returning. Time over the target was ninety minutes and this was the stream returning. In the event, thirty-one bombers were lost that night.

Gradually the various aircraft made their way to their respective airfields and the mass thinned out until it seemed that there was just us left, circling our base, getting lower with each circuit, waiting to be given the instruction to land. The Wellington touched down with a bump and I watched as the landing strip sped away underneath me, slowing as it did so, then another bump and the tail was down. I had completed my first mission but could not think how I would manage another twenty-nine or so like that. We had made it, though; we were back and that was all that mattered for now. It was a quarter to five, nearly five and a half hours since we had taken off.

I leaned round and unlatched the turret doors behind me and, removing my intercom cable and oxygen lead, I clambered out of my seat, leaning back into the turret to pick up my flask and what was left of my chocolate ration. Outside on the ground once more, it was wonderful to feel the cool fresh morning air on my face even though it was chapped from where my oxygen mask had rubbed during the night. The skipper handed the Wellington back into the charge of the ground crew who looked sorrowfully at the state of her. For the first time since getting out I looked at the damage caused by the flak and particularly by the fighter's cannon shells. We had been lucky not to have had a fire and the aircraft looked as tired and relieved as we were to be back home.

The truck sent to pick us up stopped a few yards away and we climbed in carrying our parachutes and various bits and pieces. At debriefing we recounted our experiences and what we had seen, which was very little of the target area, whilst volunteer WAAFs brought us mugs of steaming hot tea, laced with rum. In fact the raid had not been as successful as the Cologne raid because so many crews had been unable to clearly locate the target and had dropped their bombs over a very wide area. So much so that the Germans did not actually realise that Essen was the intended target and reported the night as widespread raids over the Ruhr area, which probably wasn't too far from the truth.

Afterwards we breakfasted on bacon and eggs, a real treat kept only for operational aircrew. I suddenly felt exhausted. The strain of my first full mission washed over me, my eyes were sore from staring out through the Perspex canopy for over five hours and my head was sore from twice being thrown up against the turret roof. Despite these discomforts, I was slightly elated; we had pulled together as a crew and survived an attack by a night fighter. We were an operational crew with a successful mission completed and most of all we had returned home unharmed even if our aircraft carried the scars.

The early morning air was fresh and soft on our faces as we walked back to our hut and the sky promised one of those beautiful English summer days: I would try not to sleep too long. The crew laughed quietly as we walked along the connecting pathways until we reached our hut, then one by one we fell into our beds for that blessed sleep.

Later that day, with the sun still high in the sky, our crew received three important pieces of information; firstly we were to report immediately to the medical officer at Moreton-in-Marsh, there to be given various injections, secondly we were given two weeks' embarkation leave effective from that day, and thirdly our posting: No.70 Squadron Middle East Air Force based at Abu Sueir, just west of Cairo.

My leave went far too quickly. I went back to Shrewsbury to see my mum and dad rather than spend it in London.

I had started writing to Eric Chaffner's sister Dorothy and she was definitely an added attraction to return to Shrewsbury for my leave. We had a wonderful time walking in the open countryside which surrounded the town, boating on the River Severn and enjoying the dances. One day we cycled out for a picnic to a quiet spot near to RAF Montford Bridge, the satellite airfield for Spitfires of No.61 OTU, where I had taken Mum and Dad to see the aircraft on Empire Day 1936; it all seemed a long time ago now.

All too soon it was time to go and once more leave from Shrewsbury railway station: this time I felt very different, more confident, more involved. I had my sergeant's stripes up, I had been on operations, even if only one, and Dorothy was there to see me off. We stood close together at the back of the platform and I was very conscious that I really might not see either her or Shrewsbury ever again. It wasn't long before the Great Western engine, sending shrouds of steam across the platform and over the waiting passengers, gently brought its chocolate-and-cream carriages to a chattering halt. I kissed Dorothy and tried not to think about the tears which were trickling down her cheeks. I told her to look after her mother and stepped through the already open door into the mêlée of bodies and kitbags in the compartment, everyone trying to find a seat and wave goodbye at the same time. Presently the guard blew his whistle and with more steam, smoke and noise, the driving wheels of the engine slipped for a moment or two on the rails then gathered traction and the train started to gradually edge away from the crowd left behind on the platform. I hung out of the window and called goodbye to Dorothy as the steam slowly enveloped her and dozens of other tearful, waving hopefuls: hopeful that this was only au revoir and not goodbye.

At Oxford station I met up with Bill Wastney, our front gunner, as we had arranged and went for a couple of beers whilst we waited for our train to RAF Harwell. We chatted about the leave we had both just enjoyed and shared our lack of knowledge over where we were about to go. The next three days at Harwell were spent on cross-country

145

exercises with Wellington HF889, as much for the benefit of the aircraft as for the crew, since we would be flying her all the way to Egypt. Then on Friday we flew her to Portreath in Cornwall.

At seven-thirty in the morning on Sunday, 21st June 1942 we set off on a three-day-and-night flight to join our squadron. Our first stop was Gibraltar, call sign 'Sermon', and when looking down onto that notoriously short runway as we circled round, it seemed even shorter than it really was: no room for error here and I kept wishing that it was a lot longer. Touching down in the afternoon sun after over eight hours' flying was a great relief for my backside and leg muscles. I was also very hot since I was dressed in flying kit suitable for Britain, not the Mediterranean. We had a meal, managed a couple of unremarkable beers in one of the bars along the main street and got our heads down for some sleep. The next morning after breakfast we drew our tropical kit consisting of shorts, shirt and socks and then it was off for the nine-hour flight to Malta, arriving there in the middle of Monday night.

We were soon separated from HF889 and taken down into a deep shelter to protect us from the daily air raids which started at dawn. When we re-fuelled here, we must have been given some of the very last aviation fuel on the island which was a British base and of vital strategic importance to the Allies in the Mediterranean. A few weeks later by August, the island was almost out of fuel and unable to defend itself; total surrender was only days away. Despite the entry of the United States into the war on 7th December the previous year, by the summer of 1942 Britain was on its knees. One defeat had followed another. In the first six months of 1942 German U-boats had sunk over three million tons of British and Allied shipping.

Britain knew only too well of Malta's plight and a relief convoy, which became known as the 'Malta Convoy', was put together and included the largest oil tanker in the world at the time, the Texaco ship *Ohio* which, when she had been built in America in 1939, had had her plates welded together rather than riveted in the traditional way. This was to prove to be a pivotal factor and enabled the *Ohio* to reach Malta and enter the annals of naval history.

This convoy was of such strategic importance that it was not given a convoy number but became a full-blown operation, code named Pedestal. There were fourteen merchant ships assigned to the trip and the naval and air force commitment of both sides was a testimony to the importance with which the mission was viewed. The British protected the convoy with two battleships, HMS *Nelson* and HMS *Rodney* with its huge 16-inch guns, the largest in the Royal Navy, five aircraft carriers including HMS *Indomitable*, HMS *Victorious*, and HMS *Eagle*, twelve cruisers and forty destroyers. The Axis powers met this force with twenty-one submarines, twenty-three E-boats and five hundred and forty aircraft.

Leutnant Willie Wagner, Second Officer on U-73, second from left and Rosenbaum far right

The Germans and Italians knew just how important this convoy was and attacked it mercilessly all the way from Gibraltar to Malta. On the morning of 11th August 1942, U-73, commanded by Kapitänleutnant Helmut Rosenbaum, sank HMS *Eagle* with a fan of four torpedoes and, unaware of the real strength of the British force,

147

sent this radiogram to his Headquarters, *"Convoy-15 destroyers and escort ships, 2 cruisers, 9 to 10 freighters, one aircraft carrier, probably one battleship. Fan shot against aircraft carrier. 4 hits from 500 metres distance. Strongly audible sinking noises. –All clear- Rosenbaum."*

The *Ohio* was attacked repeatedly and was twice torpedoed, dive bombed and shelled almost to destruction, but the welded plates held her together and she entered Malta harbour with her valuable cargo of aviation fuel, buoyed up between two destroyers. Her Master, Captain Dudley Mason was awarded the George Cross for his part in the battle. The island itself had been awarded the George Cross on 15th April that year. But the *Ohio*'s sailing days were over and she lay in Malta Harbour until 19th September 1946 when she was towed out to sea and sunk: a sad end to a remarkable ship.

There wasn't time to refuel our aircraft and get us away before the dawn air raids started so we took the opportunity to rest at Luqa and left that brave little island at a quarter to ten the following evening, arriving eight and a half hours later at Landing Ground 224, twenty-six kilometres west of Cairo on Wednesday morning, 24th June. Although we had been flying for twenty-six hours over the last three days and were fairly tired, it was still an impressive sight to see the pyramids to the south of Cairo from such a wonderful vantage point.

*No. 70
Squadron crest
Motto:
Everywhere*

There were a number of very obvious differences to life in the desert which impressed themselves upon me within about five minutes of our arrival: flies, sand and the heat being the first and in that order.

We handed Wellington HF889 over to the ground crew and never flew in her again. Although we all referred to an aircraft as being 'ours', they did in fact all belong to the ground staff; we only borrowed them for our sorties and each pilot had to sign for his particular aircraft on every occasion and then hand it back on our return. The ground staff were very definitely the unsung heroes of the RAF. They did a wonderful job at keeping the aircraft flying and took a great deal of pride in their work to do so. They were very attached to their aircraft and took great exception to any crew which mistreated the aeroplane: damage caused by enemy action was one thing, but damage caused by negligent aircrew was not looked upon so sympathetically.

Nowhere did the ground crew perform little short of miracles every day to keep us flying more than in the desert. How those lads kept the sand out of the engines and all the pipes as well as they did, I will never know. It was quite remarkable. No.70 Squadron had been in the Middle East at the start of the war, was there when I arrived in June 1942, was still there at the end of the war, and was to remain there for fifty-five years altogether, not returning to Britain until 1975. The RAF's Desert Air Force was rather like the army in the Far East, all but forgotten about back home in Britain and starved not only of essential equipment and spares but early on, of suitable aircraft too: until September 1940, the squadron was flying Vickers Valentia bi-plane bombers!

The ground staff and aircrews alike could make a home out of the dreariest patch of desert, which was just as well since there was very often precious little else on hand and our first priority was to get settled in: it was a steep learning curve after life in Britain, wartime or not. To start with, we were billeted in small tents around the base as there was no room in the accommodation block and we quickly learned how to avoid the scorpions and the myriad of other bugs and flying insects that plague the desert at night. Our beds were the charpoy type and we stood each of the four legs in a bowl of creosote to stop the various intruders from crawling up them and feasting on us in the night. Later, when sleeping away from the base at a landing ground, we dug a shallow hole into which we pitched each tent and surrounded it with sandbags to prevent it from blowing away in the ever-present wind.

Home! [Ray Morris collection]

On occasions when there was no camp bed to sleep in, a shallow depression was hollowed out of the sand and we lay in that so that the scorpions couldn't crawl underneath. Sand got everywhere: it got into everything we ate, put a film on everything we drank, fell out of everything we put on and settled onto everything that didn't keep moving; even writing home was a task done through sand. The local Arabs who were always around the camp would steal anything that wasn't bolted down, and there were warning signs to them, in English of course, that actions considered to be injurious to our war effort would carry the death penalty, although I never saw the threat carried out. The theft of our pitifully few possessions was a problem, though, particularly if it was a piece of an aeroplane!

On our arrival at the base we had been welcomed by our CO, Wing Commander Wood. He was a very hands-on leader, as we were to find out, and didn't believe in asking his crews to do anything which he didn't do. He did, however, look just a tiny bit impressed when he found out that his latest rookie crew had at least had one full-blooded taste of operations over Germany, or maybe it was just my imagination. When I first saw him I found it hard to believe that he was our CO: strict uniform dress codes and discipline were always fairly lax on an operational base even in England, but here it was virtually non-existent. Life on an operational base out here revolved around keeping the aircraft airworthy, and nothing else mattered. Parades, proper uniform and proper channels were considered to be bullshit and for those behind the lines in Cairo: getting the job done was the be-all and end-all of every day. The ground crew worked incredibly hard and were highly respected for their work and resourcefulness by the aircrew who flew in their aeroplanes. However lax things might have been on the ground, that did not apply in the aircraft where we were as disciplined as ever: off duty there were very few rules, on operations the full book applied.

Welcome to ZANZIBAR [Wallace Jackson collection]

The first few days were spent becoming acclimatised and getting used to the ever-present wind, sand and bugs. Within a week we lost our pilot, Bob Phillips, who was

151

sent to Palestine. We flew there with him as a crew and we were very sorry to see him go. He was a good pilot and we had all trained hard together. Once more we were a crew without a pilot.

The next night we were down for operations. It was a night bombing run to El Daba and, apart from some fairly light flak, passed off uneventfully, as did the sortie to the same target three nights later. The practice was known as 'makee-learn': giving a new crew a couple of relatively easy target missions to settle in on. Well, El Daba was fine, which is more than can be said for Tobruk three nights later. There were two targets that for the bomber crews operating in that part of North Africa came up so often and with such monotonous regularity that we gave them each a nickname: Tobruk was the 'milk-run' and Benghazi the 'mail-run'.

We took off in the dark at a quarter to nine and headed west for that stretch of desert which by the end of the North African campaign would have changed hands more times than any other stretch of land anywhere in the world. We were also on our third pilot in as many trips and on this occasion it was Pilot Officer Hammerbeck. It is very unnerving for a crew to have a new pilot, since ultimately we are all in his hands and three different pilots in a week didn't go down too well as we felt that were not being given the chance to settle down as a complete crew, thus increasing our chances of coming to grief.

Sitting in the rear turret for my first milk-run, I felt quite at home as we bounced our way down the rough strip of sand that served as a runway. Just like back in England, the ground staff and off-duty aircrew were there to see us off and I returned their waves. The sortie lasted for nearly eight hours, but apart from the very heavy flak over the docks area, which was our target, the trip was uneventful, but one thing was certain; makee-learn was very definitely over.

We had no complaints about our pilot, who had done a good job and we would have been happy enough to have him in the crew, but it was not to be so. It was nearly two weeks before we were down for ops again during which time no willing pilot emerged; we were getting quite a complex that no-one wanted to fly with us, and a lot of good-natured teasing from the other crews. The two officers in the crew, Freddie Grenfell and Tom Prothero, our wireless operator and navigator respectively, went to see the CO and voiced our concerns. We struck gold. Wing Commander Wood told them that he shared our concerns and that within a month he expected to have a very good pilot for us; in the meantime, to demonstrate his faith in us as a crew he would be our skipper.

A few days later we were down for ops and at the briefing the CO announced the target as an attack on Rommel's troop concentrations to the west in what was to be the run-up to the battle of El Alamein, although we didn't know that at the time. It was to be a medium-level raid and navigators and bomb aimers had to be particularly alert as he didn't expect anyone would want to go around again for a second run-in on the target. From the informal comments around the room which greeted this observation, he was correct. Wing Commander Wood also announced that he would be leading the raid and that we would be his crew, at which a great cheer went up and offers of good luck to the CO from all the other crews in the room. For the first time I really began to feel that we were being accepted into the squadron.

It was the first time that I had flown in the lead aircraft and it was quite an experience. From my seat in the rear turret I had a first class view back over the target area as we pulled away. Our stick of high explosive and incendiary bombs had struck amongst some vehicles which looked like a row of roman candles going off as their fuel tanks exploded. I could see the following Wellingtons coming in behind us, dropping their bombs on the now very clearly visible target area as the German gunners started to get our range. The flak was bursting very close and I decided that it was time to be well on our way home. However, the CO had other ideas and as he climbed he banked our Wellington around so that he could have a good look at the scene below us and only when satisfied that all his aircraft were safe and already away did we make for base.

Once our aircraft was settled at dispersal and we were outside waiting for the truck to pick us up, the CO thanked us all for a good job done and added with a grin that it had been a pleasure to fly with us: he was a good commanding officer who led by example and involved his men.

In 1941 the Germans, having moved through Greece needed a base further out in the eastern Mediterranean: Crete. The problem was that the British were already there. In May that year, during the fighting for the island a young New Zealand 2nd Lieutenant called Charles Hazlitt Upham had been awarded the Victoria Cross for single handedly attacking a machine-gun position and causing the withdrawal of German troops from the area, thereby slowing the enemy's advance and saving the lives of many British soldiers. A year later, now with the rank of Captain and camped just down the road from us, Charles Upham was about to be awarded a bar to his VC at El Alamein. Despite two serious wounds he led his men into battle, where he was further wounded when a machine-gun bullet broke his arm. Upham carried on and destroyed a tank and several machine guns with grenades, his favourite weapon. His exploits were finally brought to a stop when he was taken prisoner. Despite his serious injuries and loss of blood he survived the war and returned to his sheep farm on South Island, New Zealand. His was the only bar to a VC during the Second World War, and one of only three ever, the other two occasions coming during the Great War to RAMC surgeons Captain Noel Chavasse and Lieutenant-Colonel Arthur Martin-Leake. Uniquely, unlike Upham and Chavasse, Martin-Leake's two VCs were from different wars, his first award arising during the Boer War.

Ultimately the Germans captured Crete and we withdrew across the Mediterranean to bases in North Africa: the Germans now had the task of defending the island, not only against us but also against the formidable local resistance. In time this resistance became very heavily communist controlled, which just goes to show how much further into the post-war years Stalin was looking than were the British or Americans. We were preoccupied with freeing Europe, whereas Stalin was preoccupied with controlling it.

Of course we were not the only squadron operating in this area even though we had been there since before the start of the war; No.37 and No.38 Squadrons had come out in November 1940 with their Wimpys and No.252 Squadron had arrived in late 1941 with their Beaufighters as a detachment before once more becoming an independent squadron in January 1942. The Bristol Beaufighter was a wonderful aircraft, known to us as 'Whispering Death'. It was an immensely strong aircraft, weighing ten tons, and equipped with impressive fire power by any standard. It had two Bristol Hercules engines set slightly forward of the nose and was armed with four Oerliken cannons, six machine guns and eight rocket rails: occasionally they would also carry two 250lb bombs. The one feature about the Beaufighter which I envied above all others, though, was the two inches of armoured glass in front of the pilot and the sheet of armour plate under his seat. By comparison the rear turret of my Wellington, and later my Lancaster, was painfully exposed.

'Whispering Death' – the Bristol Beaufighter [Ray Morris]

One of the primary roles of No.252 Squadron was to harass the Axis supply ships in the Mediterranean. Most of their squadron's missions were inevitably daylight attacks and so part of our job was to bomb the airfields from which any fighters might fly out to attack the Beaufighters. We also attacked the harbours of the islands and Crete in particular, and that was our target for tonight.

As the light began to fade on 24th July we took off in Wellington DV639 from Landing Ground 86 for my first sortie against Crete. True to his word, Wing Commander Wood was our skipper again. I locked the turret in the forward position and watched the sand being whipped up in tiny whirlwinds by the turning propeller blades of the following Wellington almost obscuring the whole aircraft, as we slowly made our way along the perimeter track to the take-off point. We turned onto the main runway and stopped, the CO holding the aeroplane on the brakes. I could hear the rising crescendo of the engines, the Wellington straining, anxious to go, and feel the churning of my stomach as I thought of what lay ahead, but still we waited. Then up came the tail and my turret with it and we were off once more, the makeshift runway of the landing ground slipping by underneath me as we gathered speed until it was just a blur and then we were up, leading the formation of aircraft which steadily climbed into the settled evening sky.

Every few minutes, I stood up in the turret and strained round, not searching for the enemy yet, but to watch the sun; we were climbing faster than it was setting and it appeared to be rising in the west, a strange illusion. Presently we reached our bombing height and the sun began to fall back once more into the western desert and the ocean far beyond. I looked down and saw the North African coastline slip into view and then gradually fade like a dwindling string of pearls dividing a golden scarf from its sapphire cape: and then it was only the sea below us. Although I would never describe myself as deeply religious, I did share the strong faith of my parents and which they had encouraged in me from an early age in Shrewsbury. Looking down from the grandstand view of

156

my turret there were many occasions when I wondered at the beauty of the natural world and despaired at the efforts of mankind to destroy it. I knew why we were at war, I had volunteered to be a part of it and was totally committed to defeating our enemies, but I still hated the destruction of this beautiful planet which seemed to be an inevitable consequence of what we were all doing.

I switched on my intercom and asked the CO for permission to test my guns and fired a few rounds down towards that flat blanket of midnight blue, watching the tracer arc away. I wanted a cigarette, but smoking was strictly forbidden on missions, not least for the perfidious glow it produced which could bring death and destruction to us all in the blink of an eye. Most rear gunners did indulge though in the last few miles before reaching base. I searched the darkening sky, slowly turning the Fraser Nash turret left to right, moving the Brownings up and down, looking for any sign of enemy fighters, seeking that tell-tale dot in the distance which would herald an attack.

The intercom crackled in my ears as Tom informed the skipper of a change in course and I knew that we were approaching Crete. Still I kept my turret moving, port, starboard, up, down, searching for an attacker, and then the flak came up at us and the shells exploded far too close for comfort for an opening salvo. The island's harbours were defended by both shore-based anti-aircraft batteries and also flak ships anchored a little way out to sea; it was these that we had over run and that were firing at us now. The skipper dropped the aircraft and turned to port, but then we were on our bombing run of the supply ships and harbour quaysides that serviced them. "Bomb doors open," I heard in my headset as the mechanism opened the underbelly of the Wellington to expose our 4,000lb load of high explosives. The flak had increased dramatically now and the searchlights were sweeping the sky, seeking us out. I could hear the sides of our Wellington being peppered with shrapnel as each shell burst seemed to get closer.

"Hurry up, Reg, for God's sake. Drop the bloody bombs,"

I whispered to myself. The aircraft bucked as a shell exploded just below us and too damned near with our bomb doors wide open. "Right, right, steady ... steady"; his voice so calm and even, portraying a man totally in control and unaffected by the lethal hail of flak which was being thrown up at us. "Bombs gone." Relief washed over me.

The skipper dropped the aircraft to gain some speed and turned away from the shore batteries, but it wasn't home just yet: we circled around gaining more height so the CO could see how the rest of the squadron was fairing. Only when he was satisfied did we turn for home: it was all right having the CO as our skipper but it didn't come without its drawbacks and hanging around in the area after our run-in was one of them. My eyes were tired from endlessly searching into the darkness for any sign of an enemy fighter, but even so it was a welcome sight when I detected a hint of another dawn breaking and the light filtering into my turret long before it would intrude upon the sleep of the villagers far below me.

Presently we joined the circuit of aircraft waiting to land, slowly descending as each one before us landed in the half light of the new day. Although unable to hear the conversation between our wireless operator Freddie Grenfell and the controller, I could hear his instructions to the skipper; we were to stay in the circuit as one of our squadron was coming straight in. Looking down I could see the damaged Wellington making its approach, a thick black stream of smoke pouring out behind from the port engine showing up clearly against the lighter colour of the desert.

Nobody said anything, we didn't need to, we were all thinking the same thing and praying that the pilot would bring her down safely. In a furious flurry of sand the Wellington touched down and immediately slewed to port as the undercarriage collapsed, sending her off the runway and spinning around, eventually coming to rest in the soft ground at the side. The fire engine and ambulance raced to the spot as the crew tumbled out of the wrecked aircraft; one, two, three, four... The scene disappeared from my view as we continued the circuit, the CO increasingly anxious to get down and see what had happened to the crew.

Presently, we landed and the skipper handed DV639 back to the ground staff, leaving to find out the fate of the crashed crew, before returning for the debrief with good news; all were safe apart from the front gunner who had broken his collar bone in the landing. All the other crews also returned safely; a good result and a happy CO. It was a good end to my operations for July. As a crew we had completed six operations so far and we had got past that psychological barrier of the first five; statistically my chances of survival had just increased, albeit only marginally, but as I went off for a week on my first operational leave, it was a comforting thought, as too was the knowledge that we were fully integrated members of the squadron: we had come of age.

Long after I had left North Africa to fly in Lancasters with No.61 Squadron in Lincolnshire, one memorable action took place on 1st June 1944 when No.252 Squadron's CO, Wing Commander BG Meharg AFC led a major attack on a well-protected convoy steaming through the azure waters of the Aegean Sea. On his first run-in to the target, close to the surface of the sea Meharg's starboard engine was badly hit and quickly became a mass of flames. Unable to control the aircraft at that height, there was nothing he could do and it flipped over and ploughed straight into the sea in a great plume of water, breaking up with the high-speed impact. The attack was otherwise a great success which resulted in the sinking of two supply ships including the *Sabine* together with a destroyer and significant damage to three other ships, whilst the protecting Beaufighters shot down two Arado Ar196 reconnaissance seaplanes, an Me109 and damaged a further Ar196 for the sole loss of Wing Commander Meharg's aircraft.

Back at their base, Squadron Leader Foxley-Norris, later to be Air Chief Marshal Sir Christopher Foxley-Norris, had to prepare himself for the unenviable task of telling Willie

Meharg's wife what had happened. He had witnessed the CO's crash, as had several other squadron members and there was even photographic evidence: he told her that there was in reality little hope of survival for her husband and his navigator. Mrs Meharg was a Wren officer in Alexandria and reportedly took this devastating news very bravely. A few weeks later, however, she contacted a slightly embarrassed, though very relieved Foxley-Norris in rather better spirits: incredibly both Willie and his navigator had survived the crash with only minor injuries. Neither of them remembered anything after the impact until they regained consciousness floating in their Mae Wests amongst the debris and wreckage of the convoy: they were now languishing in a prisoner of war camp somewhere in Germany.

Strike in the Aegean [Courtesy of Alex Hamilton, GAvA].

No.252 Squadron at work [Ray Morris collection]

CHAPTER NINE

"If I should die, think only this of me: that there's some corner of a foreign field that is forever England."
From The Soldier *by Rupert Brooke*

After six weeks we were due a week's leave which we took in Alexandria. Before going we had been given the usual information about where was safe to go and where was not, what was safe to do and what was not. Reduced to its bare minimum it condensed down to this, the state-run brothels and the bars in the main part of the town were in bounds but the brothels and the bars in the back streets were dangerous and were out of bounds. Apart from some sightseeing in the daytime, there wasn't a lot else to do in Egypt in 1942.

Enjoying a holiday in Alexandria with pals from 70 Sqn.
I'm in the middle [Neville Bowyer collection]

Somewhere decent to stay was a bit of a problem for NCOs since most of the respectable hotels and bars were signed up 'Officers only', although as aircrew we weren't too badly treated because we stuck together as a crew and with our two officers it was a case of the Three Musketeers philosophy, all for one and one for all. This was typical of bomber crews and applied equally back in Britain. Ground staff rankers had a much harder time of it and it was not unknown for an individual to 'promote' himself to a Flight Lieutenant, put up the double ring insignia and drink in the bars and hotels normally reserved for officers. On one such occasion a 'Flight Lieutenant' fitter was sitting at the bar in a hotel when one of his flight commanders came in and sat on the stool next to him. The officer's only remark to him was, "What are you having, Curly?" and he bought him a Stella Artois. Very sadly, this particular flight commander was killed over Tobruk three weeks later, the loss of a good officer and a true gentleman.

If there was no good hotel available or affordable then the YMCA Services Club at 5 Rue Fouad in Alexandria was always a safe place to stay, if you could get in, and the Maalesh bar and restaurant at 51 Safia Zaghloul Street was a pretty decent place to eat. In fact the proprietor, Mr Comninos Yavordios, had printed on the front of the menu, 'IN BOUNDS TO HBM FORCES' [His British Majesty's Forces]. He also had printed on his menus the more subjective slogan, 'ONCE YOU ENTER YOU WILL NEVER REGRET IT'. Mr Yavordios's place was designed to be cheap, cheerful and a taste of home for the British troops. A pint of Stella lager cost 7½d [about 3p today], whisky and imported soda was 6½d and a gin and It [Italian Vermouth] was 5d [about 2p today]. Every dish on the menu was chips, fried tomatoes, French beans and onions to which you could add eggs for 5d, steak for 7d, bacon and eggs for 8d, chicken for 9d or various other culinary delights such as liver, ham, fish, roast beef or sausages. Regrets? Well, once or twice.

The desert did not belong to the RAF; we were just part of a much bigger force on both sides. At this time the 8th Army was building up to the battle of El Alamein, which in itself would lead to the complete withdrawal of Rommel's Afrika Korps from North Africa. Up until Alamein, the two armies had exchanged territorial gains as they had moved back and forth along the coastline in a series of advances and retreats, mostly around Tobruk, as Rommel sought to press towards the Suez Canal zone. The canal was vitally important to the British as it provided that age-old link with the eastern countries of the Empire and saved a long and dangerous shipping trip around South Africa's

Cape of Good Hope. For Germany too it provided a vital link to her colonies in East Africa and secured the eastern end of the Mediterranean Sea, Greece, Crete, Cyprus and the Middle East oil fields.

Stopping to brew up whilst moving along the coast on the 'Tobruk by-pass'. [Wallace Jackson collection]

The British army defended North Africa in a series of 'boxes', one of which was named the Knightsbridge Box. In June 1942 the Africa Korps eventually overran the box after the British high command had failed to seize upon the opportunities to defeat Rommel when his supply lines became too extended and his troops were trapped by a minefield in what was known as 'the cauldron'. One of the last British soldiers left in the Knightsbridge box was Sergeant Walter Turnbull. Born into a farming family in Cumberland, he had been a police officer in the West Yorkshire Constabulary traffic division before the war and had volunteered for army service. By a series of coincidences he had ended up in the 8th Army, mainly because he could drive; an unusual skill in 1939.

The overwhelmingly superior German forces were gaining ground rapidly and Sgt Turnbull recognised that their own position was hopeless, so together with two other sergeants, he volunteered to cover the withdrawal of his men. The three of them moved around their defensive position as quickly and variedly as possible to slow down the attacking forces by making them believe that the British force was stronger than just these three. As the enemy closed in on their position, Walter, as the senior sergeant, ordered the other two to escape whilst they still had time, saying to them that if either got back to England, would they please look up his wife and make sure that she and his daughter Daphne were all right.

His two comrades promised to do so and left Walter to defend the ridge alone. As he watched them go he knew that his fate was sealed: he would either die or be captured that afternoon. In the event, it was a prison camp which awaited him. He was finally overpowered and forced to surrender, but he had held out long enough not only for his comrades to escape but for the delay to be noticed by the German commander General Rommel, who ordered him to be brought to his command vehicle. As he lifted his sand goggles above the peak of his cap, the General looked down upon the Englishman, smiled benignly, and asked in excellent English, "What is your name, sergeant?"

"Turnbull, sir."

"Well Sergeant Turnbull, you have done your duty and fought bravely, but for you the war is over." He then saluted his enemy and drove away. If all the German High Command had been like Rommel, there never would have been a war.

Sgt Walter S Turnbull, British 8ᵗʰ Army – the Desert Rats

Sergeant Turnbull spent the best part of a year in a prison camp in Italy and was then moved to Stalag IVB in what became eastern Germany, the largest of all the European prison camps containing some ten thousand men of various nationalities. Daily life in the camp was miserable: it was cold in winter and hot in summer, lice lived in the seams of clothing, food was scarce and the watchtower guards were not particular which way their guns were facing when they tested them each morning. Red Cross parcels from home were a lifeline and if anything needed dividing, whoever cut it into pieces was the last to choose: it ensured that all the pieces were the same size. Nevertheless, discipline was kept and they even managed to put on a drill show. The SBO [Senior British Officer] decided that it would be good for morale if the prisoners did some drill, which they duly did and put on such a show that even their German guards relaxed long enough to watch and applaud at the end.

When release finally came in 1945, it was the Cossacks who rode up on horseback, lassoed the fence posts and ripped them down, just a few hours after the Germans had left the camp in a great hurry and headed west, anxious to be captured by the British or the Americans, anyone but the Russians, whom they had treated appallingly in the camp and everywhere else.

A prison camp was not a place I wanted to end up in and yet little did I know that whilst I was enjoying my leave in Alexandria I was less than six weeks away from being shot down and having to face that possibility.

My leave went by all too quickly and soon it was time to bid farewell to the nightspots and bars of Alexandria and climb up into the transport truck for the uncomfortable ride back to Abu Sueir. At least it had been a break from the increasing strain of operations and had given us something else to think and talk about for a week. As a base Abu Sueir was amongst the best, if for no other reason than the fact that it had running water and so we could at least have showers. Some of the other bases were definitely basic whilst the advanced landing grounds were decidedly primitive with even the drinking water being stored in empty oil drums where the petrol residue still floated on the top.

John Fenton relaxing near Cairo [Adele Badiali collection]

We were back on operations straight away and on the 1st August were greeted with a milk-run operation to Tobruk. We took off at five minutes to midnight and by half past one in the morning we were back on the deck and glad to be so. Still without our own skipper, Pilot Officer Goddard was our captain on this mission and shortly after take-off it was obvious, even to me sitting in the rear turret, that Wellington DV546 was struggling to gain height. Reg Smith, our second pilot, reported that the starboard engine was running hot and that the oil pressure was too high.

We pressed on for a little while longer but then the inevitable decision came from the two pilots that to carry on to Tobruk with a failing engine could only end in disaster, and so they turned the old girl round and returned to base. I had been here before and I knew that this was never a comfortable landing, coming in with a failing engine, short of power and a full bomb bay was not for the faint hearted. So it was with much relief that we switched off the engines, clambered out of the aircraft and handed her back to the ground crew to fix the problem. The armourers unloaded the bombs and returned them to the dump. I never ceased to admire the coolness of these chaps; just one little mistake, one slip and everything ends forever in a blinding flash, and yet they were always cheerful and easy-going: perhaps those were the essential talents needed to do the job.

The experiences of Wallace Jackson typified the dangers which the ground crews faced every day. He joined No.70 Squadron just before Christmas 1940 and a few weeks later was sent up to the airfield we were using at that time. Jumping down from the truck, he was told that things were okay there. No sooner were the words uttered than the sound of approaching Me109s could be heard. As the fighters started their strafing run of the airfield everyone dived for cover. Wallace made it into a makeshift hangar and as he lay on the ground he could hear the sound of the cannon shells ricocheting around inside: the pilots were shooting straight in through the open doors.

On another occasion he was working on one of the engines of a Wellington. It wasn't a major repair and was being carried out in the open, getting the aircraft ready for operations that night. Whilst he was working on the engines, the armourers arrived with their tractor and trailer, loaded up with 500lb bombs. A petrol bowser was parked nearby ready to re-fuel the aircraft. It was nearing six in the evening and so Wallace and an Australian chum decided that what was called for was a mug of tea and a meal whilst the armourers bombed up the aircraft. After about half an hour, their meal finished, they left the canteen tent and began to walk back to the Wellington to finish cleaning the oil filters. They were barely 100 yards away when there was a blinding flash and explosion. Throwing themselves to the ground, they covered their heads with their hands as bits of aircraft and shrapnel whizzed by and debris rained down all around. They staggered to their feet and looked across to where they would have been working a few seconds later; where the Wellington had stood there was just a hole in the dispersal area and the twisted smouldering remains of the aircraft, the petrol bowser and the armourers' tractor and trailer. Nothing was ever found to identify any of the seven ground crew: they had quite literally been blown away and the smell of burnt aircraft and incinerated bodies hung over the airfield for some time. Wallace had been saved by nothing more than a cup of tea. The hand of fate rested upon ground crews just as much as it did upon aircrews.

The funeral pyre of the ground crew [WJ collection]

DV546 may not have ever flown again but that didn't stop us, and two nights later we were back in the air, this time to Fuka with Flying Officer Fawcett at the controls. Over the next fortnight we flew the milk-run three times and to Rhodes once, each time with a different pilot including the CO. The missions were fairly straightforward from our point of view insomuch as we did not sustain any serious damage, although the squadron did suffer some losses. On two of these missions I changed places with Bill and flew as the front gunner getting a completely different view of the trip. In one way it was very pleasant to see where we were going, but I missed the view from the tail, looking back over the target.

Luck, and to a large extent superstition, played a very important part in the survival of a crew and anything which disturbed the rhythm of good luck could unsettle a crew and become a self-fulfilling prophecy. As a crew we had now completed eleven operations and had had to turn back from a further two, but were still without a permanent skipper. In itself it seemed like a good luck charm even though we were known as the odd crew out. So it was that on the morning of Wednesday, 19th August we had some unspoken misgivings when the CO introduced us to our permanent skipper, as he had promised.

Flying Officer Elliot was an easy-going chap, younger than me with an air of competence but without arrogance. "The CO has told me that you're a bloody good crew, and a lucky one, but has warned me that you chaps don't suffer pilots very long," he said, smiling. "I shall have to be on top form or you will be dropping me out with the bombs."

We looked at each other and then at the new pilot. "Don't worry, we'll give you a fair crack at it, but keep your parachute on just in case," quipped our cheerful wireless operator, Freddie Grenfell. We laughed and the ice was broken; it was a good start. We were to come to owe our lives to Flying Officer Elliot's skill.

That night it was the milk-run again. After the briefing Ron Elliot called us all together and asked us about the target, knowing that we had been to Tobruk several times already, most recently the previous night. That boded well. We were confident in him because he was confident in us and wanted us to share our experiences with him. We gathered around HX523 and talked easily. He had received the now customary good luck from the other crews at the briefing when the CO had introduced him as the new skipper of our crew. It must have been difficult for him at first, coming into an established crew as their captain but he was a good pilot and we would very soon be grateful to him for his flying skills. We stayed together as a complete crew until the end of our tour.

As the two opposing armies in the desert continued to move towards the decisive battle of El Alamein, we were detailed to attack the German troops and equipment, in particular their motor transport parks and supply dumps. The desert war was carried out over vast distances and the army without the means of transporting its troops and supplies would be most likely to lose: our job was to make sure that that was the Germans.

On 23rd August we took off for the first of three strafing operations in four days against the German troop and vehicle concentrations. These were always difficult and dangerous missions because it meant low-level flying across relatively flat and featureless desert, and when engaging the enemy we were well within the range of the light weapons as well as the medium and heavy anti-aircraft guns. I had checked and double checked my guns and the bullet channels to make sure that there was nothing to cause a blockage, the ground crew had polished the Perspex of the two turrets until they were spotless: we were ready to go. This was our third sortie as a full crew and I could feel the skipper weaving the Wellington slightly as we neared the target area just in case there were any fighters about. By and large we had air supremacy at this time and the main object of this exercise was for the front and rear gunners to shoot up as much of the enemy as possible as we flew low over their transport bases dropping 250lb bombs and 40lb anti-personnel bombs. By the time we arrived, the leading aircraft had been in and lit up the area with flares as well as their bombs and the ground defence gunners knew exactly what was coming; according to Bill in the front turret they were firing a lethal curtain of death up into the sky in front of us. I was glad that I couldn't see it yet.

The skipper talked us through the approach and, watching for the concentrations of flashes, jinked the Wellington to avoid the fire. Then in my headset I heard him say, "Okay Bill, Trev, here we go. Good shooting." The aircraft, flying so low, seemed to flash over the shadows of the features on the ground showing up in the fires started by the crews ahead of us. Suddenly there were the flashes of the guns below me and I squeezed the twin triggers of the four Browning guns, watching the tracer bullets streak downwards and weave back and forth as I rotated the turret to swing the guns across the target area. Behind me

I saw small explosions erupt like a firework, to die down and then flare up again as a vehicle, gun emplacement or store burned in the night. Flak and cannon shells were pouring up at us, exploding all around.

The Wellington bucked with each near miss and then a shell exploded right underneath my turret. I was thrown back against the rear doors, banging my head on the turret roof. Simultaneously I opened my mouth to curse at the searing pain that went through my skull and in that instant, my face mask was ripped away by a single cannon shell from the burst which struck the fuselage and shattered the Perspex turret. It took me a few moments to realise that had I not been thrown back in my seat that cannon shell would have taken my head off instead of just my face mask.

I was badly shaken by the closeness of death but was still focused upon the job we were there to do. The whole incident had lasted no more than just a few seconds and the aircraft was already turning away from the enemy positions. I pressed the triggers of my guns once more and again the tracer bullets streamed down towards the enemy. Then we were climbing and I became aware of a conversation taking place in my earphones.

"I think Trev's okay, Skip. I heard his guns firing again as we pulled away."
"Are you sure, Freddie?" replied the skipper. Then, "Trev, are you okay? Are you hurt?"

Although I could speak, I had no way of communicating with the rest of the crew; the shattered remains of my face mask lay somewhere on the floor of the turret; little more than an empty strap hung from my helmet.

For the next two hours HX523 droned steadily eastwards through the moonlit sky as we headed towards Abu Sueir, and I felt the cold night air rushing through the smashed Perspex panels of the turret. The air felt good blowing against my face, even the familiar whiffs of oil and fabric dope smelt good: I had missed death by a whisker. I slipped

171

up a prayer of thanks to God and looked out through the broken turret windows at the world around me. On each side of me and some way off I could see the ghostly shapes of other Wellingtons returning home, the moonlight dancing along their outer edges now and then stabbed by the yellow-orange flash of an exhaust flare. The ground beneath us drifted by like a pale silver cloth slipping slowly from the table over which it had been laid.

Before long I felt the Wellington gradually begin to lose height and then heard Freddie talking to control, asking for permission to land straight away as we had wounded crew. Permission to land must have been given because we lost height quickly and I locked the otherwise undamaged turret in the forward position. Then came the familiar first bump as we touched down and ran along the sand runway, followed by the second bump as the tail brought me down to the earth. We taxied off the runway and on to the perimeter track, whilst I watched the fire tender and ambulance rushing up behind us. Presently the aircraft stopped and with great relief I disconnected what was left of my intercom and was just about to unlock the turret doors behind me when they suddenly flew open and anxious voices were asking me where I had been hit.

Standing outside and looking at the tail of HX523, my crew could not believe my escape, and looking at the cannon holes in the fuselage and the mess of the turret windows, neither could I: it had been a close call, far too close, but I had survived.

We had just done four operations in six days and there was more to come. August 1942 was a very busy time for the squadron and the pressure was kept on us, but we had the night after my narrow escape off and celebrated my survival in the best way we knew how, with beer. For the next two nights it was more of the same and more attacks on the German motor transport bases and supplies, then the milk-run, then Fuka again. By the end of the month we had done thirteen missions since it began and nineteen in all, we were almost halfway through the thirty-nine operations of our first tour.

Two more sorties at the beginning of September and then on Tuesday 8th we were down for ops, Tobruk, the milk-run, a trip which would normally take just under eight hours to fly up to the target area, bomb it and fly back again. There was nothing unusual about the briefing or the target on this operation, we had done it many times before and after I had been out to our aircraft to check the guns, the turret hydraulics and the bullet channels, I settled down to wait for the time to come round.

Take-off was a little later that night and I took the opportunity to write home to Mum and Dad and let them know that I was doing fine and well out of harm's way; I had not told them about the face mask incident. I also replied to Dorothy's last two letters and then I joined the others and got ready.

The transport dropped us at our aircraft and we stood about having a last cigarette whilst the skipper signed for the Wellington and we temporarily took her over.

"Look after her, Sir, won't you, and bring her back safely?"
"Of course we will, Flight," said the skipper with a quiet laugh and gently slapped the Flight Sergeant on the back.

One by one we heard the engines from around the airfield start to fire up: it was time to go again. Slipping in to my familiar position in the rear turret I automatically looked to see that the armourers had filled the bullet channels and did a last check around the turret; in a few minutes it would be too late to find out that something was wrong. At ten to nine that evening we moved to the head of the runway, the power building in the engines and then, slowly at first, we moved forward. The ground crews were there to wave us all off and as I returned their waves, the tail came up and the Wellington gathered speed, straining to lift the weight of a full bomb load from the desert sand.

Looking down on the receding airfield I could see the

173

clouds of dust which betrayed the remaining aircraft on the perimeter track and the next one hurtling along the runway. I thought about my friend Dennis Bebbington who had been shot down the previous night and was missing. Soon all six aircraft detailed for the raid that night were up, had gathered at the meeting point and yet again were starting the four-and-a-half-hour flight to Tobruk. The crews and especially the aircraft were enduring the strain of a period of abnormal operations and six aircraft was the meagre total serviceable for tonight's operation: mechanical failure but particularly the accurate flak was taking a heavy toll on the squadron. The outward trip was uneventful and even though the weather was good my main concern was to watch out for the other Wellingtons in case they drifted too close and risked a collision. Presently Tom gave the skipper a new bearing and I felt the aircraft turn; we were nearing Tobruk.

It was past one o'clock in the morning when we began our approach and the flak was even worse than usual, the heaviest I had seen since coming to the desert. The Operations Record Book [Form 541] afterwards noted our intelligence that it was intense and accurate and it certainly was. Our target was a large supply ship anchored in the centre of the harbour; secondary targets were the jetties. German supplies were pouring into the port in readiness for the battle ahead and it was as vital to the enemy that they defended them as it was to us to destroy them. They had already suffered significant losses of supplies and equipment coming across the Mediterranean, courtesy of our friends in No.252 Squadron and others, and now we were causing more damage. The flak shells were bursting around us and a lattice work of searchlights wove a web in which to trap us as we crossed the sky. Once more I heard the calm voice of our bomb aimer guiding the skipper into the target, then, "Bombs gone," those welcome words were accompanied by an appreciative lift of the aircraft as 4,000 pounds of high explosive slipped out of her belly and streamed down towards the ship in the harbour below. I watched the water spouts reach up to us from both sides of the ship and then cascade down again all over the decks; we were so close, so close. Perhaps the shock waves from the explosions had caused some underwater damage to the ship. In the event only ourselves and 'P' Peter managed to find the ship and attack it.

Ron Elliot banked the Wellington and dived to gain speed, turning inland away from the main concentration of guns. As he did so my turret was filled with a blinding light, one of the strands of that web had caught us and held us in its grip as others swung onto the aircraft. We were coned. The skipper threw the Wellington into a series of turns and dives as he fought to rid us of the glare from the searchlights. The flak intensified out of all belief. I had never experienced anything like this before and could do little other than hold on whilst the aircraft pitched and turned, buffeted even further by the exploding shells. Then we were hit. The Wellington shuddered, paused as if gasping for breath under the shock of the shell burst, and then stumbled on in a fight for life. By standing up and leaning round I could just see that our starboard engine had stopped, but thankfully it was not on fire.

The skipper had managed to release us from the web of light and we were now heading out into the blessed darkness of the desert. I looked back towards the port area we had just left behind and saw the jetties ablaze from the fires started by Wellingtons 'U' and 'Z'; it made up a bit for our oh-so-near miss on the ship. Whilst making a mental note of the success of the attack for the debriefing, I became conscious that we were gradually losing height. The port engine was doing all the work and I knew that at this rate we were not going to get back to Abu Sueir. We were still far behind enemy lines, and a prison camp was beginning to beckon.

As if reading my mind, the skipper's quiet voice came over the intercom, "Okay, everybody, we only have the port engine at the moment, but Reg is doing what he can. There's no fire, so with a bit of luck we'll make it back. Tom, Freddie, Bill, throw out anything we don't need, please."

I knew that he wanted to lighten the aircraft and would be struggling to keep the Wellington going on one engine; by reducing the weight he would ease the strain on the port engine and help to prevent it from overheating.

With great skill and strength, the skipper nursed the Wellington nearer to home, but the loss of height became inexorable. We had flown for around two and a half hours since leaving Tobruk and were over Matruh. We were down to 1,800 feet and the skipper was in the middle of telling us that we were going to have to prepare to bale out when, to everyone's surprise, the starboard engine picked up and gave some real power. The sense of relief felt by the whole crew was almost audible, but we were all wondering the same thing: how long would the engine hold out?

Steadily we climbed above the desert and reached 6,000 feet from where the first thin hint of the new day could be seen stretching out grey fingers to chase the night away into the western sky. A sense of optimism had crept over us as the starboard engine had ticked along fairly steadily. I searched the sky intensely for any sign of the Me109s which I knew would be up at first light, all the while wondering whether we might make it back home after all. But it was not to be. Less than an hour after it had fired up again, the starboard engine died, this time for good. We couldn't be in a worse place: we were over that featureless, endless expanse of the Qattara Depression.

Once again the Wellington began to lose height and we knew that this time we were going down. There were two simple options facing the skipper, order us to abandon the aircraft and bale out, or risk a crash landing. The worry for him in ordering us to bale out was that we would inevitably all get to the ground at different places and quite far apart. In the Qattara that could mean death for us all, our best chance of survival would be to stay together, but that meant a risky crash landing. The skipper asked for our thoughts on the matter whilst we had the luxury of time to express them, and to a man we wanted to stick together, but ultimately it was the captain's decision. With a combination of landing lights and the approaching daylight making the ground vaguely visible, a crash landing it would be.

Well, I had been here before that day at Tain, but this was in the middle of nowhere, with no ambulance or fire tender for comfort. Presently, the skipper ordered me out of my turret and into the body of the aircraft. I locked the turret in the forward position and engaged the safety catch on the guns before opening the doors behind me and scrambling into the fuselage. It was only then that I realised how much damage the old girl had suffered. There were holes in the fabric sides everywhere from the shrapnel, but thankfully no-one had been injured.

Crouched on the floor of the Wellington with my back against the main spar, I felt the first crunch as we hit the ground, bounced, hit it again and then slid, turning sideways throwing up such a cloud of sand that I thought we were on fire. We came to a grinding sudden halt as the aircraft stopped its forward motion, tipped up, then fell back and finally settled in the wilderness of the Qattara Depression. The skipper had done a great job and we were all outside the aircraft in double quick time in case she caught fire. Tom Prothero, our navigator, had plotted the descent and calculated our position to be behind the Germans lines and some thirty miles west of our own. Despite coming down in Qattara, the starboard engine had at least given us a good chance of getting home.

Each of us gathered his emergency escape kit, including as much water as we had on board, a first aid kit, the Very pistol and flares, local maps and a compass. We were ready to start walking: there only remained the sad but essential duty of destroying 'O' Oscar before we left. It did occur to us that the ensuing fire might bring the Germans down on us before our own chaps, but that was a risk we had to take. We needed to get going before the sun got too hot, so the fuel taps were opened and, standing well back, the skipper fired the Very into the pool of petrol on the ground. The flames quickly ignited the canvas fabric of the Wellington and within a few moments had engulfed her. Time to go. Just before she was finally lost to our view I looked back at our faithful aircraft in time to see that there was already little left except Barnes Wallis's geodetic frame. I suppose that she is still lying there to this day.

All that day we tried to put as much distance as possible between ourselves and the crash site, but as the sun rose higher in the sky it took its toll upon us. We were tired from the previous night's mission and the slog under the desert sun soon wore us down. There was no proper shade to be had in that unforgiving terrain but we did find some scrub on an east-facing slope and took some welcome rest, taking it in turns to keep a watch; none of us wanted to be prisoners of war. As the day wore on into late afternoon and the sun began to lose its fierce heat we set off again, resolved to walk through the night whilst the air and the sand under foot were cold. Just before dark I saw an armoured vehicle in the distance. It was travelling west and since none of us could positively identify it as one of ours, we hid and let it go.

Darkness came and wrapped its shroud of secrecy around us. As we walked steadily along, stumbling occasionally over the rocks which littered the ground, I began to think of all the creatures which lived in this God-forsaken place and called it home: I hoped that they could hear us coming and had moved out of our way. I don't think that any of us gave a thought to the possibility of getting lost, the sky was clear and we had our navigator with us; we simply trusted him to get us back. The next day was the hardest. We stopped walking at about ten o'clock, again on an east-facing slope and covered our bodies from the punishing glare of the sun. Our water supplies were by now running low and only the man on watch had a drink. Once more vehicles were seen during the course of the day and whilst we were more confident that they were our own we couldn't be sure and were not yet so desperate as to take the chance.

A second night of walking followed and although the dawn found us tired and seriously low on water, we were confident that we were not too far from our own lines. The sun was beating down upon us and we stopped to discuss whether to try to push on further in the heat or to stop and lay up for the day.

"Quiet. Listen," said the skipper.

Then we heard it too; the unmistakable sound of vehicle engines coming closer. In front of us was a small rise, above which we could see the dust thrown up by whatever was approaching. Our ragged band of a crew, unshaven, unwashed, tired, hungry and thirsty stood helplessly awaiting our fate: surely we hadn't got so close only to be taken prisoner now. We squinted into the sun at the three armoured vehicles which gradually grew in size and took form as they bore down upon us. The closest vehicle pulled up in front of us and the engine started to idle,

"It's all right, chaps, they're ours. How long have you men been out here?" the voice enquired.
"This is our third day," replied the skipper. "Are we glad to see you chaps. We were shot down and crash landed out there somewhere. How far are we from our lines?"
"Not too far, we'll give you a ride back."

Painfully we climbed onto the hot metal of the armoured vehicles and my lasting memory is of the sweetness of the water which I poured down my throat through sore and cracked lips.

Thank God for the 11th Lancers.

By pure chance the Lancers had come across us about five miles out of Alexandria. Our navigator had done a wonderful job guiding us back, but it was such a relief to be able to have a ride for that last few miles. We were fed and watered, had a shave and shower followed by a medical check-up and duly pronounced fit for duty. The Operations Record Book noted our late arrival and its cause, ending thus, "after a two days trek they were picked up by an advanced patrol of the 11th Lancers and returned to base little the worse for their adventure."

Our little adventure did at least qualify us as members of the Late Arrivals Club, an unofficial and highly prestigious club of the 492 airmen who had returned from behind enemy lines during the North Africa campaign. We were awarded the certificate and little golden boot lapel badge. I wore it for years and was very sad the day it disappeared.

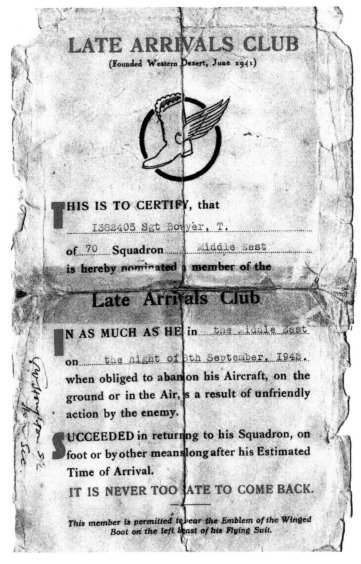

LATE ARRIVALS CLUB
(Founded Western Desert, June 1941)

THIS IS TO CERTIFY, that

1382405 Sgt Bowyer, T.

of 70 Squadron   Middle East

is hereby nominated a member of the

Late Arrivals Club

IN AS MUCH AS HE in the middle East

on the night of 8th September, 1942,

when obliged to abandon his Aircraft, on the ground or in the Air, as a result of unfriendly action by the enemy.

SUCCEEDED in returning to his Squadron, on foot or by other means long after his Estimated Time of Arrival.

IT IS NEVER TOO LATE TO COME BACK.

This member is permitted to wear the Emblem of the Winged Boot on the left breast of his Flying Suit.

My prestigious Late Arrivals Club certificate [NB collection]

The squadron had lost two of its precious few aircraft in as many days: ours was the second. The night before we were shot down, Wellington Z8976 had taken off on the milk-run but had not returned. Ten aircraft had been sent out to attack the jetties in the harbour but, as we had found out to our cost the following night, the flak and the searchlights had been much more intense than usual. Back at base we had no news of the fate of the crew, which included my friend Dennis Bebbington, flying as second pilot. Dennis was another Shropshire lad from Wrentnall near Pulverbatch and by chance had arrived on the squadron a couple of days after my own arrival. Although we had not known each other before the war, we knew many of the same places back home and it cemented our friendship.

Wellington Z8976 'T' for Tommy, captained by Sgt Carter, had been caught by the searchlights and intense flak over Tobruk and had just managed to bomb the target when both engines cut out. As the aircraft began to lose height, the starboard engine had picked up and the crew were able to fly on for some little time towards the south-east. Like us they had jettisoned everything they could to lighten the strain on the remaining engine, but a crash landing was inevitable: the Wellington came down 350 miles behind enemy lines.

All the crew were safe and set out to walk back to base. The senior crew member was Pilot Officer Johnson, their Canadian wireless operator, who took charge and formulated a survival plan, including a strict water ration. With the help of their local maps, walking by night and sheltering under the sparse scrub by day they reached the old Libyan border with Egypt within a week. They were given food by friendly Arabs, who hated the Germans, and were able to refill their water bottles.

After twelve days, we had already been back at base for a week following our own adventure and all hope for Dennis and the crew of Z8976 had faded: we were resigned to their loss. They, however, were not, and had reached Sidi Barrani, although not without their problems.

181

Flight Sergeant Croisiau, the rear gunner, was suffering terribly with his feet and could not walk any further. By a combination of good luck and good leadership, the crew arrived at a well close to a main road just before dark. P/O Johnson went forward to reconnoitre the position and saw two Italian trucks parked at the side of the road not too far away. Assessing their situation, low on food and with F/Sgt Croisiau unable to walk any further, Johnson decided to await nightfall and then attack and attempt to steal one of the trucks.

When it was sufficiently dark, leaving the navigator and front gunner at the well, Johnson led the other four in the attack. They crept up to the first truck, with Johnson and Croisiau, who had been a guerrilla in the Spanish Civil War, taking the cab and Dennis and Sgt Carter the rear. In the ensuing fight, the driver of the truck managed to grapple Croisiau's revolver from him and a fire fight started, which aroused the Italians in the second truck, about 50 yards away. These troops rushed the first truck, firing as they came and Croisiau was hit and not seen again. Meanwhile Dennis had got into the driver's seat of the first truck and started it up, although by now surrounded by Italian troops. Fortunately his beret had fallen off and in the darkness and the general mêlée, the Italians failed to see that he was an RAF sergeant! Recognising the hopelessness of their situation, Johnson ordered a withdrawal, Sgt Carter providing covering fire. They managed to meet up with the other two crew members at the well and melted away into the dark, making good their escape.

The Italians organised a search party to go after the intruders and Dennis willingly joined it, taking the first opportunity to also slip away into the dark. He followed the others and after twenty-four hours on his own in the open desert he caught up with them.

Luck stayed with the crew, who over the next few days met several groups of friendly Arabs. They were given food, re-filled their water bottles and learned where to get past Rommel's troops. Turning south-east, they entered the salt marshes of the Qattara Depression just as a torrential rain storm hit the area, allowing them to once more fill their water bottles. It was twenty-six days since they had been shot down.

Three days later, just after dawn, they were intercepted by two jeeps of an advance South African Armoured Car unit; their ordeal was over. The official report noted that, "It is never too late to come back," whilst, somewhat laconically, the Intelligence Officer made a one-line note in his diary, "After being missing for a month Sergeant Carter's crew turned up at base having walked back."

On the strength of their safe return we had a good party in our improvised mess: the Erks [ground crew] had taught us how to keep the bottled beer cold by hanging the bottles in the petrol bowsers. Six weeks later when the crew had returned from a well-earned rest we all had another party to celebrate the award of the Distinguished Flying Cross to Pilot Officer Johnson and the Military Medal to Sergeants Dennis Bebbington and Ivor Davies, the navigator who had guided them across 350 miles of enemy territory. The citation concluded, "Pilot Officer Johnson acted as leader throughout, being excellently supported by Sergeants Bebbington and Davies. This officer and the airmen displayed resolute courage and fortitude throughout the hazardous operation." Some time later news filtered back that Sgt Croisiau, who was actually a Belgian but had claimed to be a French-Canadian in order to get into the RAF, had indeed been shot in the fighting but had survived and was a prisoner of war in Germany.

On 25th November 1942 Dennis became captain of his own aircraft. By now the squadron had moved westwards behind the retreating Afrika Corps to El Daba, an airfield less than ten miles from the wreck of 'T' for Tommy. It was with great sadness that I later learned that on 22nd March 1943, after I had returned to England, Dennis's aircraft had been lost without trace on a bombing mission. He and his crew are commemorated in column 269 of the Alamein Memorial for the Missing.

Flying Officer Dennis Bebbington, MM

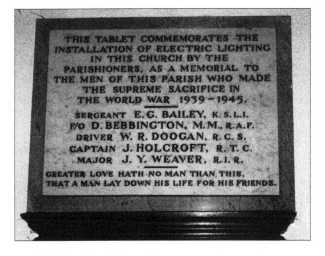

THIS TABLET COMMEMORATES THE
INSTALLATION OF ELECTRIC LIGHTING
IN THIS CHURCH BY THE
PARISHIONERS, AS A MEMORIAL TO
THE MEN OF THIS PARISH WHO MADE
THE SUPREME SACRIFICE IN
THE WORLD WAR 1939–1945.

SERGEANT E. G. BAILEY, K.S.L.I.
F/O D. BEBBINGTON, M.M., R.A.F.
DRIVER W. R. DOOGAN, R.C.S.
CAPTAIN J. HOLCROFT, R.T.C.
MAJOR J. Y. WEAVER, R.I.R.

GREATER LOVE HATH NO MAN THAN THIS,
THAT A MAN LAY DOWN HIS LIFE FOR HIS FRIENDS.

& Memorial plaque in Pulverbatch church
[Neville Bowyer collection]

CHAPTER TEN

"This is not the end; it is not even the beginning of the end. But it is perhaps the end of the beginning."
Winston S Churchill, 1942

Life in the desert was just so totally different from life in Britain that it took a little time to adjust. However, once into the mindset it was not too uncomfortable and definitely had some distinct advantages. As I have already mentioned, discipline on the ground was very lax by any standard but, as the story of our own walk back and particularly that of Dennis Bebbington's crew demonstrates, that did not mean that as a fighting force we were sloppy, quite the opposite: we were totally focused upon the job we were there to do and nothing would get in the way of that; unnecessary bullshit simply fell into that category.

When I had first arrived at Abu Sueir, I was struck by the open spaces, even for an airfield, but also by how close everything was. The date palm trees which gently rustled in the mid-afternoon breeze provided shade from the blazing sun. They also provided the location for the tents in which everyone lived, usually four or six to a tent, and convenient posts from which to tie washing lines. The bunches of dates looked so wonderfully tempting and appetising as they hung, swaying with the tree, especially to men who were short of any sort of real variety in their diet. However, unless one was suffering from severe constipation, they were to be avoided at all costs; they were a very effective laxative as those who were tempted found out.

Bully beef and soya sausages formed the basis of our fairly monotonous menus. There were a few local variations, such as bread which, once it became unfit for human consumption as bread, was made into rissoles. Not all the Arabs in the area were untrustworthy, some were very helpful and kind to us and in the final analysis were just doing their opportunist best to get by in very difficult circumstances made worse by war and a real fear of the

Germans. One of the delights which they did bring to us was chicken's eggs. Unsurprisingly they could sell as many of these to us as their chickens could lay. At first this seemed to me to be such an incongruous activity; I had not associated chickens with the desert, but of course few Arabs lived in the open desert, most lived in small settlements close to water and the trading routes. We simply became part of their trading route, and were very glad to be so as fresh eggs were a real treat back home in Britain, never mind out here. A few of the ever-enterprising ground crew, who were out here for much longer than the aircrew, even kept their own chickens.

Al Fresco desert kitchen [Ray Morris collection]

Water was of course severely rationed. It was brought to the camp in bowsers and had to be boiled before virtually any sort of use, not just drinking. I did sometimes wonder why we bothered to boil it, since it was then stored in old petrol cans which had barely been washed out, consequently all the water had a film on the top and tasted of petrol. Ground crew and aircrew generally had separate messes at base camp, but mucked in together when sent up the desert to an advanced position. The only reason for this separation at base camp was that the ground crew were generally there for the duration, whereas the aircrews tended to come and go on a regular basis. The completion of a tour, injury, capture or death were usually the four possible fates which by and large awaited all aircrew and so their time in the desert was much shorter than that of the ground crew staff, for whom this was home.

Beer and cigarettes were provided as rationed items, although the beer allocation was restricted to one bottle per airman per week; hardly enough to have a party, but we did have our own local supplies which we kept cool in the petrol bowsers. Most of the food was dehydrated because it was virtually impossible to keep anything fresh in the heat. The milky white service biscuits which were rock hard and fairly tasteless could be soaked overnight and made into a passable porridge the next morning, providing of course that all the hungry indigenous night hunters were kept out of it.

Me enjoying a well earned drink at Abu Sueir
[Neville Bowyer collection]

The flies and the sand got everywhere. We regarded sand as natural roughage in our diet but drew the line at the flies. One new arrival in the desert sat and watched an experienced campaigner carefully remove all the round black items from the bowl of rice pudding which he had just collected. Upon asking why he was removing all the currants from the pudding the newcomer was told that they were not currants but flies, and this was a daily practice at which he too soon became adept.

Of all the natural hazards which we faced, the sandstorms were probably the worst. They could blow up very quickly and largely without warning other than the sight of a wall of sand approaching from the upwind direction. The ground crew had to quickly cover any exposed engines and everything was literally shut and strapped down until it passed. We lived in dread of being caught in the air by a sandstorm because the sand which was whipped up by the wind was so fine that it got into everything and could clog the fuel lines in an aircraft and bring it out of the sky as easily as a flak barrage.

Inevitably there were some strange characters amongst the squadrons and particularly the ground staff, some of whom had been in the desert for several years already. These ground staff were, however, a source of great support to us because not only did they repair the aircraft, patch up the holes and get them back in the air fully armed, they were also the fountain of so much knowledge about how to survive in the desert. One trick we quickly learned from them was how to make a desert stove in order to brew up anywhere: take an empty petrol can, cut it in half, fill half of the remaining can with sand, tip petrol onto the sand, apply a lit match and place the pot of water over the flame: the desert stove.

Was it me who gave Tommy Cooper the idea of the Fez?
Relaxing between operations [Neville Bowyer collection]

A sense of humour was, and remains, an essential quality for survival in wartime and most people can recall specific examples from their own experience, but often the funniest stories are told at the expense of the anonymous establishment. In his book *A Lighter Shade of Blue*, Air Marshal Sir Christopher Foxley-Norris recites a wonderful story concerning the Atcherley twins, both of whom were Air Commodores at the time of the incident. Having a brother in the service is often quite useful. Whenever anything creditable happens, one is quick to claim responsibility; discreditable incidents can be promptly disowned as cases of mistaken identity. The Atcherley twins were the acknowledged masters in this field. On one occasion in 1943, David Atcherley was flying home from North Africa for an important operational conference in London. The weather over southern England was very bad, and he had to be diverted to the only airfield that was still open, Portreath in Cornwall. As was, and remains, mandatory during flying, an ambulance and a fire tender were standing by the Air Traffic Control Tower. David, now going to be very late for his meeting, taxied in at break-neck speed, leapt out of the aircraft and into the ambulance, the engine of which was still running, and disappeared in a cloud of dust toward the nearest main line railway station, Redruth.

The Station Commander was naturally furious at this unofficial requisitioning of the ambulance. He addressed an indignant letter to Group HQ. It passed up the line to Command and finally to the Air Ministry which dispatched a stern rebuke to Air Commodore David Atcherley; unfortunately it was sent to his brother Air Commodore Richard Atcherley who hastened to reply:

> *Sir,*
> *I have the honour to acknowledge your letter of 23rd November, whose sentiments I entirely endorse. To remove without authority or permission, the emergency ambulance from an operational station, thus hampering the flying programme and imperilling the lives of crews already airborne is quite unforgivable; and fully merits the tone and content of your communication.*
> *I have to inform you, however, that I personally was in no way involved in this incident. I can only presume the officer concerned may have been my brother, Air Commodore D Atcherley.*
>
> *I have the honour to be, Sir,*
> *Your obedient servant, Richard LR Atcherley, Air Commodore*
>
> *PS Personally, I always take the fire engine on these occasions.*

Now fully recovered from our short ordeal in the desert, we were back on operations: the milk-run again. One more sortie successfully completed and we had survived for another six weeks. We had the pleasure of being flown to Heliopolis by W/Cdr Wood for a week's leave. Once more it passed by all too soon in a round of bars, girls and sightseeing, all of which seemed delightful at the time. Apart from buying a few bottles of beer in the mess or a few eggs from the Arabs, there was very little to spend any money on at base camp and even less at the landing grounds, consequently we were relatively flush when our leave came round. However, I had always been used to sending money home to Mum and Dad when I worked on the TPO and I continued to do so during my RAF service. I knew that things were hard for them in Shrewsbury and I worried about them.

Our next six operations were all to Tobruk as the build-up to Alamein gathered momentum. They all passed off without anything too untoward except that the flak barrage coming up at us seemed increasingly intense each time we visited the port. On the sixth consecutive sortie we had some difficulty with one of the engines and it took a little coaxing and nursing to get us back home. We were all thinking that this might be another crash landing in the desert, but in the event after eight and a half hours we touched down at base, safe and sound.

The next day the ground crew cleared out the sand from the engine parts and had it running as sweetly as ever, which was just as well because that night we took off once more in HX523 for the relatively short mission to Fuka. Two days later the battle of El Alamein began.

At twenty to ten on Friday, 23rd October 1942 the quiet and stillness of that warm late summer evening was shattered when the Allied artillery barrage began. Even from our own position we could hear the guns and see the flashes light up the sky away to the west as we waited to take off and join in. An hour and twenty minutes later we were once more thundering down the strip in Wellington HX523 with a full load of high explosive and anti-personnel bombs. Our job was to add to the pounding of the German guns and to break up their defensive positions. To what extent we did is perhaps best answered by the lads on the ground who were just at the beginning of two weeks intense and bloody fighting.

Every other day from 18th October until 11th November, we flew operations against the Axis forces before, during and after Alamein as they retreated westward toward Tunisia. As the ground troops would testify, the Italian forces fought with courage and tenacity and in the end, having been left to fight the rearguard action alone when Rommel's Panzers made their escape, surrendered not because they had given up but only because they had fired their last round of ammunition. As a final gesture of defiance they refused to raise their arms when walking toward their British captors, and earned genuine respect in the process.

Just before four o'clock in the morning on Thursday, 12th November 1942 I clambered out of the rear turret of Wellington HX523 for the last time. With the debrief over, we walked outside into the cool air and were met by the CO, who had been delayed and had missed our chat with the Intelligence Officer.

"How did it go, chaps?" It had the air of a rhetorical question.
"We got back, sir," someone offered.
"Just as well because you lads are finished, your tour is over. Good show."

That was it; we were tour expired. My operational service with No.70 Squadron of the Desert Air Force was over. I felt a wave of relief wash over me. We had just finished a spell of fourteen ops in twenty–four days, thirty-nine in all, plus a further two which we had had to abort. I had spent 262 operational flying hours sitting behind my Browning guns, searching the skies for enemy fighters. I had been shot down and trudged two days and nights across the desert to get home and become a member of the Late Arrivals Club and I had been within an inch of losing my life when the cannon shell blew my face mask away. I was nearly twenty-nine and felt fifty-nine: I needed a rest.

We were all exhausted from the strain of flying so many operations in such a short space of time. We had, however, been able to give much greater air support to our ground forces during the whole campaign and the battle of El Alamein in particular than the Luftwaffe had given to theirs. The German fighter pilots had rather preferred to engage in air-to-air combat than to harass our troops and airfields. It wasn't that they didn't attack our airfields; it was just that they didn't do it to any significant level. It placed a greater strain upon the RAF aircrews but eased the pressure on the attacking troops on the ground.

I had completed my first tour and I was due some leave. As a crew we were very sorry to leave our trusted pilot Flying Officer Elliot behind to complete his own tour and find a new crew. We had survived and were at the top of the squadron; there was a feeling of satisfaction, of a job well done but it was tinged with more than a little sadness: we had lost too many good friends along the way.

Heliopolis was my holiday destination again and then on 25th January 1943, the anniversary of the birth of Robert Burns, I started the long journey home to England, the first leg of which was to fly in that wonderfully ubiquitous aircraft, a Douglas DC3 Dakota operated by Pan American World Airlines, down to the Sudan. From there I flew across to Lagos, again in a Dakota, where I boarded a ship bound for Liverpool. On 1st February I was promoted to Flight Sergeant and after a short spell of home leave was posted as an instructor to No.14 OTU, RAF Cottesmore in Rutland, the station having converted from Hampdens to Wellingtons the previous autumn.

That year, 1943, was to be the year in which the tide began to turn against the Nazis. The war at sea in the Atlantic was far from won but between them Coastal Command and the Royal Navy were beginning to dominate the U-boats, which were now having measurably fewer successes along the convoy routes. Sailing in the first week of May, convoy ONS-5 had lost thirteen merchantmen but Admiral Donitz had lost seven U-boats, an average of one U-boat lost for every 9,000 tons of Allied shipping; a year earlier the average had been 100,000 tons. In April and May alone Donitz lost sixty-one U-boats; he could not sustain losses on this scale. Moreover, the deaths of so many of their comrades, coupled with the attrition of Bomber Command attacks on their Biscay bases when they were in port, drained the will of the crews to go on: as a fighting force they were effectively spent.

The great change in fortune was due to two principal events, one scientific and one a combination of unimaginable good luck and good seamanship. Royal Navy escort ships and most RAF Coastal Command long-range aircraft were now fitted with 10cm radar, the short-wave transmissions of which the U-boat search receivers could not detect. Consequently, many U-boats were being caught on the surface by aircraft and escort ships, all too often resulting in the sinking of the U-boat.

The second event had occurred two years earlier on 9th May 1941. Kapitänleutnant Fritz-Julius Lemp, the commander of U-110, was leading an attack on convoy OB-319. Lemp was carrying out a surface attack on the convoy and had already sunk two merchantmen. Going in for a third ship, not until too late did he see the British corvette HMS *Aubretia* sweeping down upon him, intent upon ramming his craft. Although he crash dived, *Aubretia*'s depth charges damaged the boat so badly that she could not escape and when the destroyers *Bulldog* and *Broadway* joined the hunt, U-110 was brought to the surface. A boarding party entered the U-boat and, amongst other things, captured its Enigma decoding machine and the associated documents. What elevated this most fortunate seizure to one of utmost importance and secrecy was that whilst being towed to Britain, U-110 sank, leading Donitz to believe that the Enigma machine had gone down with her. The experts at Bletchley Park broke the code and spent the rest of the war reading all the coded messages which the Germans were sending to and from the U-boat packs.

In his splendid book *Donitz and the Wolf Packs*, Bernard Edwards amusingly recounts that even as late as 1959 when Donitz published his memoirs, he believed that his code had remained uncompromised. It was not until 1966 that the Admiralty released the story of U-110 and the capture of the Enigma machine.

It was an attack upon a U-boat on the night of 17th/18th July 1944 which resulted in the award of a Victoria Cross to Flying Officer John Cruikshank. John was the pilot of 'Y' Yankee, an American PBY Catalina of No.210 Flying Boat Squadron on anti-submarine patrol north-west of the Lofoten Islands off the Norwegian coast when in the midnight sunshine of the arctic summer he caught U-361 on the surface. Like so many before him, Kapitanleutant Hans Seidel had no time to crash dive and decided to fight it out on the surface using his heavy deck-mounted anti-aircraft cannon for defence. John brought the Catalina round ready to depth charge the submarine but was met by a veritable hail of flak. One of the shells exploded in the cockpit instantly killing the navigator/bomb aimer before the depth charges could be released. The second pilot Flight Sergeant Jack Garnett and two other crew members were also injured.

Undeterred and with great courage, John Cruikshank brought his damaged aircraft round again for a second attack, and despite the intense flak and the loss of his bomb aimer he was able to successfully drop his charges, perfectly straddling the submarine, which quickly sank taking all fifty-two hands with her. It was only then that Jack Garnett realised how seriously his skipper had been injured in the first attack. John had received seventy-two separate wounds including two large punctures to his lungs and ten penetrating injuries to his lower limbs. A serious loss of blood was quickly draining John's strength and as he slipped into unconsciousness Jack Garnett took control of the aircraft. However, by pure willpower Cruikshank managed to pull himself back to consciousness and resume flying control of the Catalina. He knew that a five-and-a-half-hour flight in a badly damaged aircraft lay in front of his crew before they could reach the safety of the Shetland Islands and he refused the pain relief of a morphine injection until, in the absence of the dead navigator, Garnett had plotted

195

a course for them. Only then did he accept first aid, but not the morphine, and hand back the controls to Garnett with strict instructions that should he be unconscious when approaching Shetland, he was to be revived in time to make the landing. He did not sleep during the flight and helped the injured Garnett to fly the Catalina back to their base.

Landing any aircraft is a highly skilled task and the larger the aircraft, the more difficult it becomes, but landing one on water multiplies the risks significantly. Cruikshank knew that his injured second pilot was unlikely to be able to safely land the crippled PBY alone onto the choppy waters around Shetland and a little over five hours later the crew carried their skipper back to the second pilot's seat from where, despite his extreme pain and the injuries to his legs, he took over the control of the flying boat, bringing her in for a safe landing at Sullom Voe. He continued to retain great presence of mind and knew that he needed to beach the aircraft so that the injured crew could be safely taken off and the PBY could be salvaged rather than allowed to sink.

As soon as the aircraft came to a grinding standstill on the stony shore, the Medical Officer and his team came aboard to treat the four injured crew members. John had bled so heavily on the flight back to base that he was given an immediate blood transfusion and only when his condition had stabilised a little, was it thought safe enough to remove him from the cockpit and transfer him to hospital.

The award of a Victoria Cross to Flying Officer Cruikshank was announced in the London Gazette on 1st December 1944. Of the four Victoria Crosses awarded to Coastal Command during the war, John was the only living recipient. The courage of Flight Sergeant Jack Garnett was also recognised and he received the Distinguished Flying Medal.

By comparison, U-361 had fortunately had a very undistinguished career. She had been commissioned on

18th December 1942 and had neither sunk nor damaged any Allied shipping.

Five months later, by December 1944 John Cruikshank had recovered from his multiple wounds, but was unable to return to flying duties. He was promoted to Flight Lieutenant and remained in the RAF until 1946, after which he returned to his pre-war profession in banking which took him to different destinations around the world including the Calcutta branch of Grindlays Bank, long since swallowed up by one of the big international conglomerates.

Born in Aberdeen in 1920, today John is the last surviving Scottish VC, the last surviving RAF VC and the last surviving British VC holder from World War Two. Until recently he was the president of No.210 [FB] Squadron Association.

Whilst I was having a break from operations, Bomber Command embarked upon what undoubtedly became one of the best-known missions of the entire war, the Dambusters' raid upon the Mohne, Eder and Sorpe dams by the newly formed No.617 Squadron. That great British inventor Barnes Wallis had developed the idea of a bouncing bomb, which was actually a cylindrical mine, to skip across the water of the great industrial reservoirs like a skimming stone. The chances of destroying the dams by conventional high-level bombing were considered so remote as to be impractical. The value of Wallis's concept was that the bomb would bounce over the defensive torpedo nets which protected the dam walls, hit the wall and then sink to the critical level before exploding.

The Air Ministry liked the idea and the plan became a reality. So much has been written about the raid that there is little point in repeating it all here other than perhaps to remember and pay tribute to the fifty-three members of the squadron who died on that night. In particular a very sad loss was that of Dinghy Young, Squadron Leader Henry Melvin Young, DFC and bar. His father was English, his mother Amercian and he had married Priscilla Rawson, also American, only a few months earlier. He had been to Trinity College, Oxford in the 1930s and had then joined the RAF. He had done a tour on Whitleys in northern Europe and another one on Wellingtons in North Africa. He was a very experienced pilot and it is easy to see why Gibson chose Dinghy Young as his second in command. Whilst at Trinity, he had rowed at number two for the winning Oxford crew in the 1938 boat race. They had won the contest, held on 2nd April, from Cambridge by two lengths in a time of twenty minutes and three seconds. It was the ninetieth boat race but was particularly notable as the first occasion on which the BBC televised the event. He gained his nickname of 'Dinghy' after having twice ditched his aircraft in the sea and been picked up in his dinghy, these two latter events giving him membership of The Goldfish Club. The club was exclusively for those airmen who had ditched or baled out into the sea and been rescued from the waves, whether by the RAF Air Sea Rescue Service, the enemy or anyone else. Inevitably many members of the Goldfish Club are also members of the Caterpillar Club, a club reserved for whose lives had been saved by their parachutes in an enforced bale-out.

The contribution of Dinghy Young to the successes of the night of 16th/17th May has largely been overlooked. As one of Gibson's two flight commanders, he had the great responsibility of much of the preparation for the raid as well as training his own inexperienced crew. After the Mohne dam had been breached, Young flew on to the Eder dam with Gibson to give cover to those aircraft attacking the dam and to be ready to assume command if necessary. Perhaps more significantly, it is often overlooked that it was Young's mine which fatally cracked the Mohne dam.

Squadron Leader Young's aircraft was the fourth to attack after Gibson, Hopgood and Martin, but whereas the first three had mixed fortunes with their mines, Young's struck the dam perfectly, sank to the optimum depth of thirty feet and exploded against the wall, thus fatally damaging the structure. Gibson's mine did not explode against the wall of the dam, Hopgood's bounced over the top and Martin's veered off and exloded near the southern

198

shore. Thus it was Young who delivered the fatal mine. If Gibson had turned away for the Eder at that point, rather than asking F/Lt David Maltby to drop his mine, the dam would have collapsed anyway as a result of the damage caused by Young's strike.

The Mohne Dam the morning after No.617 Sqn had visited

The Mohne Dam 11ᵗʰ November 1956. The darker centre section shows the extent of the damage [John Ballantyne]

After Pilot Officer Les Knight, who would later be killed attacking the Dortmund-Ems canal, had breached the Eder dam, the remaining aircraft of the first wave turned for England. Flying low across Germany and then into Holland, as they had done on the way in, Sqn Ldr Young skilfully piloted Lancaster ED877/G AJ-A toward the Lincolnshire countryside and the safety of RAF Scampton. As he crossed the Dutch coast at Castricum-aan-Zee, less than an hour from home, their aircraft was hit by flak at two minutes to three in the morning on 17th May and crashed into the sea, killing all seven crew. Over the next two to three weeks, the North Sea gave up their bodies and the crew are buried in Bergen General Cemetery in north Holland: Squadron Leader HM Young, DFC and bar lies with two crew each side of him and a little way off lie the two remaining members, whose bodies were recovered some days after their comrades.

The raid was undoubtedly a great strategic success and an even greater propaganda success. It was also a testament to the very high level of skill and courage which the crews of Bomber Command demonstrated, but it was terribly costly in lives and aircraft. Of the nineteen Lancasters which took off from Scampton for the raid that night, eight were lost and of the fifty-six aircrew brought down, only three survived as prisoners of war, including Sgt Fred Tees the front gunner in ED910/G AJ-C captained by Pilot Officer WHT Ottley, DFC. The aircraft, flying at tree-top level as they all were, was hit by flak on the way out to the dams and crashed near Hessen, 1¾ miles north north-east of Hamm in Germany. Incredibly, Sgt Tees was thrown clear of the Lancaster as it ploughed into the ground of the Boserlagerschenwald.

Wing Commander Guy Gibson was awarded the Victoria Cross for leading the mission and for his courage at the dams by repeatedly flying alongside the attacking aircraft with his navigation and landing lights on to draw the fire from the defending anti-aircraft gunners on the Mohne dam. His was the third Victoria Cross at Scampton and probably the best known VC of the war. However, the other two VCs at Scampton are both notable in their own right, above and beyond the outstanding courage which gave rise to the award in the first place.

On 12th August 1940 Bomber Command earned the first of twenty-two Victoria Crosses awarded to Bomber Command crew [the VCs of Flying Officer Garland and Sgt Gray were awarded whilst they were serving with the AASF although they are often included in overall Bomber Command statistics]. F/Lt Roderick 'Babe' Learoyd of No.49 Squadron, flying a Hampden, was attacking the Dortmund-Ems canal when his aircraft was badly damaged by ground fire. He had seen most of the aircraft ahead of him brought down by the lethal barrage of flak which the defenders were putting up, but despite the prospect of almost certain death he pressed home his attack and dropped his bombs on target, causing substantial damage to the canal. He then managed to fly his crippled aircraft back to Scampton.

Scampton's second Victoria Cross, which was also Bomber Command's second, was and remains to this day, given to the RAF's youngest recipient for aerial operations. In September 1940, Britain was in grave danger of invasion and Fighter Command was stretched to the limit in the running battle with the Luftwaffe in the skies over southern England. Bomber Command was given the task of destroying as many as possible of the barges which were being prepared in the Channel ports for that invasion.

Shortly before ten-thirty on the night of 15th September, Sergeant John Hannah, a Scot from Paisley near Glasgow and a wireless operator/air gunner in a force of fifteen Handley Page Hampdens of No.83 Squadron, took off heading for the port of Antwerp. As the bombers approached their target, one by one they were caught in the dazzling beams of the defending searchlights and the intense barrage of flak began. A few moments after Hannah's aircraft, which was being flown by Pilot Officer CA Conner, released its bombs it took a direct hit in the bomb compartment which just a few moments earlier had been full of high explosives and incendiaries.

The aircraft was also hit by bullets and shrapnel which pierced both port and starboard fuel tanks: an intense fire quickly engulfed the fuselage, leaving the rear gunner no option but to bale out when the floor beneath his feet melted. The pilot struggled to bring the aircraft round and headed back out to sea and away from the flak. However, his burning aircraft was like a flaming beacon in the sky. The fourth crew member, the navigator/ bomb aimer also now baled out and John Hannah would have been wholly entitled to follow him, leaving Pilot Officer Conner to almost certain death. The Scot had other ideas, though, and quickly reached the two manual fire extinguishers, emptying them onto the fire. But his difficulties were about to get much worse as the ammunition in the gun trays started to detonate inside the aircraft, exploding in all directions. He quickly disposed of these cases through the holes in the fuselage and returned to fight the fire, this time with his parachute. The intensity of the fire, which was fanned by the air rushing into the damaged aircraft, melted the aluminium floor he was standing on, leaving him only the struts for support. Already badly burned and almost blinded by the intense heat, he continued to attack the fire until he had nothing left to use but his bare hands, which he did sustaining further burns.

After ten minutes he had incredibly overcome the fire and extinguished the flames. Crawling forward through the cramped fuselage he reported to a shocked Conner that the fire was out and handed his captain the navigator's log and maps. When the Hampden landed back at RAF Scampton later that night, it was the last of the fifteen to do so and provided Bomber Command with a clean sweep for the night: 155 aircraft out, 155 aircraft back.

John Hannah received his Victoria Cross from King George VI at Buckingham Palace on 10th October 1940: he was only eighteen years of age. He was too badly injured to return to flying duties and never properly regained his health. Very sadly, weakened by his injuries, Glasgow's first RAF Victoria Cross holder died on 9th June 1947 suffering from the tuberculosis he had contracted whilst still in the RAF.

Sgt. John Hannah, VC

Scampton church where there is a memorial garden to John and a special rose named after him.

In August 1943, No.14 OTU moved to RAF Market Harborough and on 1st September I reported there not as an instructor but on my aircrew refresher course: I was being prepared for operational duties once more. In some ways the break from operations had been enjoyable; I had been able to get up each morning and not wonder whether I would be killed that day, although some of the training trips as an instructor had been more frightening than the milk-run! On the other side of the coin, I had missed the close companionship of a bomber crew and the adrenalin of operations; goodness knows why really because it was unbelievably dangerous.

It felt strangely reassuring to climb back into the rear turret and sit behind the guns again: comfortably familiar. At the end of my gunnery course I passed out with a score of 82 per cent, and noted on my record as above average; clearly my months on operations in the desert had done my shooting skills a world of good and not only had I gained the experience my original instructor deemed I needed, but I had gone from below average to above average. I felt vindicated.

In late October I was approached by a pilot a year older than me, who was putting together a crew before we moved on to No.1661 Heavy Conversion Unit at RAF Winthrope, and was looking for a competent rear gunner.

That Pilot Officer was Basil Montague Acott, who after the war went on to have a successful career in London with the Metropolitan Police, rising to the rank of Commander. His career would probably have gone largely unnoticed outside the confines of the police service and the London criminal underworld had it not been for a notorious murder case in 1960, the details of which rumbled on for another forty years: the A6 murder.

James Hanratty was accused and subsequently convicted of murdering Michael Gregsten and raping and attempting to murder his girlfriend, Valerie Storie, in a lay-by on the A6 near Bedford. Hanratty was hanged on 4th April 1962 and since then much has been written about the part Bob Acott, as we knew him, played as the investigating officer, in the evidence put before the jury. In 2000, the case came before the High Court to test whether Hanratty's conviction had been unsound on the basis, amongst other things, that material evidence had been withheld from the jury by Acott. The tests which the Court of Appeal applied were of course based upon the rules of evidence, practice and procedure as they are now and not as they were in 1961 when Hanratty's trial took place. After a careful examination of all the evidence put before them by very eminent lawyers, including Michael Mansfield, QC for the Hanratty family, the Court of Appeal concluded that the conviction had not been unsound and that the verdict should stand. When all else was swept aside, the modern science of DNA evidence from the car and from Valerie Storie's underwear which had been forensically preserved, proved Hanratty's guilt beyond all reasonable doubt, which was fitting really since Michael Gregsten was a scientist. It was perhaps a pity that Bob Acott did not live to see the final chapter in the case.

All that, though, lay in the future, for now there was a war to be fought and we were busy with our refresher training. The general practice was that those crews who had completed a tour would be sent as instructors for about six months to give them a break from operations. At the end of that period of instructing, each individual would return to operations, but six months was a long time to be out of the front line and techniques, equipment and tactics had moved on. The need for further training was obvious.

With a complete crew we moved to No.1661 HCU and trained on Stirlings before transferring to the Lancaster Finishing School [LFS] at RAF Syerston, five miles south-west of Newark. By the time I got there at the end of January 1944, No.61 Squadron had not long moved out to RAF Skellingthorpe only to be moved again to Coningsby to allow for runway repairs at Skellingthorpe, but at the time I did not know that it would be my posting after LFS.

A few days later I was promoted to Warrant Officer, had a more comfortable uniform to wear, a pay rise and some home leave before joining my squadron. I was posted to No.61 Squadron, the Squadron which holds the honour to have dropped the first bombs of the war to fall on German soil. On 19th March 1940, the Squadron's Hampdens attacked the Hornum seaplane base at Sylt in the North Frisian Islands. I reported for duty to B Flight, at RAF Coningsby, part of No.5 Group Bomber Command: it was Sunday, 13th February, the start of my second tour.

CHAPTER ELEVEN

"They sowed the wind and now they will reap the whirlwind."

Air Chief Marshal Arthur T Harris

My crew L to R with our faithful Lancaster, QR-T. Duggie May [BA], Dickie Ward [Nav], Bob Acott [pilot], Bill Rudd [FE], me [RG], Arthur Atkinson [WOP], Al Breynton [MUG]. I was known as Charlie after the actor Charles Boyer and because I was a rear gunner.

We gathered together as a crew and then after a few minutes' chat went to our respective messes which, for the duration of our stay at Coningsby, we were sharing with No.619 Squadron who had moved there from Woodhall Spa in January, swopping places with No.617 squadron. We had a few days to settle in and, looking around the mess, it was obvious that the lads on 617 had certainly let their hair down between operations. We were welcomed by the CO, Wing Commander RN Stidolph, who told us that we had joined the squadron at a very busy time and that they were at full stretch on operations. I was soon to find out that he wasn't joking.

The squadron was actually based at Skellingthorpe, just outside the city of Lincoln and not far from Coningsby. In 1937, when the squadron had been re-formed in the run-up to the war, it adopted the Lincoln Imp as part of the design of its crest. However, for the time being we were stationed at Coningsby whilst the runways at Skellingthorpe were repaired and also to relieve a little of the congestion in the skies over the city.

At breakfast the following Sunday I looked at the notice board in the mess to see what was happening that day and to look at the Battle Order list: I was down for operations that night. I felt my stomach tighten: that deep fear wondering whether tonight would be my last. Everyone was the same but nobody showed it: we all had different ways of covering it up, but it was there. Although new to the squadron, I had already completed a first tour of thirty-nine operations and so was certainly not a rookie, nevertheless I still felt nervous, probably because, thinking back to the thousand-bomber raid on Essen, I knew what was awaiting us.

Later I wandered down to the Flights to see if an air test was on; it was very relaxed as usual with the aircrew sitting around. Even though I had just had breakfast, I helped myself to some of the raisins from one of the cartons which were lying about.

I used to take a good walk around the perimeter track in the afternoon and breathe in the fresh air. It helped me to remember what I was fighting for. It had been more difficult in the desert because it was too hot to walk about in the middle of the day. We also did so many ops in such a short space of time, on one occasion doing two in one day, that I mainly concentrated on getting some sleep before a mission.

My own crew was still not operational, but I was down to fly as rear gunner with another crew, that of Flight Lieutenant Fitch, whose regular gunner was suffering from frost bite. Later in the day I cycled out to Lancaster QR-S for Sheila, standing at the dispersal point. The ground crew were already preparing her for the raid that night. I climbed into the fuselage, slid down over the tail spar and settled into my seat as I had done a hundred times before. I checked that everything in the Fraser Nash turret was working properly and that all the condensation was wiped clear of the guns to prevent it from freezing once we were airborne. The gun breach blocks were heated as was my intercom microphone to prevent my breath freezing it up. The temperature in the rear turret got down very low, usually to around minus fifty degrees centigrade at 25,000 feet. I also checked that the wires were attached to the sliding doors behind me. In the event of my needing to bale out in a hurry, all I had to do was turn the turret through 90 degrees to the fuselage, push down on these two wires with my elbows and the doors would slide open and I could fall out backwards: that was the theory anyway.

A year later, a young sergeant with No.50 Squadron, H James Flowers after landing back at Skellingthorpe from a mission over Germany, pressed down with his elbows only to find that the wires were missing. He now found himself trapped in the turret, prevented by his thick clothing from twisting round to reach the door lock which was behind him and level with the centre of his back. The intercom had been switched off and the crew were beginning to leave the aircraft. Despite his shouts for help, the others did not hear him over the noise of other aircraft landing and taxiing around the track. Left to get himself out, he forced his upper body round to reach the door catch in the cramped turret but just as he had almost reached it, his right knee suddenly flicked out of its socket.

Just to add to the misery of the excruciating pain, he then saw the rest of the crew climbing into the transport to take them back to debrief and the mess, leaving him alone out in the gloom of the airfield at dispersal. With no other choices he then twisted around in the opposite direction with the same result; just as he was about to reach the catch, his left knee popped out too. Eventually, in excruciating pain he managed to reach the catch and get out of the aircraft, but then, having put both knees back in, had to walk across the airfield to the debrief hut, only to be met with, "Where the hell have you been, James?"

The great lesson he learned from this little escapade was to religiously check that the wires were in place before every trip. If he had needed to bale out on that mission, he would not have had time to do so.

Around two-thirty in the afternoon all crews had their separate section briefings; pilots and navigators, wireless operators, bomb aimers, flight engineers and gunners, and then teatime arrived at last and we went back to the mess for a good meal of bacon and eggs. Only pilots and navigators knew the target before the main briefing. As we entered the briefing room, we all emptied our pockets into a tray and our possessions were kept by the intelligence officer until we returned. If we didn't return then they would be given to our next of kin; either way, the Germans didn't get them. At the far end of the briefing room, there was the familiar wall map still covered, hiding its secrets for a few more minutes, then when everyone was assembled, the curtain was drawn back, revealing the target for tonight. God, it's Stuttgart. There was an audible groan from around the room. Stuttgart is in southern Germany and it would take us over four hours to get there, fully laden, and we would be prey to the night fighters for most of that time; and then we had to get back.

The plan was that there would be a sweep over the North Sea and also a diversion raid to Munich to draw the fighters up early and use their fuel before the main bomber force arrived. It sounded good; I just hoped that it would work because we were going to be flying over German territory for a long time.

As the time for the mission drew close, the tension and feeling of foreboding seeped through the station: it affected everyone, whether the WAAF drivers or the CO, we all felt it, it was always the same. At tea there had been little chatter amongst the crews; nobody was feeling good. We were not going off on some adventure, we were going to take off in a few hours and the lives of each and every one of us would hang in the balance until we landed again. Looking around the mess, we all knew that perhaps tonight would be another night that some of us would not come back: it didn't leave much room for humour. The previous night two crews had failed to return, all but two having been killed. Twelve more young lives snuffed out.

Presently it was time to draw our parachutes from the stores. I checked mine automatically; it was second nature to me. I lifted the studded flap to expose the wire from the D-ring and made sure that the red cotton binding was intact. This told me that it had not been tampered with or accidentally pulled and just stuffed back into the cover.

The free parachute, that is where the ripcord is pulled by the airman during descent rather than being attached to the aircraft as it is for paratroopers, was invented in 1919 by the American born Leslie Irvin, who at only nineteen years of age tested his own invention in front of the US Military. In 1921 Lieutenant Harold R Harris became the first person to be forced to bale out of a doomed aircraft and have his life saved by an Irvin parachute. Since then over 45,000 men have come to owe their lives to Leslie Irvin's invention. Membership of the élite Caterpillar Club is reserved for that group of people whose lives have been saved by their parachutes in an enforced bale-out.

In the event, the overall plan for the raid did work. We didn't see any fighters and I didn't see any of our own aircraft go down. When we returned to Coningsby and touched down at seven-thirty next morning, we did so knowing that we had managed to bomb the Bosch factory and cause a lot of damage, despite cloud cover over the target. Nevertheless, of the 598 aircraft which took off, 9 failed to return, 7 Lancasters and 2 Halifaxes, 63 more airmen lost.

We did not fly the next night and so took advantage of the chance to go to the pictures. Each night, the station transport ran to the village of Woodhall Spa, about five miles away, where the Kinema in the Woods was located. This cinema, spelt with a 'K', is now the oldest continuously running picture house in the world and during the war was a great favourite with RAF personnel. The village of Woodhall Spa is a Victorian Garden Village, set amongst woodland. It grew up because of the spa waters there and the railway which brought the guests to the Royal Hotel and although the hotel, the railway and the spa have all long since gone, the village remains a quiet backwater of great charm.

Kinema in the Woods at Woodhall Spa

The spa baths which have seen better days

Standing at the crossroads in the middle of the village is the memorial to the 204 members of No.617 Squadron whose home was RAF Woodhall Spa. It is a beautiful memorial in the shape of the breached Mohne dam and stands on land donated by the East Lindsay District Council and was the site of the former Royal Hotel and Winter Gardens which were destroyed by a German land mine on the night of 17th/18th August 1943. In 1986, the squadron committee was trying to raise the £20,000 that was needed to build the memorial. F/Lt Chan Chandler, DFC and bar, who had been a rear gunner on No.49 Squadron at Scampton and No.617 at Woodhall Spa, offered to sell his medals together with citations through Sotheby's. The press got hold of the story and on the morning of the sale he went on the BBC Breakfast television programme to explain why he was selling his medals. He had barely left the set when a telephone call was received from John Paul Getty who, astonishingly, had been watching the programme. Mr Getty offered to pay the full cost of the memorial on the condition that Chan did not sell his medals. Typical of Mr Getty's generosity, there is nothing on the memorial to say that he was its benefactor.

No.617 Squadron memorial at Woodhall Spa

But all that was still years away; in February 1944 we were in good spirits simply because the squadron had not lost any aircraft on the previous night's raid. Aircrew socialised together, irrespective of rank and it was not unusual for one member to go home on leave and take another one or two of his crew along with him, especially if they were from Canada, Australia or New Zealand and so unable to get home themselves. Sometimes, bar staff not familiar with aircrew culture would try to restrict the lounge to officers only, with disastrous results. One such occasion involved a new barmaid at a regular aircrew haunt. The pub was already fairly full when this particular crew arrived in the lounge. The Flight Sergeant attempted to get served only to be told by the barmaid that the lounge was for officers only. The entire room put down their drinks and everyone crushed into the bar which, it was said, was now so full it was breathing by numbers. The senior officer present made the situation known to the landlord who was upstairs having his tea. He rushed down, apprised his new member of staff of the rules relating to aircrew and normality was restored. It was another example of the closeness of aircrew.

Four days later it was Schweinfurt. This was to be Bomber Command's first attack on the vital ball-bearing factories in the town and the plan was to split the force into two waves, two hours apart. No.61 Squadron was to be part of the first wave: oh what joy. The squadron had taken a battering and had lost twenty-two crews in eight months: it had been a very dangerous time for Bomber Command crews and it wasn't getting any better.

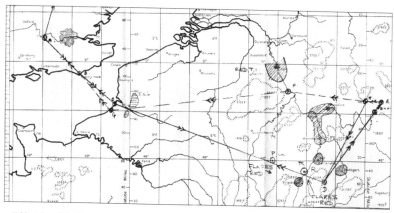

Pilot's flight map to Schweinfurt showing the target and turning points [Bernard Fitch collection]

Once more I was detailed to fly in Flight Lieutenant Fitch's aircraft. Bernard Fitch was a very experienced pilot and when he completed his tour in April, he became the first person to complete a tour with the Squadron since August 1943 and was subsequently awarded the DFC. He left us when posted to No.5 Lancaster Finishing School at RAF Syerston on 27th April.

F/Lt Bernard Fitch, DFC [Bernard Fitch collection]

After our tea, we left the mess and went to the crew locker rooms to collect our flying clothing and parachutes. We tested our oxygen masks and helmet intercom, earpiece and microphone. It was a routine but vital check: now was the time to find a fault, not when being attacked by a night fighter or missing the order to bale out. Then it was time to collect our escape kit: Belgian and Dutch francs should we land in those countries and food rations to eat whilst on the run – compressed fruit and Horlicks tablets. We also had sandwiches and wide-mouthed flasks of hot coffee to drink during the mission, and chewing gum to help with concentration. Today's football managers have not the slightest idea of what it is like to chew gum at times of real tension! Duly dressed and kitted out, it was time to go.

It is difficult to describe just how cold it got in the aircraft, but especially in the rear turret, which was not really part of the fuselage, but stuck outside it at the end. I was dressed in my thick long johns, a thick vest, a shirt, a sleeveless jersey, a scarf, a thick polo neck jersey, battledress, my Taylor flying suit, which would be heated once I was in the aircraft and plugged it in with my Sidcot suit over the top, heated slippers, fur-lined boots down which I tucked a commando knife and a torch, helmet, goggles, and of course my parachute and harness. On my hands I wore silk gloves, then a pair of chamois gloves, then fingerless woollen mittens and finally a pair of thick outer leather gauntlets which plugged into the heated suit. They didn't always work any more than the heated slippers did, but they were good when they did.

All the Perspex from the front of the turret had been removed, giving the gunners a better view of the sky outside and so helping us see night fighters sooner; it did, but it also increased the feeling of being perched out in thin air. As a guide, the temperature dropped about two degrees centigrade for every thousand feet of height and since it was already well below freezing at sea level, I could expect the temperature in my turret to fall to about minus thirty degrees centigrade that night. Despite the heating links, my oxygen mask and helmet would freeze onto my face and leave a burn mark, so to try to protect my skin a little I would smear it with Vaseline and stuff cotton wool around the edges of the mask and helmet. I may have looked comical but it certainly helped.

Sgt Jimmy Huck in his flying kit, giving some idea of how many layers rear gunners had to wear before squeezing into the turret. The picture also shows the open front of the rear turret! [Ted Beswick collection]

Anyone who has ever sat in the rear turret of a Lancaster will know just how little room there is. Most of the space is taken up by the four Browning machine guns, the hydraulic mechanism and the bullet channels which feed the guns with 12,000 rounds. The rear gunner had to squeeze in behind all this and then close the doors, and many a lad had to be literally crammed into the turret by another crew member before take-off. No-one was fat in those days, but the rear turret was definitely for thin aircrew.

That night the Coningsby Base Commander, Air Commodore Bobby Sharp, joined us as an unofficial addition to the crew. It was against orders but many COs did this to give leadership and support for the crews they were sending out, sometimes several times a week. For some COs it was their last sortie as they were shot down and died with their crew. The Air Commodore spent most of the trip sitting on the step which led down from beside the pilot to the bomb aimer's position in the nose of the aircraft, although at times the skipper did organise him to busily throw out bundles of 'window', strips of tin foil used to confuse the enemy radar signals.

The air was bitterly cold as we clambered out of the truck in front of Lancaster QR-S. A lazy wind was blowing off the North Sea and across the Lincolnshire flats and it cut like a knife, even with all our kit on. It had snowed earlier in the day and the light dusting gave the airfield a spectral appearance. In peacetime it would have been pretty, but not tonight. For a little while we stood outside the Lancaster, huddled in a small group, having a last cigarette whilst the ground crew fussed around their beloved aeroplane. Aircrew thought the world of their ground staff. They looked after the aircraft and they looked after us. To have a Lancaster bomber ready to fly night after night, involved thirty-eight people, of whom the aircrew were only seven. The other thirty-one were ground staff ranging from the fitters and armourers to the controller and the invaluable WAAF who packed our parachutes. They are the forgotten and unsung heroes of Bomber Command because without their skills we would not have had so many aircraft to fly and the damage to the German war machine would have been that much less.

Presently, F/Lt Fitch signed for QR-S from the ground crew and she became our responsibility for the next few hours. Then all too soon the rockets went up signalling us to get aboard and start up. From around the airfield the noise of the engines grew to a deafening crescendo as one by one the Lancasters of two squadrons fired up and started to move. Some thirty aircraft, four great Rolls Royce Merlin engines each, all running together. Just before eight o'clock we joined the line of shadowy figures and bobbing navigation lights taxiing around the perimeter track towards the head of the main runway. I watched the vague shape of the Lancaster behind us as it followed our faint tracks through the powdery dusting of snow, the flurries thrown up by its churning propellers obscuring my view with a shroud of white mist.

The tightening in my stomach had eased now; there was a job to be done. I checked that the turret was locked in the forward position, slipped a wakey-wakey Benzedrine tablet into my mouth, grimaced on the bitter taste and followed it with a piece of chewing gum. A few moments later we had reached the end of the track and waited to turn onto the runway. There to wave us all off was a group of some fifty people; ground staff, airmen and WAAFs, standing around the chequered wagon in that bitterly cold wind to wish us all God speed and a safe return. We got the green on the Aldis lamp, the brakes came off and we moved onto the runway. The engine revs began to build and I could feel the airframe vibrating heavily, then we started down the runway. I returned the frantic waves of the well-wishers and then, in a moment, they were gone, lost in the dark and the swirling snow of our slipstream as once more the runway opened up in front of me and the lights flashed by faster and faster.

In my headset I could hear the navigator counting out our speed to the skipper as we slowly gathered momentum towards the 125 miles per hour that was critical if we were to get into the air. Seventy-five, eighty-five, ninety-five, "Come on, Sheila, lift off, we're running out of concrete," I muttered to myself. The tail had come up and then the noise of the runway under the wheels was suddenly gone.

There was the reassuring clunk as the undercarriage locked up and we gradually climbed into the night sky in a long circuit to our meeting point whilst I looked down onto the snow-covered countryside of Lincolnshire, easily able to pick out the hedges and narrow lanes dividing the fields over which the dark shapes of other Lancasters were passing, their navigation lights still twinkling.

The crew called each other up through the intercom to make sure that it was working all right and that we were all in touch, and I asked the skipper for permission to test my guns. By now we were at about 8,000 feet and climbing all the time to the bomber stream meeting point. Then, navigation lights off, we set out across the Home Counties towards Reading and then Beachy Head, aiming to cross the French coast at about 20,000 feet, above the level of the light flak, on the long leg towards the turning point south of Schweinfurt. I switched on my heated suit and felt the comforting tingle as it began to warm me.

Then the warning in my headset, "Enemy coast coming up," and from now on we could expect an attack at any moment. I had been searching the sky for some time already, but now my efforts doubled. We had tricked the night fighters last time but I didn't think it would work a second time, not since we were in the first wave of the attack. I stood up in my turret and peered out into the darkness of the night and searched back as far as I could see.

There was safety in the numbers of the bomber stream, but there was also the ever-present danger of collision. 'Don't be proud – stay with the crowd', was the slogan on the posters in the Flights which urged crews not to drift off on their own and become easy targets for the night fighters, directed onto them by the ground radar stations along our route. More flak was coming up now as we penetrated deeper into Germany, momentarily lighting up a patch of sky, then welcome darkness again. A change of course and then the steady motion of the aircraft resumed, allowing the mid-upper and me a constant view around us.

Suddenly, over to one side a burst of orange lit up the shape of a Lancaster I hadn't even known was there, its wing on fire. The flames spread quickly and soon engulfed the aircraft as it turned over and plunged towards the earth. It was too far away for me to see whether anyone got out and I was intent on ensuring that the fighter which had brought death to that crew didn't do the same to us. The Ju88s and Me110s with their upward firing cannon would enter the bomber stream and slowly fly beneath an aircraft, shoot straight up into the petrol tanks in the wing, not the fuselage in case the bombs exploded and brought them down as well, and then slide away in the dark to do it all again. We hated them.

Another Lancaster very close to us was going down with flames streaming out behind and then yet another a little way to the rear. The desert had been bad but this was terrifying. I knew that we were nearing the target because the flak batteries were getting more active, and then we were on our bombing run.

"Left, left, left, steady; bombs gone," the quiet calm voice of the bomb aimer guiding the skipper on to the TIs [target indicators.]

I felt her lift fifty feet straight up as if pulled by a piece of string when the weight dropped out; felt the skipper hold her straight and steady for the photographs, those seconds ticking by like hours; heard the thump of the bomb bay doors closing; saw the searchlights weaving across the sky, thin stabbing fingers of light that could mean disaster if they coned us. The flak was exploding all around and looking down I could see the outline of several Lancasters and Halifaxes silhouetted against the fires burning in the city far below, as they flew across the aiming point.

Then it was over and, free of our bombs, we picked up speed and headed into the darkness beyond the target for the first turning point of our homeward leg, always fearful of turning too soon and colliding with another aircraft in the stream. It was speed which was taking us away from that cauldron of death and destruction to which we had added and were a part of, into the blessed cloak of darkness: but now the fighters would be arriving to take their revenge for what we had done. I looked back across the target and could see that the fires were spread out a long way but they faded by the minute as we left them further and further behind. The long dangerous flight back across the seemingly empty, treacherous skies over Germany, the only voice in my headset that of our navigator giving course changes to the skipper as we droned ever nearer to the Dutch coast and the North Sea, our gateway to safety. On and on we flew into the darkness, the hydraulics constantly rotating my turret from side to side, the guns up and down, flying steady, straight, level, the shortest route home, the bomb bay empty, our job done; the freezing air blowing through the turret, my oxygen mask rubbing hard on my face where the cotton wool had slipped, grinding the frozen condensation into my cheeks, reminding me that it was not quite over.

A searchlight flicked on and some more flak came up but it was a long way off; some other poor crew had strayed into the defensive box and were being punished for it. I wanted to watch, hoping that they would get through as we had done, but it was too dangerous to lose concentration now, although I was vaguely conscious that there had been no fateful splash of orange and it wasn't long before the light went out. On we flew still, the steady rhythm of the engines a reassuring companion. Then far below, tiny pinpoints of light and a moment later the flak came up, light-coloured puffs of smoke betraying the shell bursts, the smell of cordite seeping into my turret. Then, just as I thought we had escaped, the port wing lifted from the force of the shell that exploded just beneath it, but the Lancaster hardly winced and then we were through the predictive flak.

The intercom sparked into life again, "Coast coming up, skipper." At long last, and a few moments later I looked down to see the thin string of cotton threads that were the lines of waves breaking along the shore of the French coast slowly receding into the darkness, into nothing. We had made it to the English Channel and although it was no time to relax, a great feeling came over the aircraft; we were nearly home, had nearly made another one safely. We crossed the coast of England at Beachy Head once more and I relaxed just a little, enough to pour a cup of coffee from my flask, the steam making the raw flesh on my cheeks smart as I took a welcome sip of the sweet fluid.

We were losing height steadily now and I knew that we were dropping down to join the circuit over Coningsby. Called in by control in the order of our arrival, we stepped down 500 feet at a time on each circuit until at last it was our turn to land and I felt the reassuring clunk as the undercarriage locked down. We were gliding in now but the Lancaster hesitated, floated and hung breathless for a moment as if unwilling to leave the sky and return to earth. Then she was down, contact with the concrete and racing past the lights at the edge of the runway as again it unfolded in front of me into the distance, just a blur at first but then becoming clearer and soon each light had an identity of its own as the brakes squealed and slowed her to a more sedate pace. It was like watching a film being run backwards, the view the reverse of the one I had had a few hours earlier. We turned in and taxied to dispersal where our faithful ground crew were waiting to welcome us, and their aircraft, back home. It was still snowing.

The Lancaster settled on the 'frying pan' dispersal, the Merlins quiet, save for the clicking of the metal which had glowed so hot for the last eight and a half hours, contracting quickly now in the cold night air. One by one we stumbled out of the fuselage and down the ladder to the firmness of the ground.

"Well done, chaps, bloody good show. Let's get a mug of hot tea." It was Bobby Sharp, the CO; I had forgotten all about him being with us as I turned towards the WAAF driver waiting in the transport to take us back for debrief with the intelligence officer. As I did so I glanced up at the port wing to see the hole left in it by the shrapnel; another job in the morning for the ground crew.

When we walked into the debriefing room, there were already several crews home and everybody was talking at once, just adrenalin-driven babble. One of the volunteer WAAFs brought us each a mug of steaming hot tea whilst we waited to be called over to one of the tables, all eight of us. Mostly it was F/Lt Fitch, the navigator and the wireless operator who reported, but the mid-upper and I made a contribution about the attack and how many of our own aircraft we had seen go down and the CO reported on window and flak. Many of the crews had a black mark over their noses where the rubber of their oxygen mask had melted a bit with the heat and sweat – everyone except the rear gunners whose faces were red from the ice which had formed around our masks and rubbed our faces raw.

We got rid of our kit, went for a breakfast of bacon and fresh eggs, the treat reserved for aircrew, and then it was blessed sleep for those who could close their minds to the horrors we had seen and the friends we had left behind. That night we lost QR-E. F/Lt Webb's crew all died when she went down, apart from Sgt Brown who managed to parachute to safety but was captured soon afterwards. We had survived, though, another mission completed. I eventually drifted off into a land of troubled dreams: it had been another long night.

The first half of March was very good for the squadron. On the 10th we were part of a thirty-strong force which raided the aircraft factory at Chateauroux and all the crews returned safely. Indeed of the 128 aircraft that took off that night, only one was lost, the Lancaster of Squadron Leader Pike from No.207 Squadron over Clermont-Ferrand; sadly all the crew were killed. Five days later we were back to Stuttgart and this was the first operation I did with my new crew including Bob Acott as our pilot. QR-T for Tommy was our aircraft, and a very good one she finally proved to be but sadly an inevitable fate awaited her.

The raid was not a great success. The wind had caused the Pathfinder marking to fall back and most of our bombs fell in open country to the south-west of the city. When we got to the target the fighters were waiting for us and although QR-T was not attacked I saw two other Lancasters going down.

However returning home we had a close call. The aircraft generator had failed causing the loss of our master compass and radio transmitter. After we left the target we headed back to England, but drifted too far west. If it hadn't been for the vigilance of the ground crew manning an isolated flashing beacon site in Somerset, we would have continued across the Bristol Channel, using up the last dregs of our fuel, and crashed into the mountains of south Wales. In response to our distress calls we were thrown a lifeline; the runway lights of RAF Westonzoyland, which was now directly below us, flicked on and reached up to us through the darkness. But we were not safe yet; as we made our first approach the hydraulics failed and neither the wheels nor the flaps would lower. We had to overshoot. With our nerves stretched even tighter and our fuel almost gone we went round again whilst Bill Rudd worked feverishly to lower the flaps by hand and the emergency compressed air tank provided the power to the undercarriage. Following a tense nail biting circuit we at last touched down. We learned later that the lights had almost been switched off after we had failed to land at our first attempt. Without our radio transmitter to call for them to be switched on again, we would have crashed.

The rest of the squadron aircraft returned safely and together with other raids, Bomber Command put up 1,116 aircraft that night, a new record. But there was no room for complacency. In three raids, Leipzig on 19th February, Berlin on 24th March and Nuremberg on 30th March we lost 245 aircraft over Europe, over 1,700 airmen, most of who never came home again. At Leipzig we lost seventy-eight aircraft, the worst losses on a mission in the war so far. At Berlin we lost seventy-two aircraft, surely it couldn't get any worse; at Nuremburg it did.

Quite simply, the raid should never have gone ahead. It was a full-moon period, which would normally have meant a stand down and although the early weather forecast suggested that there would be high protective cloud for the outward journey, later reconnaissance by a Mosquito of the Meteorological Flight reported that the cloud would probably only be over the target. To add to the full moon, the lack of cloud and badly forecast winds, to make matters even easier for the fighters, the route included one long straight leg of over two hundred miles across Germany to Nuremberg. Everything was against the mission but it was not cancelled and 95 aircraft from the main force of 795 were lost: most of the men flying in those aircraft were killed. We lost eighty-two aircraft on the way out, sixty on that long straight leg alone. It took an hour to fly and the fighters shot us down at the rate of one every minute; one every three miles.

For those still able to look down, the track of the bomber stream was clearly visible from 20,000 feet; the bright gashes of burning aircraft on the black ground, filled with bombs and fuel, marking the funeral pyres of so many of our friends. The fighters had an easy time; every one of our 795 bombers left a deep and wide condensation trail as it sped on its way, a perfidious invitation pouring out from the engines, gleaming straight and clear in the moonlight, showing up a deathly pale against the deep navy blue of the night sky. It was so easy for a fighter pilot striking from below to pick out a target and our bombers were being shot down quicker than anyone could count. Those like wireless operator Sgt Reg Payne in F/Lt Michael Beetham's crew of No.50 Squadron who survived the Nuremburg raid, will never forget the images of that night.

The raid was an unmitigated disaster; the attack was not a great success and the losses were Bomber Command's heaviest of the war. Moreover, it came less than a week after the last heavy bomber raid to be launched against Berlin, in which seventy-two aircraft had been lost. Losses on this scale were simply unsustainable.

Nuremberg brought an end to the Battle of Berlin. It also brought the battle's only Victoria Cross. Pilot Officer Barton was the captain of a Halifax from No.578 Squadron. His aircraft had been attacked and badly damaged by a fighter on the way to Nuremburg and following a communication misunderstanding, three of his crew, including his navigator and wireless operator

224

had baled out. Despite having also lost power from one of his engines, he carried on to Nuremberg, bombed the target and set course for home. Fate was against this brave young man, though, because an unexpected wind pushed his Halifax up the North Sea and he did not cross the English coast until he was over Sunderland, by which time his fuel had run out and he was forced to land. Although his three remaining crew members were only slightly injured in the crash their pilot did not survive it.

Although we didn't know it at the time, the Berlin raid on 24th March produced one of the most remarkable escapes of the war. No-one really knows how many people have survived after jumping out of an aircraft without a parachute, but six such occasions have been documented; that of F/Sgt Nicholas Stephen Alkemade is probably the most incredible. Nicholas Alkemade was the rear gunner in Lancaster DS 664 KO-D of No.115 Squadron, piloted by F/Sgt J Newman. Flying at 19,000 feet over Westphalia, they were attacked by a Ju88 twin-engine fighter. The Luftwaffe pilot fired his cannons and caught the Lancaster towards the rear of the fuselage. Two cannon shells crashed through the rear turret shattering the Perspex around F/Sgt Alkemade and driving a piece into his right leg. Despite his injury, he opened up on the fighter with his Brownings. At the same moment a blast of searing heat and flame scorched his hands and face. The whole rear section of the aircraft was ablaze and the heat in the turret was so great that it melted the oxygen mask on his face. The pilot ordered his crew to bale out as he fought to keep some control over the aircraft.

Nicholas Alkemade opened his turret doors to reach into the fuselage behind him for his parachute, but the intense heat forced him to quickly close them again, but not before he had caught sight of his parachute blazing in its container. Facing certain death, he could choose one of two ways to die: he could stay where he was and be roasted alive as the Lancaster dropped nearly four miles to earth, or he could open the turret doors and drop out, being assured of at least a quick death when he hit the ground. He chose to jump. He turned the turret sideways and dropped out backwards, but as he did so his flying boot became jammed, causing his knee to twist badly as the slipstream buffeted him about.

A few seconds later his foot came free and he began his fall of three and a half miles, glimpsing the burning torch of the Lancaster as he tumbled through the air. Three hours later Sgt Alkemade opened his eyes, not in Heaven but on a hillside in Westphalia. By an incredible chance he had fallen through some pine trees and into a snow drift, which between them had cushioned the impact.

Having accepted that fate did not wish to claim his life that night, he pulled himself out of the snow drift, took off his parachute harness and tried to walk away. However, he was in too much pain and although he was uninjured by his fall, his wounds from the Ju88 attack prevented any realistic chance of escape. He made little progress and with no further choices he began to blow on his whistle until he was found. The Germans, of course, simply did not believe him at first, believing him to be a spy, but when Luftwaffe officers interrogated him they found that he had a twisted right knee, splinters in his thigh, a badly bruised back, a deep head wound and first-degree burns on his hands and face. The search party then found his harness in a four-foot depression in the snow drift and a few miles away, the wreckage of KO-D with the charred remains of Alkemade's parachute still inside.

On 25th April 1944 F/Sgt Alkemade was presented with the following certificate by the Stalagluft commandant:

> *"It has been investigated and corroborated by the German authorities that the claim made by Flight Sergeant Alkemade is true in all respects, mainly that he made a descent from 19,000 feet without a parachute and made a safe landing without injury, the parachute having been on fire in the aircraft. He landed in deep snow among fir trees."*

And despite all that, he didn't qualify for the Caterpillar Club! Not long afterwards, all rear gunners were issued

226

with pilots' parachute and harness; this design allowed the gunner to sit on the parachute at all times, rather than having to recover it from the fuselage and clip it on their chest before baling out.

My crew possibly survived the war simply by the sheer luck of having our leave delayed and so not being available for operations on the nights of the Leipzig, Berlin and Nuremberg raids; such is the hand of fate, for the squadron lost two aircraft on each mission. Pilot Officer Carbutt's crew in QR-W and Flying Officer Cox's crew in QR-G were lost over Berlin, whilst on the Nuremburg raid Squadron Leader Moss's crew in QR-P on their twentieth operation were shot down by Hauptman Rudusch in an Me110. Pilot Officer Haste's QR-V was shot down on the way home from Nuremberg by Major Rudolf Schoenert in a Ju88. Sgt Jim Fulker was the only survivor from the twenty-eight lads in those four Lancasters. The optimistic and successful start to the month had been ravaged over the skies of eastern Germany.

There was, however, light at the end of the tunnel. Although we didn't know it at the time, the successes of the German night fighters had passed their peak. As D-Day approached, Bomber Command was assigned to attack small military targets in France in preparation for the invasion. The targets were designed to deny the troops in the Normandy sector any rail link supplies and also were part of a deception to make the Germans believe that the invasion would come in the Pas de Calais area, in northern France. Overlaying that strategy was a need to weaken the Luftwaffe to give the Allies control of the skies over the invasion beaches.

The crews who had taken such a battering in the disastrous Berlin and Nuremburg raids were given a break, and upon our return from leave we were naturally at the top of the list for these new targets, the first of which was Toulouse on the banks of the river Garonne, one of France's largest cities with a population of around 250,000 and home to a large aircraft repair plant. Along with eleven other aircraft from No.61 Squadron we took off from Coningsby at seven-thirty in the evening and headed for the south of France as part of a relatively small force of 144 Lancasters and one Mosquito from No.5 Group.

The raid was particularly successful and it was mainly the flak which caused us the problems rather than night fighters. Along with the rest of the force, we dropped our bombs right on the target from around 13,000 feet. The target had been marked very accurately by Wing Commander Leonard Cheshire, CO of No.617 Squadron at the time, flying in the Mosquito, on his third low-level pass over the factory. Although the factory was heavily defended, the Mosquito was simply too fast for the flak gunners. This was the first time that a Mosquito had been used for target marking, instead of the Pathfinder Lancasters of No.8 Group and the bombing had been so accurate that within a few hours Air Chief Marshal Harris ordered No.5 Group to act as an independent force, using its own marking methods. All the aircraft on operations that night returned safely except for the Lancaster of Warrant Officer Senior from No.207 Squadron, which was hit by flak and blew up over the target, killing all the crew.

Five days later we were once more down for operations, this time the ribbon on the wall map led to Tours in central France, south of Paris: the target was the huge railway marshalling yards. We were then told by the briefing officer that our bombing height would be between 5, 500 feet and 7,500 feet.

"God, Al, I hope to hell that we are on the top deck when we get there," I whispered to my mid-upper. "The flak is going to be lethal at that height."

It had been a very pleasant early spring day and I had enjoyed my walk around the perimeter track in the afternoon. My thoughts had, as so often before an operation, been of home and life before the war. My relationship with Dorothy Chaffner had not really taken off even though we had enjoyed some good times during my leave, and we did remain friends. I had thought about Lydia and wondered where she was and what she was doing and of course I had thought about my mum and dad. I had turned thirty in January and was beginning to think that if I survived this war, it was perhaps time to settle down, but not just yet. I hadn't met the right woman and I could so easily be killed on my next mission: I could so easily be killed that night. I shuddered and pushed the thoughts out of my mind as I had done many times before.

With the briefings over, that feeling of quiet foreboding descended upon the base as the tension began to mount with each passing minute towards take-off. At last it was time to get ready and climb into the transport to be taken to dispersal. A last cigarette and then it was time to go. One by one we ascended the short ladder and ducked through the doorway at the rear of QR-T. The rest of the crew turned right and took up their positions whilst I turned left, checked that the bullet channels were full, clambered over the tail spar and struggled into the rear turret. Once satisfied that everything was in order, the doors were locked behind me, I plugged in my intercom and called up the skipper. We went through the turret rotation drill and then I fixed it in the forward position, checking the safety catch was still on. It wasn't cold enough yet for my heated suit; I would turn that on once we were airborne.

Merlin engines were starting up all over the airfield and we edged out of the frying pan dispersal onto the perimeter track that I had walked around a few hours earlier. Then we were at the head of the runway and I was returning the frantic waves of the men and women at the chequered wagon. It was eight o'clock.

We climbed into the late evening sky and as I looked through the side windows of the turret, I could see the strip of evening light far out to the west grow wider until we reached our cruising height. Only a little sporadic flak spoiled an otherwise uneventful trip across France although no-one was relaxed. The skipper weaved the aircraft gently from side to side to give Al and I chance to see below, should a fighter try to creep up on us; they weren't all defending Germany.

After some three hours we started to descend to our bombing height and I knew that 180 Lancasters squeezed into that small target area was going to bring with it the risk of collision. The searchlights flicked on and the anti-aircraft guns started, "Bomb doors open. Steady, right, right, steady, bombs gone." The familiar quiet tone of Duggie's voice sounding in my ears seemed to drown out the noise of our engines. We were just holding on for the photograph when out of the darkness behind us loomed the shadowy image of another aircraft. "Dive port, go," I yelled into the intercom. In an instant QR-T dropped like a stone and I was thrown forwards and upwards over the guns and yet again I struck my head on the turret frame. Despite the sickening pain, I looked up to see the immense ghostly black silhouette of another Lancaster slide gently by barely fifty feet above us, its great yawning bomb bay doors gaping wide, the engine exhausts glowing in the dark and their thundering, reverberating roar drowning out our own engines. The saliva had drained out of my mouth in the few seconds of the incident and the chewing gum stuck rigid and hard to my palate.

"Didn't make it to the top deck then, Charlie!" quipped Al. The skipper's terse reply soon put a stop to anything I might have said. He was very strict about having no idle chit-chat on the intercom, especially over enemy territory. It was part of the discipline that helped to keep us alive. I had seen aircraft collide; it was a frightening sight. It had been a very close encounter that I never wanted to repeat and yet when we eventually got back to Coningsby, there were other crews who had also had near misses over the target and at the first turning point. It was a miracle that no-one had collided over Tours.

The next night we were down for ops again: Aachen, just on the German side of its border with Belgium. It was another very successful raid and we dropped our bombs right on the target indicators, although there were more fighters about here than further south. We bombed from around 19,000 feet above the scattered cumulus clouds. This was one of those diversionary raids to make the Germans believe that the invasion was coming at Calais.

On our homeward leg, I saw the broken cloud below us but knew that this would offer little protection from the anti-aircraft fire, and as if the gunners down there read my thoughts, a coastal flak ship opened up. Little pin points of light far below followed a few moments later by the shell bursts, but they didn't trouble us for long and we were quickly through it and heading for the outer reaches of the Thames Estuary.

The squadron lost QR-W that night, which failed to return. Flight Sergeant Anderson managed to get out and parachute to safety but was taken prisoner: he was the only member of Flying Officer Williams's crew to survive. On the other side of the airfield, No.619 Squadron had fared even less well and had lost another two aircraft and both crews.

The hazard and obstacle of fire in the tight, cluttered and confined space of the fuselage together with the possibility of injuries having been sustained from a shell burst or cannon fire, made the window of escape for crews little more than a few seconds. It was barely long enough to clip on a parachute and move to the front hatch or aft doorway before the G forces started to make movement all but impossible. The bomber, which was so much a part of the team and had carried her crew so far, now out of control and spiralling towards her own destruction on the earth beneath, so often refused to let her crew go and trapped them inside.

Sgt Reg Payne, Wireless Operator [Reg Payne collection]

CHAPTER TWELVE

"Oh, to be in England now that April's there, and whoever wakes in England sees, some morning, unaware, that the lowest boughs and brushwood sheaf round the elm-tree bore are in tiny leaf...."
From **Home Thoughts From Abroad** *by Robert Browning*

The runway repairs and extra buildings at Skellingthorpe were completed by the middle of April and on 15th we returned to share the airfield with No.50 Squadron. These were two remarkable squadrons and it is perhaps apposite that they should have shared the same base. After the war, when the statistics were being compiled, No.61 Squadron was found to have flown on more raids than any other Lancaster squadron and had flown on the second highest number of raids in the whole of Bomber Command's heavy squadrons, the highest number of raids in Bomber Command's heavy squadrons being flown by none other than our friends in No.50 Squadron.

RAF Skellingthorpe was a very friendly base and the local villagers had a great affection for their squadrons, and still do. The base was situated on the edge of the village from which it took its name and lay about three miles to the west of the centre of Lincoln. I had acquired a bicycle whilst at Coningsby and brought it with me to Skelly, as we all called the base. Bicycles required identity papers just as much as we did and if you took it into Lincoln and were seen by the RAF police, you could be stopped, and usually were, and asked to show the bicycle's ID card. Not having the card was a chargeable offence, even for aircrew. Having a bicycle was really a necessity, though, to get around the camp from our billet, to the sergeants' mess and the flight offices.

Skellingthorpe was a satellite airfield for RAF Waddington which was a couple of miles away and probably because it was so close to Lincoln, it had no NAAFI or other entertainment on the site; everyone went into the town. Strictly, Lincoln is a city with a magnificent cathedral standing on top of the hill and visible for miles around, which of course was the idea when it was built in the Middle Ages. Indeed, until about 200 years ago it was the tallest building in the world. During the war, however, it acted as a navigational landmark for the German bomber crews making their way to the industrial heartland of Yorkshire, to the north.

The main attraction on the base was when there was a dance in the sergeants' mess or in the officers' mess. These were always held during a full-moon period when there were no operations planned. They were wonderful evenings, civilian guests were invited, everyone let their hair down and a lot of drinking was always involved. If we didn't have a local band to play for us, the music was broadcast over the wireless. Anne Shelton and Vera Lynn were the favourite singers and we danced to the tunes of the day from Carroll Gibbons and the Savoy Orpheans, Geraldo, Ambrose, Benny Goodman, Artie Shaw and of course Glenn Miller. Sometimes, the morning after one of these dances, we would find that an air test was necessary on an aircraft or a training flight was planned. Heavily hungover and with a very thick head many an aircrew member would climb aboard the aircraft and make full use of the therapeutic benefits of the oxygen supply to clear his head before taking off.

During the war there were more airfields in Lincolnshire than any other county in Britain and Lincoln was surrounded by them: Coningsby, Skellingthorpe, Scampton and Swinderby; Wickenby, Waddington, Digby and Kelstern; Metheringham, East Kirby and Woodhall Spa are just some of the names I remember so well. Consequently the streets were always full of RAF personnel at night and whilst some pubs were favourites with aircrew, others would be favourites with ground staff. The local girls, the WAAFs and the ATS certainly had the time of their lives with all those RAF boys on hand; although sometimes things didn't quite work out so well. At Skellingthorpe there were two or three very attractive blonde WAAFs who were at first in great demand. However, it seemed that as soon as an airman started to take one of them out on a regular basis, he got the chop and failed to return from a mission. It wasn't long before these WAAFs became known as 'the chop girls', demand drained away and nobody risked taking them out more than once if at all.

One of the favourite meetings places for couples was under the Stone Bow, a huge stone archway, part of the Guildhall. It still stands in the middle of Lincoln, at the junction of High Street and Saltergate near the River Witham and in the war provided shelter from the rain and winter winds whilst waiting for your girlfriend or boyfriend to turn up. During the war, the local girls referred to this archway as 'the Snake Pit'. Sometimes it was quite sad to see a girl left waiting for a lad who didn't turn up; more often than not it was because he had been shot down the night before and she didn't know it yet. Not far from the Stone Bow, on the corner of High Street and Clasket Gate, was Boots' restaurant. Up the flight of stairs, we would be met by a waitress and shown to a table and a pretty decent meal could be bought at a reasonable cost whilst being entertained by a string quartet.

Just below the Stone Bow on the other side of Saltergate was the Saracen's Head Hotel, which was the main drinking place in Lincoln, especially for officers. It was always full of airmen and their girlfriends. I had many an enjoyable evening in there, but never with a chop girl! For those airmen who had a steady girlfriend, the Unity on the corner of Broadgate and St Rumbold Street was a favourite, or the Crown, as these pubs were less crowded, but still very busy. There were canteens especially for the Forces at the YMCA in St Rumbold Street and the NAAFI in Saltergate where you could have a wash and brush up and a reasonably priced meal as an alternative to the Boots' restaurant. Occasionally we would get into the Turk's Head, but it was up at the top of the hill in Lincoln and a little too far out, unless we were going to a dance in the Assembly Rooms afterwards.

The building work on the station had included a new much larger sergeants' mess, built on our squadron's side of the airfield, close to the Doddington Road and although not as cosy as the old wooden one on the other side of the runways, it was large enough for both squadrons to use. It had new showers and ample washing facilities for us all, although from time to time we still had to go through a rather uncomfortable exercise. After our daily shower and shave, we would all hang our canvas wash bags on a peg; every few weeks we were told to remove our bags from these pegs between eleven and one o'clock. Just before the two hours were up, a ground staff airman would come along with a trolley and take down all the remaining bags, their owners presumed to have failed to return from a mission.

Hartsholme Park lake where we did our dinghy training

Hartsholme Park has a lake in one part of it and since the park was very near to the base, the lake was an ideal place to take us for dinghy survival training. In the event of a ditching, each member of the crew had certain jobs to perform so that a proper routine on leaving the aircraft was followed, and nothing was forgotten. The dinghy was thrown into the lake, always upside down, and we had to get into it. It was the job of the mid-upper to get to the dinghy and turn it the right way up, and then everyone else got into it. In the lake we had to do this in full battledress, although we were allowed to take our shoes off. It was always a perishing cold training exercise and a very smelly one too. However, for those crews who did have to ditch, nothing could prepare them for the biting cold and cramped misery in an aircraft life raft the size of a tractor tyre. More than anything, it was the wind that chilled the survivors. Even if they had got into the raft dry, they were soon wet from the sea spray and hypothermia would very quickly set in. The role and rapid response of the Air Sea Rescue Service was vital. No.279 Squadron based at Bircham Newton patrolled the North Sea and was responsible for saving the lives of many airmen by finding them, dropping a larger dinghy to them and then guiding in a rescue craft.

On 12th February 1944, Lancaster W4119 VN-Q Queenie took off from Skellingthorpe on a routine training flight for fighter attack assimilation. The aircraft was to meet up with a Spitfire over south Yorkshire near the Humber estuary and practise evasion methods and corkscrewing in particular. Flight Lieutenant Michael Beetham with his full crew together with Pilot Officer Jennings and his two gunners made up the ten occupants of Queenie. They met the Spitfire and for the first twenty minutes all went well, F/Lt Beetham rolling the aircraft through the corkscrew manoeuvres whilst his gunners used their cine guns on the Spitfire, recording the success of their attempts to shoot it down. The two pilots then changed places, as did the gunners.

The exercise continued and as the Spitfire dived in to attack Queenie, the rear gunner shouted, "Corkscrew, port, go." P/O Jennings put the Lancaster into a steep dive to port, then a climb to port followed by a roll over the top and a dive to starboard, but as he started to do so someone shouted, "Port outer on fire." Sgt Reg Payne was the wireless operator and looked out of the window to see a mass of flames streaming out from the outer port engine. The pilot cut the engine and activated the fire extinguisher, which seemed to douse the flames, but as soon as the extinguisher was empty the fire burned up again and quickly engulfed the engine and the wing around it.

Realising that it was only a matter of seconds until the wing broke away and dropped off, P/O Jennings gave the command to abandon the aircraft, but their troubles were getting worse as each of those seconds passed. They had ten crew in the aircraft instead of seven and it was getting crowded around the rear entrance door.

From his wireless compartment, Sgt Payne could see that all four gunners together with the bomb aimer, who had been taking photographs of the Spitfire from the astrodome, were now gathered around the rear exit. He had also seen that the whole port wing was on fire and so he left the wireless compartment having firmly fixed his parachute to his harness.

The bomb aimer, Sgt Les Bartlett, had already opened the aircraft door and rolled out. Reg Payne quickly moved to join the four gunners who, together with Don Moore, the flight engineer were hesitating by the open hatch. The next out was Jock Higgins, the mid-upper, but he forgot to remove his helmet and intercom lead. Luckily as he went out, the lead pulled his helmet off but he still hit the tail plane and was held there for a few precious seconds until his unfurling parachute whisked him away. Unaware of the intensity of the fire and of the very few seconds remaining before the wing fell off, the three gunners seemed too frightened to jump and beckoned Reg to go next. Reg sat on the edge of the open doorway and, thinking of the cold water of the Humber estuary waiting below him, rolled out, only to be thrown back into the aircraft by the slipstream. The others quickly pushed him out again and at that moment the port wing broke away sending Queenie into a spinning dive to the ground, taking Don and the three gunners with her. Don Moore was destined to die. His fate had been sealed the moment he had stepped into Queenie that day: because it was only a training flight he had left his parachute behind.

Moments before Sgt Payne had left Queenie, F/Lt Beetham and his navigator had managed to leave the stricken aircraft through the forward escape hatch, followed by P/O Jennings. Meanwhile, Sgt Payne had quickly counted to three and then pulled on the ripcord of his parachute: nothing. Again he pulled and still his 'chute wouldn't open. In desperation he pulled again and again as he plunged through the cloud layer, knowing that he too was about to die. Finally he prayed to God to save him and as he did so, he realised that he was not pulling on the ripcord, but on one of the harness handles. In an instant he gave a quick pull on the D-ring and with an overpowering sense of relief felt that life-saving tug as his parachute ballooned above him, slowing his fall to earth to a more sedate pace. He was already below the cloud base: his prayer had been answered with just moments to spare and he was also coming down over land rather than the cold sea.

Now that he had time to take in what was happening, he looked up to see the outer section of Queenie's port wing floating down behind him but fortunately drifting away from him; there was also another parachute a little way off. Queenie hit the ground with a bright orange flash followed by a pall of black smoke, instantly killing the four men trapped inside her. A few seconds later the sound of the crash reached Reg as he floated quietly towards the earth. His guardian angel was still with him and he landed unhurt in a ploughed field whilst he saw the other parachute drift on a little further only to crash into a dense wood: Pilot Officer Jennings was cut and bruised but otherwise unhurt. The remaining crew all survived the crash and became members of the Caterpillar Club. Afterwards as they gathered at the RAF East Kirkby buildings, they were asked to identify the bodies, but no-one volunteered; they just couldn't bring themselves to look at what was left of their friends.

Flight Lieutenant Beetham and his crew flew thirty operational missions with No.50 Squadron from RAF Skellingthorpe, most of which were during the Battle of Berlin. They survived ten missions to the German capital as well as sorties to Leipzig and the infamous Nuremburg raid. He was awarded the Distinguished Flying Cross and the Air Force Cross, remained in the service after the war and, following an outstanding career at home and abroad, was appointed Chief of the Air Staff, becoming the longest-serving officer in that post since Lord Trenchard. He was knighted and made Marshal of the Royal Air Force, a post in which he still actively serves today.

Fl/Lt Michael Beetham, 1944 [Sir Michael Beetham]

*Marshal of the Royal Air Force Sir Michael Beetham,
GCB,CBE,DFC,AFC,FRAeS,DL, 2007 [H James Flowers]*

Queenie had crashed near the perimeter track of RAF East
Kirkby and in 1979, together with a local villager, Reg
Payne returned to the site, now part of the Lincolnshire
Aviation Museum. At the side of the field, the local man told
Reg to stay where he was and, picking up an old bucket,
walked up and down the rows of potatoes, stooping every

few yards to pick something up. After several minutes he returned with a collection of items in the bucket including numerous pieces of Perspex and small metal parts from the Lancaster. Also in the bucket was a large piece of bone which Reg took to a friend who worked at Kettering General Hospital and had it analysed. It was blood group A and part of the pelvis of one of the crew who had died in Queenie; it had lain in that field for thirty-five years. A little imagination will give an idea of the force with which Queenie hit the ground.

The crew of Queenie just before her final flight [Sir Michael Beetham]

The preparations for D-Day were gaining momentum and Bomber Command was particularly busy disrupting the German defences, supplies and communication network. On 18th April, three days after the squadron's move back to Skellingthorpe we were listed for operations, the first of which was to Juvisy, just outside Paris. The mission was considered a complete success and the Intelligence Officer's report records that almost three hours after take-off, we bombed two red spot fires and that the bombing was concentrated around the markers. Although I was preoccupied looking out for fighters, I did allow myself a moment's reflection upon the fact that it was almost exactly six years since Peter and I had been down there, 10,500 feet below me amongst the cafés, patisseries and night life of Paris in the early summer of 1938. How different life had been for the people of Paris then. Well different for most anyway, others would still be selling the same commodities; the café owners, the restaurateurs, the girls in the night clubs; only the nationality of the paying customers had changed during the intervening years. I was glad that I had gone when I had the chance; it wouldn't be a very pleasant place now.

The next mission two days later was also to Paris, this time to the railway marshalling yards at La Chapelle. Split into two parts, the force bombed each half of the yards and caused significant damage. The Group did its own low-level marking with Mosquitoes and we achieved extremely accurate and concentrated bombing. There was no sign of night fighters, although, since we were bombing from 7,750 feet, the flak was fairly intensive and some of it came close enough to rattle through the fuselage. After dropping our bombs and incendiaries, we weaved our way through the searchlights which were all around the marshalling yards and headed for home. Once more, all the squadron's aircraft returned safely.

The weekend brought no relief, it never did, and on Saturday, 22nd April we were back in the air; this time the target was Brunswick in northern Germany. Although the initial marking by 617's Mosquitoes was once more very accurate, a thin layer of cloud obscured the target and faulty communications between the bomber controllers conspired to frustrate our efforts, with the consequence that many bombs were dropped away from the main target area at first, but later became more concentrated. We hated that thin layer of cloud. The defenders would shine their searchlights onto it and although the light couldn't penetrate it, it lit up the cloud below us and made a silver backdrop; when the fighters arrived, flying above the bomber stream, they could see us silhouetted against that backdrop.

With our bombs gone, we turned away from the target and landed back at Skellingthorpe without incident at twenty-five past five in the morning. Unhappily though, QR-P flown by F/Lt Bird, DFC, failed to return, with only him and Pilot Officer Davies surviving to become prisoners of war. There but for the Grace of God went I, because after my two missions with F/Lt Fitch, I had filled in for the sick rear gunner on another crew, when we raided the aircraft factory at Chateauroux; it was F/Lt Bird that I had flown with.

After breakfast on Monday 24th, together with Al Bryenton, our mid-upper I cycled down to the Flights after seeing on the notice board in the mess that we were on ops again that night. The ground staff had QR-T ready to go, wherever it was that we were to be sent and around mid-morning we had a chat with them to see how much fuel was going into the aircraft and what the bomb load was like. This was always a good indication of how far we were going to have to go. The tanks were being filled, 1,200 gallons; we knew that it was going to be a long way that night.

Later at the briefing, all was revealed. The red tape on the large wall map at the end of the room stretched from Skellingthorpe right across to Munich, almost on the Austrian border. Dear God, it was going to be long night and an uncomfortable return flight.

Around seven-thirty we clambered on to the bus with all our kit and were driven across to the far side of the airfield where the ground staff were carrying out their last-minute checks and top-ups on our Lancaster, standing on the frying pan dispersal.

"Good luck, boys," said the WAAF driver as a few minutes later and with equal difficulty, we clambered back out of her bus.
"Thanks a lot, Pat," we returned, each of us occupied by our own thoughts of the mission which lay ahead.

It was a pleasant spring evening and the birdsong from the trees behind us resounded in the still air around the silent aircraft. The base was quiet, waiting for the signal that would start up the Merlin engines and send us on our way. We sat for nearly an hour under the Lancaster on the armourers' trolley, now empty of its load, chatting quietly and smoking. Gradually, as the light began to follow the sun and fade into the west, the birds fell silent, save for one lone song thrush that sang its little heart out, encapsulating everything that an English evening should be.

Then once more it was time to go and we mounted the familiar step ladder into the body of the aircraft, each to his designated location. I checked again that the bullet channels were full: 12,000 rounds to feed my four Brownings at a rate of 1,200 rounds per minute, and scrambled over the tail spar and into my turret. At nine o'clock, we had the green on the Aldis lamp from the controller's van, and in the rapidly fading light I returned the eager waves of those we were leaving behind. Once more I watched the runway unfold in front of me as, slowly at first, we thundered down that concrete strip, and at 125 miles per hour lifted into the evening sky.

Barely had we left the runway when the Skellingthorpe Road, seemingly just a few feet below us, slipped into view and there a small group of well-wishers with upturned faces and waving arms counted us out and on our way. They would count us back in again in the early hours as they lay in bed or busied in the kitchen at the start of the new day. A few moments later the three great square towers of Lincoln cathedral, with the red warning light on the top eased into my view just a little below and off to the right. It was always an anxious few moments until we had climbed above that cathedral on the top of the hill, standing in the way of our heavily laden Lancasters, but oh what a wonderful sight it was when we were returning, empty, safe, home.

The great towers of Lincoln cathedral

243

'Home on Two' by Reg Payne. A Lancaster struggling back on only two engines with the welcome sight of Lincoln cathedral [Reg Payne]

The sky was becoming black with bombers as we began our circuit towards the meeting point and then the stream set course to the west of London on the first leg of the long flight to Munich. The main force for the night was targeting Karlsruhe, but we were going on for about another eighty miles, another hour into Germany, another hour to be attacked by the fighters, another hour in which to die.

We crossed the south coast of England near to the Isle of Wight and far below was the black cloth of the Channel, full of ships busy with invasion preparations, coastal defences and no doubt German E-boats seeking out a target, but all this was hidden to my gaze from 12,000 feet as we continued to climb steadily. "Enemy coast ahead," the familiar warning broke through my concentration. The skipper began to weave gently and all our nerves stretched a little tighter. From a cloudless sky, I could see the long white threads of the waves breaking on the French coast as it slipped by underneath and then felt the Lancaster bank and turn again on the next leg of our route. We had come in south of Le Havre, passed below Paris then another turning point to the Franco-German border. I searched deep into the black recesses of the night, fearing the stealth of a fighter slipping into the

244

bomber stream and firing up into our heavily loaded fuel tanks, bringing certain death.

Then, 20,000 feet below me I saw the tiny pinpoint pricks of light that betrayed the flak coming up at us. "Flak coming up, Skip," I reported and almost simultaneously we ran into the box barrage. The blinding orange flashes exploded all around us and I could feel the Lancaster being tossed from side to side as if it were a toy; whichever way we turned, the flak was there and the closer to Munich we got, the more intense the barrage. Then the searchlights came on, those thin groping fingers weaving and probing the sky, ready to betray us. For one crew it was their last mission as the lone pale blue pencil beam of the radar-controlled light locked onto their Lancaster and within seconds eight or nine other beams held it fast, gripped in the dazzling glare. I watched the aircraft fall and turn trying to escape from the web which held it, then a blinding flash and that fine aircraft was no more and nor were the seven young lives inside it.

I could feel sweat forming on my face, only for it to freeze, and the condensation from my oxygen mask made icicles below my chin. Despite the bitter cold in the turret I was too hot and turned the heat down on my Taylor suit, all the time looking, looking for the danger of fighters or collision. Eventually we started our bombing run. The Mosquitoes had marked the target well and we ran up to the centre of Munich.

"Left, left, steady." The Lancaster rocked violently and the starboard wing was thrown up as a shell burst just underneath it. "Hold it, Skipper, steady, bombs gone." QR-T rose sharply as she parted company with the 1,950 4lb incendiary bombs which we had been carrying, followed by that long, long minute for the aiming point photographs to be taken, then with the bomb bay doors closed we headed towards the cover of darkness and the turning point for the start of our homeward journey.

It was never a good idea to look down at the mayhem and destruction which was unfolding below us and to which we had added because it took away my night vision. The glare was so bright I could feel my eyes smart after so many hours of darkness; but how could I not look? I was drawn to it. After all, it was why I had come all this way, why I had endured the cold, the discomfort of my little turret, the fear of attack. This was what it was all for. Every few moments another line of explosions, another line of grey clouds would rise up from the city beneath and the already-raging fire would spread a little further until the whole carpet of buildings seemed to be engulfed. But that was the whole purpose; to drain the enemy of its will to go on fighting, to go on killing us. The war could end tonight if they would just say so. None of us really wanted to be here, doing this. There were many more enjoyable ways that we could all be spending this Monday night. We were here because we had to be. Our armies would soon be invading this land below us, and we were doing everything we could to help and make sure that they were successful.

Clouded by guilt that I had let my attention slip for a few moments, let my defences drop and put my aircraft and friends at risk, I stared hard out into the darkness once again, my night vision returning, the rhythmic up, down, side to side motion of my Brownings focusing my attention on the world outside, searching for that tell-tale speck or exhaust flare that would betray an attacker. Generally, Lancasters flew on the top deck of bombers, with the Halifaxes below us and so the night fighters were our greatest threat.

"Aircraft approaching from starboard quarter," the voice of our wireless operator, his eyes never leaving the green cathode ray tube of the radar set; sentinel, urgent, sending another blast of adrenalin through us all. I searched hard through the night sights on my guns. "Corkscrew, starboard, go," as the words were falling out of my mouth I pressed the firing buttons on the Brownings, at the same moment seeing the tracer from the fighter coming at us. The skipper's reactions were instant and the Lancaster dropped like a stone. I was lifted out of my seat and my head thrown against the turret roof as the cannon fire lazily zipped through the space we had just left behind, followed a moment later by the dark shape of a twin-engine fighter, an Me110. We were corkscrewing for our lives and for a moment I was disorientated with the reverse pressures of the fall and rise of the motion. I could feel the vomit coming up into my throat as once more the aircraft plunged, climbed and rolled over the top, and I had to swallow hard to keep it down.

Eventually we levelled out and resumed the gentle weaving motion. I had lost sight of our attacker as he broke away, but was filled with fear that he was still out there, waiting for us to settle down and then try again. It was like playing three dimensional chess where check-mate was fatal. I searched the void like never before, convinced that the German was still there. Total concentration and vigilance were what kept us alive; never drop your guard, always stay alert. The words from my first days of training three years ago were still resounding in the back of my mind. I might be an experienced air gunner but I was not a complacent one; too often I had seen how quickly disaster and death could come.

It wasn't long before we were targeted by the predictive flak of the German ground defences. The light-coloured puffs of smoke showing where each shell exploded were getting very close now, and I felt the Lancaster buck as this time the port wing was hit by shrapnel. But almost at the same time we were through it and from my rear seat I could tell we were out of range of the battery as the explosions fell behind and then stopped altogether. The engines continued their steady rhythmic drone as we swept on across the blanket of darkness beneath us.

We had been flying for over six hours now and my legs hurt, I had cramp from sitting too long in one place and my bottom was numb, even though I was sitting on my parachute. I stood up and tried to stretch my aching muscles a little. I leaned forward over the guns and felt the blast of cold air through the open front. I also had an overwhelming need to relieve myself; it was always the same on long missions.

There was an Elsan chemical lavatory provided at the back of the fuselage, but nobody used it, it was too much trouble. The intercom had to be unplugged, the oxygen feed disconnected and then you had to grope around for the emergency oxygen supply bottle, stumble in the dark to the Elsan, remove two or three pairs of gloves, terrified that some exposed skin would touch the bare metal because to do so meant leaving that skin behind, frozen to the aircraft by the sub-zero temperatures. Then there was the flying suit to unzip and trousers to unbutton and finally to fumble about feeling for the body-part which had long since shrunk to pre-puberty proportions to escape from the cold. It just wasn't worth the effort and most crews simply passed a can around: to all but the two gunners that is. For us there was no choice, we were never allowed to leave our guns, even for the few minutes needed to attend to the calls of nature. It was too dangerous; the threat of attack by night fighters was ever present: we simply had to let it go and get cleaned up in the showers back at the mess later on. It was not an issue or a subject for debate or comment; it was simply a fact of life in a bomber, particularly on long sorties where the whole crew ran on adrenalin from before take-off until after landing.

At 23,000 feet it was getting light at around four o'clock in the morning. We were still over enemy territory and had another two and a half hours to fly before seeing Lincoln cathedral. Whilst the daylight made it easier to see the fighters, it also made us easier to be seen and the advantage was definitely with the other side. We had lost the cover of darkness and our best hope was that the fighters had all landed to refuel and wouldn't come back up again, fearing attack from our own Fighter Command squadrons.

After some eight hours of flying we were over the English Channel once more. The sun was fully up now; it had been up with us for some time, but as I leaned forwards in the turret and looked behind me I could see the Sussex coast shining in the morning light, nearly home. Within a few minutes we were crossing the rolling hills of the South

Downs and away to the west I could see the expanse of the New Forest cloaked in the fresh spring green burst of new leaves. An hour later and it was Lincolnshire that I could see below me. It was on mornings like this that I felt that I had the best seat in the aircraft.

The sun was sending its warm rays to probe between the shadows on the land, causing the mist to rise up from the still wet grass after the heavy overnight dew on the patchwork quilt of small fields bounded by hedges two hundred years old. The little villages of gentle cottages which had seen so much go by their doors since they had been built all those generations ago nestled into the soft rolling countryside, each with its own church, whose tower or spire stood out as if to welcome us back. This was the land that we were fighting for, this was what we were trying to preserve. I was looking down upon part of a picture, a way of life that belonged to us and was familiar to us. Someone was trying to destroy it and we were not about to let that happen.

If the sun was quietly announcing the start of another day then the arrival of several hundred Lancaster bombers was the early morning call which would shatter the peaceful tranquillity of the scene which lay beneath me. There were very few mornings throughout the war that Lincolnshire did not awake to the sound of heavy bombers returning from operations, and very few evenings that the villages and towns did not shake to the thundering roar of those aircraft labouring into the night sky heading for another strike at the enemy: another dawn, another dusk.

We had been steadily losing height for some time and I knew that Bob Acott would soon be calling up Black Swan, the Skellingthorpe call sign announcing our imminent arrival. We would be given a number and told to join the circuit of waiting aircraft at a particular height. The skipper and our wireless op, Arthur Atkinson, would listen out as each aircraft touched down, cleared the runway and the next one came in on its approach: "No.8 clear" [landed and clear of the runway]; "No.9 touching down"; "No.10 funnels" [turning in to land]; "No.11 downwind" [on the downwind leg, ready to turn in to land]. As each aircraft landed, those circling were told to descend to the next height level, so that each one came down like a giant corkscrew until the last Lancaster was safely down and taxiing to its dispersal. In the days before radar, this method enabled the control tower to know the position in the circuit of each returning aircraft.

Soon it was our turn and I knew that we were coming in. The clunk of the undercarriage locking down, the fields and hedgerows slipping past with gathering pace as we floated lower and lower, then the road flashed by underneath the turret, the solid thud as the tyres made contact with the runway. We raced along its unfolding surface, slowing as the Lancaster gobbled up the yards until sated, then we were turning onto the perimeter track and into the dispersal pan to the welcome of our ground crew. I clambered out of the turret and down the ladder into the fresh morning air, and as I lit a cigarette I looked up at the peppered holes where the shrapnel had pierced the sides and both wings of our aircraft. We were tired and glad to be back.

But this morning there was no aircraft to welcome home for the ground crews of QR-B flown by Pilot Officer Newman and VN-Z flown by Flying Officer Durham, DFC; they would not be returning. Some weeks later, though, it was a cause for celebration when F/Sgt C Trottner reported back to the squadron having survived QR-B's crash and evaded capture.

We had done four ops in seven days, twenty-four hours in the air, every one of them spent watching, waiting and expecting the moment of attack; the cannon shells, the flak, the searchlights, our nerves stretched taut. I was ready for my bed, but sleep did not come easily and when it did I was made to relive too much of what I had seen.

CHAPTER THIRTEEN

"The sea is calm tonight. The tide is full, the moon lies fair upon the straits; - on the French coast the light gleams and is gone; the cliffs of England stand, glimmering and vast, out in the tranquil bay."
From Dover Beach by Matthew Arnold

There was to be no relief, however. Two nights later on Wednesday we were back in the air heading for Schweinfurt near the Czechoslovakia border once more. At the briefing we had been warned by the Met officer of a moderate headwind and it was not long before we ran into it. The rear turret was never a comfortable place to be but in bad weather it was dreadful.

A gentle breeze blew across the airfield at Skellingthorpe, driving the drizzle into our faces as we got out of the bus in front of QR-T. We waited in a little huddle in the shelter of her wings whilst the minutes ticked by; a cigarette, a joke that wasn't funny, a vain hope that the mission would be called off, until at last it was time to go.

Soon after crossing the French coast, I could feel the skipper struggling with the aircraft to keep it on course and having to make frequent changes as we were buffeted about by the increasing strength of the wind. Being blown off-course could mean the end for a crew as it would leave it prey to the fighters. Other than that, it was fairly uneventful until we reached Nancy where the flak came streaming up at us with a vengeance. We were flying at about 16,000 feet and right into the main area. The skipper was trying to weave us through it and hold the Lancaster against the wind. It must have been a struggle every mile of the way.

The flak was intense and I felt that familiar tightening in my stomach, then suddenly there was a massive explosion above us and some way off to starboard. For a few moments all the unseen aircraft for miles around seemed to be lit up by the vivid greens, yellows, blues and reds of the scarecrow hanging in the air. At the time we thought that these were shells fired up at us to simulate an aircraft exploding after taking a direct hit in the bomb bay and designed to scare the hell out of us. They certainly succeeded in doing that, but it is perhaps just as well that we didn't know that that was exactly what had happened; a direct hit on the bomb load. It was to be hoped that the crews would have known nothing about it, but my heart was racing just the same at the sight of this immense explosion.

As we crossed into Germany the defences picked up the bomber stream and marked our route with red and green sky flares fired up from the ground. That brought the fighters in and during the next forty minutes I saw three more aircraft going down, mainly away to port. We were now near to Schweinfurt but having to make small dog-legs whilst waiting for the Pathfinders to mark the target. The Mosquitoes had struggled even more than we had against the wind and without a navigator to act as wind finder, they were late, a delay which cost some crews their lives as the fighters were able to pick off any bomber which was blown out of the main stream.

My eyes were sore and I had a searing pain across the front of my head from staring out into the dark looking for an attacker. Eventually the markers went down and at half past two, five hours after take-off, we dropped our bombs from 15,750 feet. The searchlights were there too, criss-crossing the sky, probing the darkness for us; I felt that it was us alone they were looking for, of all the bombers over the city, we were the only one they were sweeping the sky for. At last, photographs taken, the doors of our thirty-three-foot-long bomb bay closed, and I felt the skipper turn and dive into the darkness away from the fires and lights below. As he turned the Lancaster for the French border, a great gust of wind caught her and seemed to lift her up, then sent us speeding on our way home: the headwind that had plagued us all the way to the target was now our best friend as we raced for the safety of Skellingthorpe with a hundred and twenty-five mile an hour power booster behind us. The wind was so strong that it even blew in through the open front of my turret, despite the slipstream. I wasn't about to complain, though, this wind was speeding us home, helping us to cover every mile back to Skellingthorpe in record time. Every minute over enemy territory saved was a minute less in which to be shot down. I hardly dared to think about that welcome back at base; the feel of the wheels on the runway, the engines silent, the light of the debriefing room, the young WAAF bringing us mugs of hot, sweet tea laced with rum, the bacon-and-egg breakfast, the cool, cotton sheets of my bed, blessed sleep.

Daylight. I had to look down now, to watch for fighters coming up at us, but there were none; they too had had enough. Instead I could see the complex patterns of shapes along the top of the clouds. It reminded me of pictures I had seen as a child at school of a glacier, not smooth and flat but twisted and broken. Over there a great valley, hundreds, maybe thousands, of feet deep and fifty miles long carved between the piles of churning cloud; below me billowed folds, motionless it seemed, yet imperceptibly changing shape, stretched away behind us as far as I could see, no sunshine here to brighten their grey, dismal mass, as full of foreboding as the European lands they covered. Then, as if with the stroke of a brush, they were falling away and there beneath us was the English Channel, the crests of breaking waves no more than thin strips of white paint on a blue canvas.

The sea gave way to land with London away to the east, then the fields and villages of the Home Counties catching the early rays of sunlight. Constant vigilance for the unexpected attack or collision produces a sixth sense of danger, in the same way it produces a sense of when it is safe. On this morning as we flew home, I had an overwhelming feeling of safety and tranquillity. It was going to be another beautiful day and the heating of my Taylor suit was keeping me warm, as was the coffee I was drinking. Soon below me once more was the gently rolling countryside of Lincolnshire. I suddenly realised that I was terribly tired and despite the cold air rushing through the gaping hole in the turret where the Perspex had been removed, I could have slept. My wakey-wakey tablet had just about worn off. I gave myself a shake and concentrated on looking out for other aircraft as we neared the crowded skies around Lincoln where all the airfields were receiving returning aircraft. We had survived another mission and so had all the other aircraft which had taken off from Skellingthorpe the night before.

The raid did produce a Victoria Cross for Sgt Norman Jackson, though he did not receive it until after the war. He was the Flight Engineer in a No.106 Squadron Lancaster which was attacked by a night fighter near Schweinfurt. A fire was started in the wing fuel tank near the fuselage and so Sgt Jackson climbed out onto the wing with a fire extinguisher. Before he did so the navigator made him put on his parachute, which then unfortunately opened as he climbed out onto the wing. Undeterred, with the navigator and bomb aimer holding the rigging lines, he continued in his attempts to save the aircraft and its crew. Lying on the wing of the Lancaster, Sgt Jackson started to use the extinguisher on the fire but the force of the slipstream ripped it out of his hands. At the same time the flames started licking up onto him and the lines of his parachute. There was no choice; the two crew men inside had to let him go before he burned on the wing and a moment later saw Sgt Jackson ripped from the wing and disappear into the darkness. Although badly burned, he did land safely but broke an ankle and was captured soon afterwards. The remaining crew baled out, although the pilot, Flying Officer Miffin, DFC and F/Sgt Johnson did not survive.

D-Day was now only five weeks away and the pressure was being kept up. On the evening of Friday, 28th April we were part of a small force of eighty-eight Lancasters and four Mosquitoes which attacked an explosives factory at St-Médard-en-Jalles, just outside Bordeaux. Fifteen aircraft took off from Skellingthorpe at around half past eleven and what I remember most of this raid was having to stooge around the target for over an hour. The haze and smoke in the small target area prevented most of us seeing the markers and the Master Bomber ordered us all to return home. That was one of the longest hours I have spent because, although we were not troubled by fighters, the flak was fairly heavy because of the U-boat pens at Bordeaux; however, the greatest risk of all was colliding with another aircraft in the dark as we circled the target.

The pilots of those aircraft which had not dropped their bombs now had to land back at base with full bomb loads: we all hated doing that. The weight put a huge strain on the undercarriage and tyres of the aircraft and the potential for disaster was very high. Nevertheless, we all got down safely and the following night ten crews from Skellingthorpe joined the force which went back to St-Médard-en-Jalles and very successfully bombed the explosives factory without loss.

The month of April ended well for No.61 Squadron and saw a DSO, four DFCs, a bar to a DFC and two DFMs being awarded to its aircrew. There was also the award of a rare Conspicuous Gallantry Medal to F/Sgt Leslie Chapman, the wireless operator in Lancaster QR-Q for his actions during the Nuremberg raid four weeks earlier.

It also brought a welcome break from operations for our crew and we all started a well-deserved week's leave. I went back to Shrewsbury to see Mum and Dad. I always tried to get to see them for at least a couple of days in each leave. I knew that they worried about me, Mum in particular. At thirty years of age and still single, I was happy to spend my leave relaxing and resting, so I spent all of this one at home with my parents. Having me home for a week helped Mum with the rations as she had my card to go shopping with as well as their own. After our tea, I would go out into town in the evenings with some friends and have a few beers, many of which were bought for me. Aircrew were still held in very high regard amongst the public and I often found that when I got to the bar to order, someone had already paid for it. Sometimes they would say something like, "Have that on me. You boys are doing a wonderful job," or words to that effect; at other times I would have no idea whose kindness provided my drinks.

On a couple of occasions during the week, I went out with a girl I had known at school; it was just a friendship but we went to a dance one night and to the pictures at the cinema in Castle Gates on another. From time to time people would ask me what it was like in a bomber. I didn't particularly want to talk about it and would say that it was all right for me because I was still alive; it was the lads who had been killed who had really suffered. In truth, if I had told people just how frightening it was to be attacked by a night fighter at 20,000 feet or what the flak was like, or how it felt to see another aircraft going down in flames knowing that your friends could be in it and the next one might be your own, they wouldn't have believed me. I was on leave and wanted to forget all these things for a little while. If I was lucky enough to survive I would have plenty of time to remember in the years to come.

Mum and Dad didn't ask me; that was the main thing. I couldn't have lied to them but my dad knew how it was, he had been in the trenches of the Western Front during the Great War. Nevertheless, each evening before I went out, we would sit around the wireless set and listen to the mellow tones of Alvar Lidell reading the news and putting a gloss on the Bomber Command losses. Whilst he reported the number of aircraft which had failed to return from the previous night's raid, he didn't say anything about their crews who failed to return; that most of those missing aircraft were carrying seven young men who had taken off from England the night before never to return.

Once again my leave rushed by all too quickly and once more I was standing on Shrewsbury railway station waiting for my train to take me back to Skellingthorpe. I remembered the enthusiasm, almost excitement, that people had still felt about the war when I first came home from my initial training at RAF Bridgnorth in early 1941, but all that had evaporated now. Looking at the faces around me, I could see they were war weary. Most were service men and women and all but the youngest looked strained and serious. The older civilian population wore every day of the war on their faces. People were cheery enough, but it was a cheeriness born out of resolution not happiness; years of worry, of rationing, of struggle and heartbreak, had taken their toll.

The night after our return from leave, the whole crew scrounged a lift into Lincoln and descended upon the Saracen's Head at the corner of Salter Gate and High Street where we started celebrating our skipper's promotion to Flight Lieutenant. After a few beers we made our way up Steep Hill to the County Assembly Rooms where there was a dance on. Although a fairly unpromising building from the Bailgate entrance, inside the eighteenth-century Assembly Rooms were beautifully decorated, but in 1944 we were more interested in the decorations on the floor than on the ceiling! Halfway along the left hand wall of the main room there was an alcove in which a three-piece band was playing. As usual, there were no chairs and so, having got another drink at the bar on the way in, we simply joined the mass of bodies lying on the floor. WAAFs, ATS, a few WRENs and plenty of local girls, all mixed in together with dozens of airmen: we had many a good night in the Assembly Rooms.

At breakfast the next morning, in between reliving some of the events of the previous evening, Al our mid-upper asked me what it was like in the rear turret, apart from being bloody cold, and if I would like to try his mid turret for a change. I rather fancied a change of view and the chance to see where we were going rather than only where we had been and so we decided to see if we could change places for the next operation; today seemed as good a time as any to ask the skipper. As a result I flew our next three operations, to Lille near the French/Belgian border, to the German military camp at Bourg-Léopold in Belgium and to Tours in central France, in the mid-upper turret.

It was to Tours that the ribbon stretched when, on the 19th May we had gathered once more in the briefing room and the map was uncovered. We had been there before, on 10th April, to attack the railway marshalling yards from 5,000 feet. The Germans had repaired them and so, according to the CO who was now standing in front of the map and pointing to the railway connections of the town, it was vitally important that we returned and destroyed them again. We were always told that the raid was vitally important; it was part of the patter, but although we didn't know it then, the railway links through Tours would have poured thousands of German troops and tons of supplies into Normandy when in little more than two weeks' time the D-Day landings took place, had we not destroyed them. It was to be another low-level raid which we were to carry out with great accuracy to avoid civilian casualties and we were instructed only to bomb on the instructions of the Master Bomber.

At the end of the briefing, the RAF police opened the doors of the room and we spilled out into the bright May sunlight. As we slowly cycled over to the mess for our pre-operational tea of bacon and real eggs, Al and I had another chat about our change of positions in the aircraft once more and for the umpteenth time since the change had been approved I reminded him that port and starboard in the rear turret were the other way round, because he would be facing backwards.

"Aye, Charlie, I think you said," his easy Canadian accent laughing at me. Since this would be his third sortie in the rear turret, he felt that he had got the hang of that one and no further reply was necessary for this quiet country lad of few words.

At a quarter past ten the brakes came off QR-T and we started down the runway of RAF Skellingthorpe. From my grandstand position in the mid-upper turret, I waved back to the crowd standing by the controller's caravan to see us off. The thundering roar of the Merlin engines and the rush of the tyres on the concrete reached a crescendo and we were up, heading straight for the red light on the towers of Lincoln cathedral. It was only from the upper turret on these last three trips that I had truly realised what a huge obstacle those towers were on take-off, but I hadn't yet had that early view of them on our return because the last two missions had been fairly short and it was still dark when we touched down.

We joined the circuit and then linked up with the other 112 Lancasters and 4 Mosquitoes of No.5 Group which formed the force to attack Tours. It was much warmer in the mid-upper and since we were not flying too high anyway, I needed to keep turning the heating down in my suit. These turret guns would turn through 360 degrees and whilst looking for attacking fighters I could also see the occasional glimpse of another Lancaster which was flying directly parallel with us, but far enough away not to be a collision danger. It was the last time that we had been to Tours that the risk of collision in the turning area had been so high and it was going to be no better tonight.

After about three and a half hours of flying and experiencing nothing worse than some light flak, I could see the target area, already marked by the Mosquitoes. We seemed to be ages waiting for the Master Bomber to call us in, but he had been ordered to ensure that civilian houses nearby weren't hit. Then the bomb doors opened and our run-in began. There was plenty of flak coming up at us now, but it was fairly light and not very accurate. With the photographs taken we turned and headed back across France towards Skellingthorpe. Despite being over the target area for so long, we hadn't seen any fighters. It was my sixteenth operation; I was more than three-quarters of the way through my second tour.

Two days later, on Sunday morning, 21st May after breakfast, I wandered over to the board in the mess to have a look at the battle order for that night; sure enough, we were down again. Perhaps it would be France once more, I wondered. No operation was ever easy, but some were definitely harder than others. At the afternoon briefing my hopes of another mission to France were dashed.

"The target for tonight, gentlemen, will be Duisburg," announced the CO as he uncovered the briefing map on the end wall. "It is the first large attack here for over a year."

God no, I thought, not Happy Valley.

"All right, Charlie, Al, regular turrets tonight, please,"

said Bob Acott as we came out of the briefing.

"Okay, skipper," we replied in unison. It was what we had expected and wanted ourselves; the industrial Ruhr was the most heavily defended part of Germany and we knew that it would be a difficult operation.

"By the way, we will have an extra crew member with us tonight. Flying Officer Turner is joining us for some sightseeing in Happy Valley."

Pilots at the top of their OTU course would do a couple of trips as second pilot with an experienced crew before taking charge of their own aircraft, so that they knew what was awaiting them and could lead their crews through it; this was Flying Officer Turner's second dickie trip.

In the dwindling light of the evening, we left the truck which had brought us out to the dispersal and joined our faithful ground crew around QR-T. The skipper had a brief chat with the flight sergeant and signed for the aircraft whilst I climbed up the ladder to make sure that the bullet channels to my four Brownings were full. Then peace descended on the airfield again and the familiar sound of the last song birds could be heard in the trees behind us. Smoking a last couple of cigarettes, we took up our customary positions on the armourers' trolley and quietly chatted before dropping into an easy silence.

The time came and around the various dispersal pans crews started to climb aboard their aircraft. The familiar sound of Merlin engines starting up split the quiet of the evening and the air began to vibrate. I slid over the tail spar and settled in the familiarity of my turret, like being with an old friend. Once more we joined the line of Lancasters on the perimeter track making for the head of the runway and then it was our turn to go.

Waving to the crowd standing beside the controller's van, I watched the runway unfold into the dark and then it had slipped away beneath us and we were over the boundary and climbing up towards the red light on the cathedral. We joined the bomber stream and headed out across the North Sea. It was pitch black out there, all the navigation lights had been switched off and I could not even see the aircraft which I knew were there, never mind any others that I didn't. We crossed the enemy coast at about 21,000 feet and were greeted by a single searchlight of a shore battery, seeking us out for the flak. Sure enough the explosions came up but before long I could see it falling behind; we were through it and on across Holland.

The skipper was gently weaving the Lancaster and I moved my guns up and down, and from side to side, searching for an attacker. Dickie gave the skipper the final course change and I felt the aircraft turn as we headed for Duisburg. I didn't have to ask if we were nearing the target, the heavy flak told me that we were. The yellow flashes were exploding amongst the bomber stream, filling my turret with the smell of cordite and rocking the aircraft like a leaf floating on the breeze.

"Bomb doors open."
Just by looking down I could see that the target was obscured by cloud and it was obvious from the conversation between the skipper and Duggie May our bomb aimer that they were looking for the flares to guide them in.

"I can see a Wanganui, Duggie, but it's late. Have you got it?"
"Yes, I see it."
"Okay, we'll go in on that."
"Right you are, skipper; steady, left, left, left, steady, bombs gone."

I felt the Lancaster give that welcome lift as our fourteen 1,000lb bombs slipped out of the racks. Looking down through the open front of the turret, I could see them against the illuminated tablecloth below me, falling, tumbling; they seemed almost weightless and then they were gone, lost in the mist. The photograph failed, the bomb doors closed and we turned away from Duisburg. The thick blanket of cloud masked the explosions and fires which were burning fiercely below and I could see only a bright orange glow spreading through it, like blood seeping into a cotton sheet from the open wound it covered.

Free of our bombs, we headed away from the flak and the searchlights, into the welcome cover of darkness and I could feel us gaining a little height for the run back across Holland and the North Sea. At 23,000 feet the engines were running smoothly and we levelled out; I turned the heat up a little in my suit, tried to stretch and searched hard into the black abyss which surrounded us. In that moment I saw the white tracer strike into CF-Y Yorker and the Lancaster's port wing become engulfed by fire, its shape materialising out of the dark sky and then falling away like a fiery plume, down and down, every second becoming smaller yet brighter until, in its final act, it ploughed into the earth next to a farmhouse on the Dutch countryside and exploded; it was Russ Margerison's aircraft.

These images have remained with me, so real, so clear.

The next night we went to Brunswick again, but no-one had any confidence that the raid had been successful because of the heavy cloud cover, which cleared away an hour after the attack. I remember this raid simply because it was my last one as a rear gunner. Two days later I was back in the mid-upper turret on an uneventful raid to Eindhoven in Holland, but we brought our bombs back as the Master Bomber thought that the visibility over the target was too poor.

A few days later the notice board in the mess told me that tonight, 27th May 1944, I would be on operations; it would be the last one of my second tour. Later that day, the briefing disclosed the target as Nantes, near to the French Bay of Biscay coast and close to where the Luftwaffe had sunk the *Lancastria* four years earlier. The railway junction and workshops in the town, away from the residential areas, were the actual targets. We had a fairly uneventful flight to Nantes and arrived on time. Then, just as we began our bombing run over the railway, the Master Bomber called us off and closed the mission. The target had been marked so well and the first fifty aircraft in had bombed it so effectively that there was nothing left on the ground for us to aim at; it had all gone, the workshops and railway lines had been completely destroyed. With the attack abandoned, we turned for home, taking time to jettison four 1,000 pounders on the way to lighten the aircraft on landing; we kept the remaining ten to use another time.

We flew back as the first faint brush strokes of grey light began to appear in the eastern sky away to my right. I missed the wonderful views downwards which I had from the rear turret on homeward journeys like this, but here in the mid-upper I could see all around and in particular watch out for other aircraft, and it was warmer, well, a little anyway. By the time we were over the New Forest, the sun was shining on the returning aircraft, glinting on the Perspex of the turrets and cockpits like so many Aldis lamps flashing a greeting to one another across the sky. The vapour trails streamed out from behind the four Merlin engines, showing the position of each aircraft and its track across the sky; no wonder the Nuremburg raid had cost so many lives, the condensation trails would have been like signal beacons homing in on each aircraft to show the fighters exactly where they were.

I felt a tap on my leg and, without looking down, I extended my gloved hand and felt it being wrapped around a mug of hot coffee. In the rear turret I had been shut away from this luxury; alone, cold, vulnerable. After a while we began to lose height and once more joined the circuit over Skellingthorpe. I turned the turret and looked forward, and there in front of us bathed in the early morning sunlight was Lincoln Cathedral, rising out of the mist which still enveloped the rest of the town like a primordial friend greeting our return. The cathedral that was so difficult to climb over on our outward journey, now so warm and welcome a sight, its great towers beckoning to us.

Almost idly as I sipped my coffee, I swivelled the turret and looked in turn along each wing of the Lancaster, the engines in synchronised rhythm. To the rear I could see the twin tail fins and the top of the turret that I had sat in for so many hours. Round again I went and casually waved to our navigator who was standing in the astrodome taking photographs. It was such a peaceful scene with other aircraft above and below us in the circuit that it was difficult to remember that we were at war. I was glad that it had been like that, for it was to be my last ride in a Lancaster bomber.

Presently the intercom crackled in my headset, "Undercarriage down, full flap," as, heavily laden, we came in over the road and raced down the runway in the early morning daylight: it was five o'clock, exactly six hours after we had taken off. Bob taxied round to our dispersal where the ground crew and armourers were waiting to welcome us back and relieve the Lancaster of her bomb load. I disconnected the intercom and oxygen leads and removed my helmet. Could my second tour really be over? Had I beaten the odds again and survived another one?

I put the safety catch on the guns and slipped out of my seat onto the floor of the aircraft, almost sub-consciously breathing in the familiar smells of fuel oil and cordite. The other crew members were all tidying up their stations and getting ready to leave the place ready for the ground crew to take over. Al was struggling out of the rear turret and over the tail spar as I had done so many times before, hampered by bulky layers of clothing. I helped him out and then, carrying my flask, escape kit and parachute, I climbed down the ladder onto the concrete pan and lit a cigarette. Al joined me a few moments later and we stood beside our trusted Lancaster whilst waiting for the others. The birds were singing in the trees behind me as they did every morning, but today I noticed their presence more than usual. The skipper finished the paperwork with the ground crew flight sergeant and joined us as we walked across to the truck which was waiting to take us to the debrief.

As if he had read my earlier thoughts, he slapped me on the back and said, "Well that's your tour over, Charlie. Lucky chap. We shall miss you."
"It's not over unless the Old Man says so, skip. We've had a couple of short trips lately and he might only count

them as halves."

"I bloody well hope not, for all our sakes," he replied, laughing, as we scrambled into the back of the truck. "A couple of half trips for you will be the same for the rest of us."

I took the steaming mug of hot tea from the smiling WAAF, thanked her and walked across the room to join the others at a table, behind which sat a very attractive Intelligence Officer. We hadn't seen her before but she was definitely a sight worth flying all night for. As we each flopped down onto the wooden chairs to face her, she smiled at us invitingly, putting us at our ease and reducing the adrenalin levels that we were still running on.

"Good morning, chaps. Glad to see you all back in one piece. You know the routine. Right, where were you when the Master Bomber called an end to the raid?" The flight officer directed the question to Bob.
"Right on our run-in. Another few seconds and we wouldn't have had to land with 10,000 pounds of high explosives under our arses."
"Yes, quite so," she replied and flashed that lovely smile again, her eyes sparkling in the smoke-filled room. "Was there much flak?"
"Not really, not too bad at all. Moderate I should say," he replied.
"Were the PFF markers clear to see?"
"I saw the flares on arrival at the target so kept on the bombing run hoping for the RSFs to come up but we didn't see any. Two red Varys were fired at 01.41 so we abandoned our run-in and turned for home."

The Intelligence Officer's voice became strangely distant, detached from the scene before my eyes. What was the visibility like? How strong was the wind? Was the Met forecast accurate? Did the bombing become scattered? Was there any creepback? Were there many fires? Did you see any large explosions? Her questions carried on, mainly directed at the skipper, Arthur and Dickie. I had drifted off and my thoughts were lost in a jumble of the attractive Intelligence Officer, whether tonight was the end of my second tour and how war brings some people together and tears others apart. How, whether the hand of fate rests kindly or cruelly upon each one of us, it can turn our lives or end them in just a moment. Had she left someone behind to sit here at five-thirty in the morning and ask us the same questions we had been asked three nights ago, and five nights ago, and six nights ago and so on? Had she lost someone very close in this bloody endless war? Was that why she was sitting here asking these same damned questions? The burning Lancaster from a few nights ago floated across my mind again.

I suddenly became aware that the voices around the table had fallen silent and I realised that everyone was looking at me expectantly.

"Come on, Charlie, don't be shy. Tell the officer if you saw any fighters," the skipper prompted me.
"Yes, sorry. I saw a fighter in the target area, thought it was an Me210, but wasn't sure. It was moving away from us; didn't see it again."
"Thank you, Trevor," she almost whispered, her voice like velvet. "Did you see any of our own aircraft go down?"
"No, thankfully I didn't. Are any of ours overdue?" It was a pointless question because I knew she wouldn't reply to it.

And then that was it. It was all over again, the usual questions and answers. We got up from the table, thanked the officer and went outside. It felt good to be in the fresh morning air as we cycled across to the mess for our bacon-and-egg breakfast after having got out of our flying kit. I kept the chocolate and orange juice: I had long since learned not to hand those little luxuries back to the store keeper.

I should have gone to the billet with the others to get some sleep, but I wasn't that tired just yet and decided to walk for a little while. I took a deep draw on my cigarette and looked across at our Lancasters, standing at rest; they had all returned this morning, from both squadrons.

They were a comforting sight and looked so elegant, each within their own dispersal pan, some being worked on by the ground crews, others simply standing framed against the trees, quiet, indomitable, ready.

I vaguely heard the car come along the perimeter track and stop behind me but I was so deep in thought that I hardly noticed it.

"Warrant."
The voice cut through my reverie in an instant and I turned quickly, saluting the Wing Commander sitting in the driving seat of the little Austin.
"Sir."
"That's the end of your second tour, lad, you've done well. You're off ops as from now. Your crew will miss you. Your experience has been good for them. Sgt Bryenton will take over in the rear turret. You've convinced him that it's the best seat in the house." He smiled and then added, "Good luck, lad."
"Thank you, sir."

With a grating of the gears he drove away and left me to return to my thoughts. I didn't know it at that moment, but my war was over. I had survived after all.

When I got back to the billet, the others were already asleep. I suddenly felt very tired indeed but it was a deeply troubled sleep into which I eventually slipped, filled with dreams of burning aircraft, the smoke puffs of exploding flak shells and the tracks of tracer bullets cutting through the night sky like so many stilettos. These dreams were to haunt me for years to come and have never really left me completely.

| | | | | | | Flying Times | |
Date	Hour	Aircraft Type and No.	Pilot	Duty	Remarks (including results of bombing, gunnery, exercises, etc.)	Day	Night
					Time carried forward :-	252 55	421 40
18.5.44	15.00	Lancaster T	F/Lt. Plak	Rear Gunner	Low Level.	.45	
19.5.44	22.15	„	„	Mid Upper	Tours - Operations		6.05
20.5.44	19.30	„	„	„	Wescott - Base	1.00	
21.5.44	22.40	„	„	Rear Gunner	Duisburg - Operations		5.05
22.5.44	22.30	„	„	„	Brunswick - Operations		6.15
24.5.44	23.00	„	„	Mid Upper	Eindhoven - Operations		3.15
27.5.44	23.00	„	„	„	Nantes - Operations.		6.00
					Total Flying Operations: 384.00.		
			T.L. Bear O/C for W/CR. Commanding B Flight. May 1944. Flying Time 15.00 : 33.20 :	Total Flying Time : 706.00.		
(35)					Total Time	257.40	448.20

The last operational page in my log book. I had survived
[Neville Bowyer collection]

No.61 Squadron
crest complete
with Lincoln Imp
Motto:
Thundering
through the
clear air

CHAPTER FOURTEEN

"I doubt any single man did more in winning the war than he did. I doubt whether that is generally realised."

Field-Marshal Bernard Law Montgomery speaking of Air Chief Marshal Sir Arthur Harris

On 11th June 1944, Flight Lieutenant William Reid stepped forward in front of His Majesty King George VI at Buckingham Palace and received his Victoria Cross. Like John Hannah, Bill Reid was from Glasgow, the son of a blacksmith and on the night of 3rd November 1943 he was the captain of a Lancaster bomber of No.61 Squadron which took off to attack Düsseldorf in the Ruhr. Shortly after crossing the Dutch coast, his aircraft was attacked by an Me110 and the pilot's windscreen was blown out. The tail gunner had managed to drive the fighter off although the Lancaster's rear turret was badly damaged and the communications system and compasses were destroyed.

In addition to the loss of the pilot's windscreen, through which the bitterly cold air was now blowing like an Arctic gale, the elevator trimming tabs of the aircraft had been damaged in the attack, making the Lancaster difficult to control. However, after satisfying himself that his crew were uninjured he carried on towards Düsseldorf without saying anything about the injuries he had suffered to his head, shoulders and hands.

It wasn't long before they were attacked again, this time by an Fw190 fighter, which raked the Lancaster from end to end, killing the navigator and fatally injuring the wireless operator. The mid-upper turret was hit and the oxygen system was rendered useless. F/Lt Reid was once more wounded, but refused to abandon the mission. He had memorised the route to Düsseldorf and fifty minutes later arrived over the centre of the target area.

After releasing the Lancaster's bomb load, Bill Reid set course for home using the pole star as a guide, but he was slipping in and out of consciousness from loss of blood and lack of oxygen, the emergency supply having run out. Nevertheless, the flight engineer and bomb aimer managed to keep the Lancaster airborne even though they ran into very heavy flak over the Dutch coast and knowing that a serious hit or another fighter attack would finish them off. Once over the North Sea, they revived their skipper and got him back into the pilot's seat to make the landing, and despite the blood from his head wound flowing into his eyes, he brought the Lancaster safely back down to earth at the first available airfield with a runway long enough for the bomber.

The citation in the London Gazette summed it up as follows:

> *"Wounded in two attacks, without oxygen, suffering severely from cold, his navigator dead, his wireless operator fatally wounded, his aircraft crippled and defenceless, Flight Lieutenant Reid showed superb courage and leadership in penetrating a further 200 miles into enemy territory to attack one of the most strongly defended targets in Germany, every additional mile increasing the hazards of the long and perilous journey home. His tenacity and devotion to duty were beyond praise."*

After leaving hospital, Bill Reid was rewarded with a posting to No.617 Squadron at Woodhall Spa in January 1944, but a few days after receiving his VC from the King, whilst attacking the V-weapon storage dump at Rilly-la-Montagne, near Rheims, his Lancaster was struck by the Tallboy bomb dropped by another aircraft 6,000 feet above him. Realising that it would be only moments before the Lancaster broke up, he ordered his crew to bale out and as they did so his aircraft went into a nose-dive, pinning him to his seat. He managed to release the escape-hatch cover above his head and struggled out just as the bomber broke in two. Although he parachuted safely, he landed heavily and broke his arm. He was captured within the hour and spent the rest of the war as a POW, finally at StalagLuft III at Luckenwalde, west of Berlin.

After the war, Bill graduated from Glasgow University and followed a successful career in agriculture, retiring in 1981. He died at his home in Crieff, Perthshire on 28th November 2001, forty-eight years after being awarded his Victoria Cross.

Fl/Lt William Reid, VC

Two days after my brief chat with the CO on the perimeter track, my next posting came through. Following a week's leave, I was to join No.17 OTU at RAF Upwood as an instructor and so Monday, 29th May was to be my last on the station. By chance, neither squadron was flying operations that night; as a result I was given a very good send-off. We went into Lincoln, which was as usual full of airmen, and joined in the fun and relaxation. When we got to the Brick Makers Arms, the landlady was sporting a very uncomfortable-looking black eye. Apparently her husband had caught her in the back yard serving one young airman more than a pint of beer. Many of these pubs had dark alleys and back yards which were the scenes of various activities, including the Sally Ann which was down by the river and where we would often see a couple of the local policemen nip in and have a crafty pint whilst making their nightly rounds. I was sorry to leave Lincoln; it had been a good posting to a great squadron, but as was always the lot of surviving aircrew, I was on my way once more.

The next morning after breakfast, I gathered up my belongings from the billet, collected my travel warrant and said goodbye to my crew. I caught the train from Skellingthorpe village back into Lincoln to St Mark's LMS station, one of the two railway stations which were near the River Witham, and as I rocked back and forth in the compartment my rather sore head reminded me about the good time I had had the night before and I reflected that I could have done with our traditional cure for a hangover, a blast of pure oxygen from one of the aircraft. The train pulled up to the platform and an hour later I managed to get a seat on my connection, which was just as well since it was a long slow journey from Lincoln into Birmingham, where I had to change to get the train for Wolverhampton, then change again for Shrewsbury.

I was very glad to sit down at Mum and Dad's table once again and I could tell that they were greatly relieved to have me home for a few days. By prior arrangement, I had managed to acquire a lovely piece of ham before leaving Lincoln, and it was worth every penny just to see the look on the faces of my parents when I put it on the kitchen side. It had been a long time since they had had meat like that; there were some advantages to being aircrew, who were still thought very highly of at this time.

At RAF Upwood I was back to flying in Wellingtons, which seemed strangely small in comparison to the Lancaster, and then in July I was posted again, this time to No.10 Air Gunnery School near Barrow-in-Furness at the southern end of the Lake District, where I flew as an air gunner instructor in Avro Ansons and Martinets as well as Wellingtons. This was a lovely part of the country to fly over on a clear bright summer's day, looking down onto the grey radial massif of the Cumberland mountains which contrasted with the lush green of the little fields set in the valley bottoms and the occasional cluster of farm buildings and cottages gently nestling amongst the tangled ribbons of dry stone walls. About halfway up the coast between Barrow and Carlisle, and about three miles inland from the seaside town of Seascale is the village of Gosforth. Inevitably it has grown in size today, but in 1944 it was still a beautiful little place with a school, a very old and interesting church, a couple of pubs and just past the church, Gosforth Hall, the farm owned and worked by Isaac and Annie Hartley whilst their son John was away in the army.

It was not a grand hall in the tradition of English country houses by any means, although it was very old and well built, but it was everything that a truly English farm should be, and anyone who ate a meal there would be given milk from their cows, honey from their bees, fruit from their trees and probably a salmon poached from the local river. There was little mechanisation on the farm of course; at harvest time, the fields were cut with a reaper and binder pulled by two great Clydesdale horses, the stooks stood up in the fields to dry and later loaded by pitchfork onto a trailer, also horse drawn, before being taken to the farm where an old steam engine drove the threshing machine to separate the grain from the straw. It reminded me so much of being at home in Shropshire and of Atcham in particular.

After the war I developed a hobby of looking at old churches and the gravestones in their grounds. These were real people and their gravestones are evidence of their lives and can tell a very interesting story about those who lived in the towns and villages of Britain. Sadly we don't really care for these stone relics as well as we would if they were pages of parchment or drawings on a cave wall, but they are just as illuminating.

Gosforth church could well have been in the mind of Rupert Brooke when he wrote *The Old Vicarage, Grantchester* whilst sitting in the Café de Westens, Berlin in 1912, and in particular those very well-known last two lines, "*Stands the church clock at ten to three? And is there honey still for tea?*" Born in 1887, Rupert Brooke was a Fellow of King's in 1913 and joined the Royal Navy at the start of the Great War, gaining his commission in September 1914. He saw action in Antwerp but died of septicaemia on 23rd April 1915 en route to Gallipoli. Brooke was buried on the island of Skyros in the Aegean. Like Wilfred Owen, who had lived literally just around the corner from me in Shrewsbury, the war had stolen another great poet so young. The church yard at Gosforth also holds an item of special interest for in it stands an eight-foot-high stone cross upon which are carved both Celtic and Christian symbols. It is one of only two such crosses in Britain.

In September, I learned that I had been awarded the Distinguished Flying Cross in recognition of my courage and devotion to duty as an air gunner during fifty-nine missions through two tours on operations with the Middle East Air Force and Bomber Command. My award appeared in the London Gazette on the 19th of that month. I wrote home and told Mum and Dad, who were immensely proud of me; I was very pleased too. I purchased the purple-and-white diagonal-striped medal ribbon and sewed it onto my uniform in time for my next posting to No.11 AGS at RAF Andreas in the north of the Isle of Man where I spent the next few months, including Christmas and New Year.

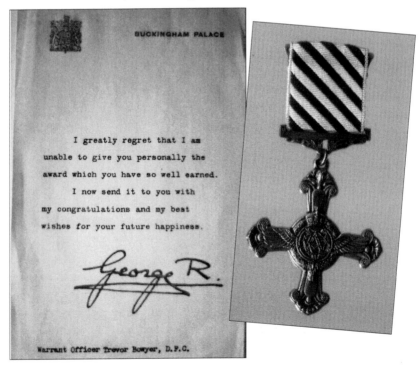

The letter from King George VI which accompanied my DFC [Neville Bowyer collection]

September was also the month in which General Montgomery devised a plan which would end the war by Christmas, but as with so many plans in so many wars before, it didn't. Operation Market Garden was all about capturing the bridges on the road to Germany to speed up the Allied advance from the west and beat the Russians to Berlin. D-Day had happened and the Allies were pushing across Europe, but we were not really told of the calamity that was Arnhem, the bridge too far. The events that conspired to prevent the capture of the bridge, despite the exemplary courage of the British 1st Airborne Division under the command of General Roy Urquhart, put an end to hopes that the war would be over by Christmas 1944. The British war cemetery at Arnhem containing 1,678 Allied graves is testimony to the sacrifice of so many, including the twins Thomas and Claude Gronert from the Parachute Regiment who joined together, had consecutive service numbers of 5511523 and 5511524 and were both killed on 17th September aged just twenty-one. They came from Carn Brae in Cornwall and were miners at South Crofty before they enlisted. In 1946 their mother Lylie Gronert visited their graves as the guest of the people of the Netherlands in recognition of the sacrifice of her sons and of her own loss.

SS Lieutenant-General Wilhelm Bittrich, Commander of the II Panzer Corps, was a professional soldier and holder of the German Knight's Cross. He had seen action across Europe throughout the war and was battle hardened even by SS standards. By one of those pure coincidences upon which such events can turn, his troops and tanks had been sent to Arnhem, well behind German lines, to give them a rest from the fighting after the D-Day landings. Their unexpected presence there was to be pivotal to the outcome of the battle.

Just how hard and bitter was the fight for the bridge at Arnhem [now known as the John Frost Bridge, named after Lieutenant-Colonel John Frost, Commander of the 2nd Parachute Battalion, who held out at the bridge virtually until the end] and the extent of the sacrifice by the British 1st Airborne Division, was perhaps most succinctly but tellingly described by Bittrich himself. At the height of the battle in a conversation with Field Marshal Model, the overall German Commander in the field, about the failure of the SS to regain control of both ends of the bridge, Bittrich said of the 1st Airborne Division, *"In all my years as a soldier, I have never seen men fight so hard."*

By comparison with the tension and the dangers, but also the close companionship of life on an operational station, things were fairly dull and routine for instructors at the training bases, although I did have a good time whilst in the Isle of Man, particularly over Christmas and New Year. There had been very little actual flying mainly because of the poor weather conditions over the Irish Sea, so much so that during the whole of December I only took to the air once for a two-hour air firing test for a group of young gunners.

Although there were many shortages on the island, fresh fish was not one of them and I made the most of this welcome change to the RAF menu whilst I was there. I also began to find out the high esteem in which genuine holders of the DFC were held by the public. I say genuine holders, because around this time, very occasionally, an officer would buy and put up the DFC ribbon and pretend to have been awarded the medal. Most were quickly found out, court martialled and spent the rest of their service as an Aircraftman 2nd class cleaning out the lavatories; they were regarded with utter contempt by everyone. However, one or two did get away with it, although as with all cheats, they were sooner or, sometimes, later found out. There were very many brave lads during the war who did not receive any sort of recognition; that did not make them any less courageous, but pretending to have such an award for having done little or nothing was wholly reprehensible and was treated as such.

The Christmas dances and parties on the base and in the capital town of Ramsay, which was only three or four miles away, were plentiful. Since I was still single and unattached I relished these occasions and found that there were plenty of girls who wanted to know what it was like to fly in a Lancaster bomber over Germany. I didn't have to shoot a line, I had really done it, but I also knew that I didn't want to talk about it yet because it brought back too many memories of lost friends and the stark images of burning aircraft. I had enough trouble sleeping as it was. However, I am bound to admit that one local girl in particular did regularly make sure that I went to sleep happily whenever I could get a pass out, which was easy enough for instructors.

The war in Europe was still dragging on and although we knew that we would win it, at the beginning of 1945 just exactly when that would be no-one could tell because German resistance seemed as strong as ever, certainly for Bomber Command, although losses were thankfully a lot fewer than in the dark days of the winter of 1943/44. Consequently, the RAF process for aircrew rolled on and I was being prepared for a return to active duty. I was selected for the 2nd Tactical Air Force [2TAF] flying in American Mitchell B25 light bombers and joined the force on 6th January 1945. The 2TAF was designed to give air support to fast-moving ground forces and was commanded by Air Marshal Sir Arthur Coningham, who had been in command of the Desert Air Force when I was in North Africa. It had been established in the run-up to Operation Overlord, the invasion of mainland Europe beginning with the D-Day landings on 6th June 1944.

I was now part of No.2 Group and in March was posted to No.13 Operational Training Unit at RAF Harwell, which was about halfway between Oxford in the north and Newbury to the south. I was back to where I had started out from so long ago in June 1942 on our way to the desert; all the operations and experiences which lay ahead of me then were now behind me and quickly slipping into the past. It was to be my final posting of the war and one which would change my life and shape my future.

In the meantime, however, No.50 and 61 Squadrons were still at Skellingthorpe and carrying out operations against strong German defences. On 14th March Sgt H James

Flowers was the rear gunner in Lancaster VN-F, one of 255 aircraft detailed to attack the Wintershall synthetic oil refinery at Lützkendorf. After an uneventful trip over to the target in eastern Germany, VN-F arrived as the whole area began to burst into light from the Pathfinder flares and early bombs. Ground and sky alike were lit up in a blaze of colour which contrasted starkly with the previous six hours of pitch darkness through which they had flown. There was no flak coming up at them but they knew that the night fighters would soon be arriving. Committed to their bombing run, James saw a fighter swoop in and attack the Lancaster following them in; had the fighter pilot chosen VN-F there would have been no opportunity to corkscrew.

"Bombs gone." Then an agonising twelve seconds, flying straight and level over the target, a sitting duck hanging in the air, waiting, counting… "photographs taken"; turn, dive, get the hell out of there. The maelstrom that was the oil refinery began to slip away in the distance, the detail became blurred, the fires just an orange glow on the black empty backdrop of German soil.

Free of its bomb load, the Lancaster sped homeward through the darkened sky, its engines singing a comforting steady rhythm, its exhausts glowing red. In the rear turret James Flowers searched the abyss for an unseen enemy, knowing that as each minute passed they were a few more miles nearer to home, to safety, and he thought of his new young bride waiting for his return. In the space of a heartbeat his world was flooded with light; the fighter flare had burst just above them. Frantically he rotated the turret from side to side, searching for the incoming aircraft that he knew was there. Then he saw it, the familiar silhouette of an Fw190 starting its attack.

"Fighter, fighter, corkscrew starboard, corkscrew starboard."

Instantly his New Zealand pilot John Lawrey, slammed the aircraft into a starboard dive, the G-forces straining James' body against the straps of his harness as he desperately tried to aim the Brownings at the approaching fighter. Knowing that only split seconds remained between life and death he pressed the firing button in the middle of his hand controls and fought to pull the line of tracer onto the fighter. In that instant, from the corner of his eye he caught a movement down on the port side; a Ju88 stealthily trying to get underneath the Lancaster's wing to use its upward firing cannon, *Schrage Musik*.

Realising that the Ju88 posed the greater threat, he turned his Brownings onto it and once more tried to pull the line of tracer onto his target whilst the pilot continued to roll the Lancaster through a succession of corkscrews. With temporary relief James saw the fighters break away, but as the light from the sky flare died, he knew they would be back. Hardly had the Lancaster levelled out than the fighters attacked again. Once more the Lancaster was thrown into a series of corkscrews so tight that the rivets were in danger of popping out. Taffy Flowers in the mid-upper turret followed the line of his namesake's tracer from the rear turret and again they succeeded in beating off the attack. Bruised and tense from the last twenty minutes of combat, James settled back into his seat, adjusting his position on his parachute, as once more the aircraft levelled out and the navigator gave yet another course for home.

"Corkscrew, port, go," shouted James and Taffy in unison as for a third time the determined Luftwaffe pilots tried to finish off their enemy. This time, with the two gunners firing at the same instant, the hail of .303 bullets was too great and the fighters quickly broke off once more.

Although the crew did not know it at the time, that was the end of the duel; it had lasted for twenty-six minutes. After they landed safely back at Skellingthorpe, James checked his ammunition channels; they were totally empty. Firing at 1,200 rounds per minute, he had used all 12,000 rounds; had the fighter pilots but known it, the Lancaster was almost defenceless. Such is the gift of fate. As Bernard Fitch had once observed, "Survival was almost entirely a matter of luck."

Sgt H James Flowers, rear gunner [James Flowers]

Following the successful invasion of Europe on D-Day and the liberation of France, the Germans were forced back behind their own frontiers. As a consequence, Bomber Command was required to carry out more daylight raids. The great advantage the bomber crews now had over the daylights raids in the early days of the war was long-range fighter escort, mainly the American P-51 Mustang. On 9th April, just a month before the end of the war, one such raid was ordered. Fifty-seven aircraft took part, mostly from No.50 and 61 Squadrons together with seventeen Lancasters of No.617 'Dambusters' Squadron. We said goodbye to some friends that day; both squadrons lost an aircraft and twelve of the fourteen crew were killed.

The target was the oil storage tanks in Hamburg and at around half past one in the afternoon, just before take-off, the CO went around to every crew as they waited by their aircraft at dispersal, "I hope you chaps have got your picnic baskets with you today, because this one is going to be a piece of cake."

Unfortunately, no-one told the Germans and though they might have been low on pilots, those that they had were flying the Me262 jet fighters. Sgt Ted Beswick was the mid-upper gunner in his No.61 Squadron Lancaster which took off from RAF Skellingthorpe at twenty-eight minutes past two and made it safely across to Hamburg. On their run-in, with the bomb bay doors wide open, the aircraft was hit in the nose by flak, slightly injuring the bomb aimer Sgt Harold Heppenstall, as the box barrage caught up with them. Having successfully bombed the target, the pilot, Ivor Soar turned for home, only to be told by Harold that there was a 2,000lb high-explosive bomb hung up in the bay.

A short but focused discussion then took place between captain and crew, as a result of which they went round again, attracting a hail of flak. Still the bomb would not drop, so round they went for a third time. This time the flak was very concentrated as they were rapidly becoming the only aircraft the Germans had to aim at, but still the HE would not release. Enough was enough and they turned for home.

Ted's Lancaster was now very near the back of the returning bomber stream, but it was not quite the last aircraft. Flying behind them were QR-J, piloted by F/Lt Paul Greenfield and VN-F. Without any warning, QR-J reared up, climbed a little and then just blew up. From underneath, an Me262 shot through the falling debris at an incredible speed; Ted's Lancaster was next in line. The rear gunner, Canadian Jimmy Huck opened fire on the fighter, but Ted couldn't get his guns to dip low enough to bring it into his sights. "Corkscrew, port, go," he called to Ivor over the intercom, but there were too many aircraft close by and all Ivor could do was make a shallow dive. It was enough. As the bomber levelled out, close by, throttled back and flying straight and level, Ted saw an Me262 lining up another Lancaster; the German was so near that he could see the pilot's face. In an instant Ted aimed and fired into the cockpit area. Black smoke poured from the stricken fighter as it dived and fell away out of sight.

"You've got him, you've got him, Ted!" yelled Gwynn Rees, the flight engineer.

There is no doubt that Ted Beswick saved the lives of that No.617 Squadron crew that sunny Monday afternoon.

Sgt Ted Beswick, mid-upper gunner [Ted Beswick]

VN-F, piloted by the twenty-five-year-old Flying Officer Berriman of No.50 Squadron, was the other loss that afternoon before the Mustang fighters arrived and shot down three of the five Me262s. Berriman had been attacked from below as the German fighters climbed at an incredible rate. The aircraft had burst into flames and broken up, falling from the sky like a stone. James Flowers had seen the attack and as he watched the burning ruins tumbling over in the sky, he saw the rear gunner bale out, somersault and then his parachute open. With relief he saw the gunner escape but a few moments later, to his utter horror he watched helplessly as the parachute burst into flames and his friend fell ten thousand feet to his death. Not for him the luck that had been handed to Sgt Alkemade who had survived without a parachute at all.

For Ted Beswick and his crew, their troubles were not yet over; they still had 2,000 pounds of primed high explosive sitting in the bomb bay. Despite several attempts over the North Sea to unload their unwelcome passenger, the bomb remained determined to return to Skellingthorpe.

Nearing home, the pilot called up the airfield, code named Black Swan, gave his squadron code Spot Nose, and broke the unhappy news that he was returning with a hang-up. The aircraft circled ready to land, the ambulance and crash wagon waited; at any moment on touchdown there could be a huge explosion and seven young men and a Lancaster bomber would disappear into eternity.

With every nerve stretched tight, Ivor Soar nursed the damaged aircraft past the towers of Lincoln Cathedral, and gently eased her lower over the fields, startling the cattle quietly grazing on the spring grass. As if knowing that this might be her last flight, these her last moments, the Lancaster hesitated on the final approach, floated, seemingly unwilling to take the risk of returning to the earth. She slipped across the Skellingthorpe Road and then with an almost imperceptible bump she was down and racing along the runway that I had watched unfold from my rear turret so many times. As she did so, with the ambulance and crash wagon chasing her on the grass verge, Ted, sitting in the mid-upper turret, heard an almighty clatter beneath him.

"Skipper, I think it's dropped off into the bomb bay doors." He could hardly say the words in anticipation of the explosion that was bound to follow.

"Okay Ted, thanks," replied Ivor Soar calmly and as they reached the end of the runway, he pulled the Lancaster onto the grass verge, to await the armourers.

As a crew I think they probably broke the record for the shortest time to exit an aircraft and as they stood a little way off the armourers arrived and carefully but almost casually removed the bomb and made it safe; it went back into store after all. What great chaps the ground crews were and yet they have had very little recognition.

On No.50 Squadron at that time was Wing Commander James Flint, DFC, GM, DFM. In the early days of the war, as a young sergeant pilot he was stationed at RAF Scampton flying Hampdens with No.49 Squadron. On one particular mission his aircraft was so badly damaged that when returning home it began to lose power and height whilst still over Holland. Another Hampden flying close by was piloted by his friend Sgt Stubbs, later to become a Wing Commander Master Bomber, who saw what was happening and, having spotted a Dutch airfield, albeit in German control, radioed his idea to Sgt Flint. "Jimmie, land on that Dutch airfield below. We'll come in behind you and pick you up."

And with that, both aircraft flew in low over the airfield with all guns blazing. Having given the resident Germans a very unpleasant shock, sergeants Flint and Stubbs pulled their aircraft up and away from the airfield and headed out over the North Sea; one of the engines on Jimmie's Hampden was running at full speed, preventing him from landing on the airfield, so foiling their plan.

However, their problems were not yet over as the waters of the North Sea glinted in the early morning light. The Hampden was once more losing height and the waves beneath them were growing ever closer. With great skill he managed to nurse the ailing aircraft to the safety of England but he couldn't reach his base at RAF Scampton and it wasn't long before he was forced to land in a field. The aircraft had barely ground to a halt and the crew disentangled themselves from the wreckage and stumbled out into the fresh morning air, when they were met by a local farmer's wife carrying a tray on which she had put their breakfast.

Not long after this incident, on the night of Saturday 5th July 1941, Sgt Flint's aircraft was once more attacked, this time by enemy night fighters. The first attack came just after crossing the Dutch coast on the way to the target. They managed to shake the fighters off and continued to the target, making a successful attack. However, on the return trip across the North Sea and just fifty miles from the coast of Norfolk, they were again attacked by two Me110s. The cannon shells ripped into the Hampden mortally wounding Sgt Benny Fitch, Jimmie's navigator, and igniting the Very cartridges. The fighters circled the Hampden and attacked again; this time the 20mm cannons took the life out of the port engine. But by now they were within sight of the English coast and in the growing daylight of that Sunday dawn, the German pilots peeled away and left Jimmie and his crew to the North Sea and their fate.

Though free from further attack, the stricken Hampden sank inexorably towards the waiting waves until it was barely skimming the breaking crests. In the fuselage behind him Jimmie knew that his navigator had been injured and he fought desperately hard with the controls to keep his aircraft flying on the remaining engine and to bring it back to Scampton where the help that his navigator needed was waiting. But ahead of him he saw the cliffs at Cromer rising from the sea and despite his efforts he knew that the Hampden would not climb over them. So with no other choice, he ditched AD856 as close to the beach as he could, and, escaping through the hatch above his head, joined his crew on the wing. He looked at their life raft lying in shreds beside them, riddled with cannon shell holes and in that moment Jimmie realised that the navigator was not with them.
"Where's Benny?" he asked of the others.

Their expressions told him all he needed to know and without hesitating he returned into the fuselage of the now sinking Hampden. He found Sgt Fitch unconscious, still in his navigator's position. Struggling against the water which was rapidly flowing into the fuselage and the weight of the injured man, he managed to free his navigator and drag him to the escape hatch. The Hampden was already completely awash and, with its tail lifting into the air, was starting to dip beneath the sea.

Determined not to leave his friend to drown in the sinking aircraft, Jimmie forced his way against the water through the open door and, despite them both wearing full flying kit, swam towards the shore as AD856 EA-P slipped out of sight. Fighting against the waves, exhausted and bitterly cold, fifty yards from the beach Jimmie felt the welcoming hands of a soldier who had seen their plight and had waded in to the sea to help drag the injured navigator from the water. Sgt Fitch never regained consciousness and finally lost his fight for life on the beach at Cromer shortly afterwards. Jimmie had done everything he could to save his navigator, including risking his own life, but the airman's injuries from the cannon shells had been too great to withstand the ordeal in the tumbling waves.

In the rarest of circumstances, Sgt Flint was awarded two separate gallantry medals for two separate incidents arising from the same action; the Distinguished Flying Medal for his exceptional courage and flying skills in bringing his crippled aircraft back to the safety of the shore and thus saving the lives of the rest of his crew and the George Medal for his outstandingly courageous actions to save Sgt JD Fitch from drowning in the sinking Hampden bomber.

Always ready to help others, whatever the risk to himself, later in the war and by now an officer, Jimmie Flint saved another airman when he dragged him out of a burning aircraft. This was an incident which happened at a bomber station when, following an explosion, the aircraft was burning furiously, trapping the airman inside. Once more without hesitation, he went into the aircraft and pulled the airman out just before the aircraft exploded.

In the worst days of the war, the survival chances for bomber aircrew were around one in four; less than they had been for a junior subaltern on the Western Front in the years 1914 to 1918. More than 55,000 young airmen died whilst prosecuting the war in occupied Europe alone, against a vicious, demonic dictatorship which was committed to the extermination of certain peoples and the enslavery of others, including the British. But as I knew only too well, the killing, the destruction and the horrors of war were not confined to Europe; in the desert, the story was the same. German aspirations of domination were compounded, aided and abetted by a series of allies who shared their values, not least the Japanese, whose treatment of prisoners of war was barbaric by any standard.

On 14th May 1940, the Luftwaffe bombed the virtually defenceless Dutch city of Rotterdam even though the government had formally surrendered, and in a ninety minute daylight bombing frenzy, 30,000 civilians died and another 50,000 were injured. In retaliation, Bomber Command attacked military and strategic industrial targets in Germany and so ended the 'phoney war'.

With the defeat of the British Expeditionary Force that same month, Britain and its Empire stood alone against the might of the world's most powerful army and air force, which now occupied northern Europe from Norway to the French border with Spain. The German forces had swept away all before them, rolled up to the English Channel and stopped. No army had successfully crossed that narrow stretch of water for nearly a thousand years. Hitler knew that he must crush the British people or lose the war, and he also knew that air supremacy was the key to that victory; and so began the Battle of Britain. In the summer of 1940, the burden of salvation lay upon the Royal Air Force, for only it stood between freedom and oppression.

Hermann Goering, a former First World War fighter pilot, had promised Hitler that his Luftwaffe would clear the RAF from the skies in a matter of days. Outnumbered more than four to one, RAF Fighter Command took on the might of the Luftwaffe during the long hot summer days of 1940. But they were not alone, because whilst the battle raged above southern England and the fighter airfields were repeatedly attacked, Bomber Command was destroying the German landing barges, the ships, the ports and the equipment that was needed for the invasion and stored along the French coast. These were mostly daylight raids, carried out at low level in aircraft which were highly vulnerable to the coastal defences and German fighters.

Whilst Fighter Command, fortunately, had cutting-edge aircraft such as the Hurricane and Spitfire, Bomber Command was operating obsolete, slow, light bombers such as the single engine Fairey Battle. The cost in the lives of aircrew was very high and daylight raids were recognised as being unsustainable. Night bombing was introduced, but the difficulty was that at this early stage of the war, aircraft had primitive navigation equipment, often only a sextant and map which were both useless in cloud. Crews were trying to find, more often than not by dead reckoning, small specific targets in the middle of a huge land mass in total darkness; it was soon shown to be totally impracticable. Indeed on one occasion a bomber crew became so lost in poor weather conditions at night that it bombed what it believed to be an enemy airfield in Holland; in fact they had bombed a fighter base in Cambridgeshire. Fortunately no-one was injured and the bomber returned home safely. However, next day a couple of spirited Spitfire pilots, upon discovering the identity of the squadron concerned, flew over its base and dropped dummy German Iron Crosses, in a gesture of good humour.

The serious side of the incident highlighted the pitiful state of navigational equipment and training; crews were being sent five or six hundred miles into enemy territory to bomb a weapons factory, often obscured by cloud, fog or industrial haze, and then find their way back to Britain again. It was simply not practical and too many crews and aircraft were being lost in crashes not caused by enemy action, but more usually through running out of fuel. Today, when technology allows computer-controlled missiles to hit a target the size of a manhole cover, it is hard to conceive how difficult it was for us. Not least because everything was pitch dark; unfortunately the Germans didn't leave the lights on to guide us in.

In the summer of 1941 the government carried out a secret survey of bombing accuracy. The resultant Butt report concluded that only 30 per cent of bombers were getting to within five miles of their target; the number actually hitting the target was considerably lower than that, whilst the loss of men and aircraft remained disproportionately high.

During 1940 and 1941, the Luftwaffe had kept up a punishing regime of bombing British cities, not just London but Leeds, Liverpool, Glasgow, Manchester, Bristol, Birmingham, Coventry, Plymouth and Newcastle in particular, in an effort to terrorise the population and break its morale. On 14th November 1940, the Luftwaffe dropped more than a million pounds of bombs on Coventry and razed it like Warsaw and Rotterdam. Over 43,000 civilians died in these raids on Britain, but the people of those cities and elsewhere stood firm. The cost to the Germans had been the loss of 2375 of their aircraft.

Nevertheless, following the Butt report, military strategists at the Air Ministry adopted and refined the 'area bombing' tactic. Essentially it was the same tactic used by the Luftwaffe, but on a greater scale and much more difficult and dangerous to execute. The idea was put to Churchill who whole-heartedly embraced it as being entirely consistent with his private views, "When I look round to see how we can win this war there is only one sure path... and that is an absolutely devastating, exterminating attack by very heavy bombers from this country upon the Nazi homeland," and also his public views, expressed in September 1940, "The fighters are our salvation but the bombers alone provide the means of victory. We must therefore develop the power to carry an ever-increasing volume of explosives to Germany, so as to pulverise their entire industry and scientific structure on which the war effort and economic life of the enemy depends, whilst holding him at arm's length from our island."

Still conscious of the appalling loss of life in the trenches during 1914–18, The War Cabinet, containing Conservative, Labour and Liberal politicians concluded that aerial bombing was the preferable strategy and approved the policy. It instructed the Air Ministry accordingly. In 1942, Bomber Command had a new man in charge, Air Marshal Arthur T Harris; it fell to him, and to us, to implement and deliver the wishes of our political masters. Harris has been consistently blamed for the strategy of area bombing: it was not Harris's strategy, it was not Bomber Command's; it was the Government's. I can think of no better example of where the messenger has been repeatedly shot.

Until the last few weeks of the war, Churchill was a strong supporter and indeed advocate of area bombing because he realised the importance of forcing the Germans to defend their homeland. Albert Speer, Hitler's Armaments Minister described it as "the greatest lost battle on the German side".

Opponents of the area bombing strategy most often quote the raid on Dresden to indict Sir Arthur Harris and Bomber Command of culpability; but it was not Harris's conception. Once more it came from the very top. Churchill was under pressure from Stalin to provide a defining blow against the Germans quickly and to help the advance in the east. The Air Ministry had selected Dresden as a target as far back as 1941, because of the railway yards there, but Bomber Command had avoided attacking it until that fateful night in February 1945 when the Prime Minister ordered that it should do so. It was one of four such selected targets which included Chemnitz and Leipzig, but when the news of the Dresden firestorm got out, public opinion soured, the other targets were largely dropped and the politicians ducked, leaving Bomber Command and Arthur Harris to take the blame. I believe we stand acquitted.

As aircrew, we were not given the luxury of picking over the moral ethics of our orders in the quiet calm of peaceful surroundings. We were at war; we were fighting for our very survival, for the survival of our families, and the RAF was the only arm of the services which was able to strike at the German homeland on a regular basis. The whole purpose of area bombing was to disrupt industrial production, wear down morale and to force the enemy to divert resources, including troops from the battle areas, to the defence of Germany. In this latter respect it was very successful in that 55,000 guns and a million men were engaged upon that defence; but the price paid by the young men of Bomber Command was desperately high.

We were at war with the German people. It was total war. It was irrelevant whether they were in uniform or not, they were all part of the German war machine, producing munitions and materials with which their army, air force and navy sought to dominate Europe and beyond. It is surely a fallacious distinction to separate civilians and service personnel in such circumstances. It was civilian scientists who developed Hitler's Vengeance weapons, the V-1 and V-2, which killed thousands of civilians in London; it was civilian workers in the factories who produced the fighters and the flak shells which shot down and killed more than 55,000 RAF aircrew; it was civilian shipbuilders who built the *Bismarck* which sank HMS *Hood* with the loss of all but three Royal Navy sailors; it was civilian workers who made the torpedoes which sank the evacuation ship *City of Benares*, drowning all but six of the children on board, and which sank hundreds of merchant ships, claiming the lives of thousands of Merchant Navy sailors like Blake Turner; and it was civilians who made the guns and tanks which killed our soldiers in North Africa, Italy and Normandy, at Dunkirk, El Alamein and Arnhem. In the final analysis, it was the Nazi administration which developed its war manufacturing base in civilian built-up areas.

Of course it was exactly the same from the German point of view. British civilian workers were equally employed busily making all the same weapons for us to fight them with. What it demonstrates is the wasteful futility of war, but also that total war cannot make distinctions between the clothes which people choose to wear. A nation at war is just that, together as a nation, whatever individuals within that nation might think about it.

Many of us knew exactly what it was like being bombed; Ted Beswick was bombed out of his home in Birmingham three times and his last house was set on fire twice.

Looking down from my rear turret at the destruction and carnage that we had wrought upon the enemy beneath me did not fill me with any joy. I took no pleasure from knowing what the effect of six or seven hundred bombers dropping 14,000lb of high explosive each would be on the people of that city far below. But if we did not do it to them, they would certainly do it to us. They had done it before and would do it again. The irony was that we were preventing the Germans manufacturing bombers with which to attack Britain; instead they had to make fighters with which to attack us over Germany.

Bomber Command aircrew were all volunteers, every one of us. We had an average age of just twenty-two and many gunners, like John Hannah, were only eighteen when they flew out to face the most terrifying battle conditions imaginable, not once but time and time again. For many, it only stopped when they were killed. The Lancaster and Halifax were great bombers in their day, but they were also noisy, cold, cramped, smelled of oil and aviation fuel and were highly dangerous places. Too many of my friends and tens of thousands I never knew died in burning aircraft, trapped by the G-forces as they spiralled 20,000 feet before crashing into the earth, their last few minutes of life a terrifying realisation of inevitability.

Many lads took off from their operational station in the dwindling light of a summer evening and never returned. Reg Payne tells of two young wireless operators with whom he trained, who were both killed in the early months of 1944. Their parents came to Reg's house to see his parents because Reg's brother, who flew with No.48 Squadron, was still missing from a raid over Düsseldorf on 3rd November the previous autumn. Reg's brother was a POW, being one of only three who survived when their Lancaster had been hit and blew up; the two young wireless operators were not so lucky and as the weeks and months went by with no news of their fate, both their mothers were so grief stricken that they were committed to a mental institution in Northampton; only one later came home and then not for eighteen years. The consequences of area bombing were felt far and wide on both sides.

292

Whoever may have been to blame for causing the Second World War, I know that it was not the young men and women who served in Bomber Command. When we dropped our bombs on German cities, we were not criminals; we were doing what our own country asked us to do and had to do, however unpalatable, in order to win because winning was the only way to survive. As we flew across Europe and bombed our targets, we were targets ourselves, as more than 55,000 graves can testify. Every mile of the way we were the hunted enemy of the German people and they used every means to kill us. There was no-one in a bomber crew who would not have much rather been at home with his family or out with a girlfriend, than spending hours at a time flying 18,000 feet above occupied Europe, constantly only moments away from death. It was not enviable, it was not enjoyable, but nor was it avoidable. It was so dangerous a task that only volunteers did it and we did it to secure freedom for our children.

Sadly, the British people, led by its politicians, turned their backs upon those who, in the dark days of 1940 to 1944, when the country was in mortal danger, were treated as heroes, 'our brave bomber boys'. The same nation which readily embraced the peace which we had helped to secure quickly grew squeamish about the harsh reality of how that peace was secured; they forgot that when two men say, "Let's go to war today," people die.

Although life on the ground on an operational station is often depicted as all beer and laughs, it was much more complex than that. Certainly we enjoyed ourselves whenever we could, because we never knew whether our next mission would be our last. But such times were the result of living on adrenalin and fear, tainted by physical and emotional exhaustion, relief at having survived another mission when others did not, and recognition that respite lasted only until the next mission.

When I arrived at Coningsby and went to my billet, the locker next to the bed I was allocated had not been cleared from the last occupant. There was a photograph of a nice-looking girl on the top, signed with a message: "Peter, with my love forever. Beth", and the sort of personal belongings which we all carried around were in the drawer. Peter had not returned from operations the night before.

That was what it was like. A small but relentless loss of crews, week after week; some would be good friends, others only acquaintances, others still new to the squadron and on their first mission, but all kindred spirits. We felt their loss, but then had to move on; another mission, another target, another night of fear and death. It is now in my later years that I have missed the people I knew so well. Their faces still float through my mind, faces that were so young, lives that had lived so little. Some of those young men had never even kissed a girl; they didn't know the pleasures of a relationship: they were killed too soon to have had that chance.

There were other stark reminders around the station which would point to the loss of this or that crew: a vacant dispersal area the next morning; an empty table at breakfast; a wash bag left pegged on the line; a bicycle left propped up outside the briefing room; a motor car remaining unmoved outside the mess; a new CO. Each a symbol of finality which struck hard at us no matter how often it was repeated, but then they had to go into the box of dark memories and the lid closed tightly upon it; we had to function as a crew for our own survival and dwelling upon the loss of others was not a luxury we could afford. The cars which were left behind were impounded and awaited instructions from the next of kin once the owner's fate was known. If he was never going to return, the family would often let it be sold to someone else on the base for a very reasonable sum, the money usually going into the airmen's benevolent fund. Some cars changed hands many times.

CHAPTER FIFTEEN

LIFE'S DUTY DONE

"Oh, I have slipped the surly bonds of earth and danced the skies on laughter-silvered wings; sunward I've climbed and joined the tumbling mirth of sun-split clouds – and done a hundred things you have not dreamed of;.....put out my hand and touched the face of God"

From High Flight [An Airman's Ecstasy] *by John Gillespie Magee*

As my time at Harwell progressed, it was fairly clear that the war would not last much longer. The training regime carried on but the urgency had gone from it and as a result there was very little flying practice for air gunners taking place; most of the training was being conducted on the ranges. As April advanced, so the emphasis was turned towards recovering our troops who had been held as prisoners of war. During the last week of April and the first week of May, Bomber Command was focused on two humanitarian operations, *Exodus*, to bring back our POWs and *Manna*, to drop food and supplies to the Dutch in Western Holland. The area was still under German control but there was such a food shortage that the local population were dying of starvation. Through an agreement with the local German commander, operation *Manna* went ahead without the Lancasters being attacked.

However, Bomber Command continued operations until the night of 26th/27th April when 115 Mosquitoes attacked various military targets, mainly airfields, without loss. The last airmen from the Command died on the night of 2nd/3rd May when a Mosquito was shot down whilst attacking a Luftwaffe airfield, killing both crewmen. Later in the night two Halifaxes collided over Kiel losing thirteen of the sixteen crew. These fifteen airmen are all buried in the Kiel War Cemetery.

Hitler committed suicide in his bunker with Eva Braun on 30th April and when the news reached us a few days later, there was a real sense that the war in Europe would soon be over; and so it was. On the morning of Monday 7th May 1945 the mess was bustling with expectation as we gathered around the Marconi wireless set which sat on the table in the corner and was carefully tuned to the BBC Home Service. Presently, Alvar Lidell, who had read so many news bulletins during the war and was the most familiar voice on the wireless, introduced the Prime Minister, Winston Churchill. The room fell totally silent in a moment.

"Yesterday morning at 2.41am, at General Eisenhower's Headquarters, General Jodel, the representative of the German High Command and of Grand Admiral Donitz the designated Head of the German State, signed the act of unconditional surrender of all German land, sea and air forces in Europe, to the Allied Expeditionary Force and simultaneously to the Soviet High Command... Today this agreement will be ratified and confirmed at Berlin. Hostilities will end officially at one minute after midnight tonight, Tuesday 8th May..."

For a few seconds after Churchill had finished speaking we were all silent as the realisation of what he had said sunk in, and then a great cheer went up. We had made it; we really had won the war, in Europe at least. Five years earlier in May 1940 after Dunkirk, no-one had given Britain a hope against the might of the Third Reich. But we had come through it victorious and those of us standing there had lived to see that day. The bar was open and in a moment of solemnity we raised a glass to all our comrades who had died to make this victory possible. The war was to have cost the lives of more than 305,000 British servicemen and women.

Inevitably, the party which had been planned for a few days was given the go-ahead for that evening. It started fairly early on most stations up and down the country, and Harwell was no exception, particularly since we were not an operational base. I was standing by the bar with a couple of pals at about half past seven, when I noticed two young women come into the room, one of whom I recognised from an earlier dance on the base. I had wanted to speak to her then, but for one reason or another I had not managed to. I had thought about her several times since then and wondered who she was and where she worked since I knew she was not one of the WAAFs on the base. Tonight I wasted no time at all, went straight across to her and asked if they were meeting anyone and if not, could I get them each a drink.

Elsie Minshall, the girl I married
[Neville Bowyer collection]

Elsie Minshall was in her mid-twenties, actually she was twenty-five but I didn't know that until later, a little older than most of the single women who were usually at the dances and since I was now thirty-one I felt more comfortable talking to her. We had a wonderful evening, dancing to the band music which played on well into the night; being VE Day all added to the pleasure because there was such a great feeling of relief everywhere. Of course the war wasn't over, it was only the Germans who had surrendered, the Japanese were still fighting on in the Far East and we had many troops from all the services out there. But for one night at least, we could believe the war was over.

I arranged to meet Elsie again the next night and our relationship grew from there. By one of those strange coincidences of real life, Elsie had been born just five miles away from my home in Shropshire, at Wytheford forge in Shawbury, but it had taken the war to bring us together. Elsie's father George, who had also been born at the forge, had left Shawbury at sixteen and moved to London to work as a plate layer on the Southern Railway. He made a career with the Southern, met Elsie's mother Florence, married and settled in Deptford. However, when Flo was expecting Elsie, her second child, in the winter of 1920, she went to stay at the forge in Shawbury with George's parents, taking Elsie's sister with her, and that's how she came to be born in Shropshire.

Wytheford forge in Shawbury, Elsie's birthplace
[Neville Bowyer collection]

Although Elsie was brought up in London, the coincidence of our birthplaces was just one of the early bonds which we had and also helped endear me to her father, with whom I always got on very well. Elsie had four sisters and one brother. By the 1930s her father had been promoted to Permanent Way Inspector for Charing Cross and Waterloo, a post which during the war, and the Blitz in particular, was to put him in considerable danger and require him to be at work for days at a time with hardly any sleep between air raids. The Luftwaffe bombers did all they could to disrupt the transport network of London during the Blitz, and it was George's job to supervise the repairs to the railway track and bridges to get the trains running again as soon as possible. He was also the first person to be out to inspect the damage after the raids, which was an especially dangerous job particularly where bridges and delayed fuse bombs were involved. He worked hard and he worked his gangs hard, but he had also come up from the bottom and so he brought real experience to the job.

In the King's Birthday Honours List of 1942, George Minshall was awarded the British Empire Medal in recognition of his dedication to his work during that time and for the personal danger he had faced in doing so. His award appeared in the London Gazette on 5th June 1942. I later found out that even after the war, he still went to work wearing starched collars, a bowler hat and a pocket watch and chain of which he was very proud.

Ready for Buckingham Palace, Elsie's father George Minshall, BEM [Neville Bowyer collection]

A year or two before Elsie left school at fourteen, the family had moved from Deptford to Catford when George bought their own home at 103 Sandhurst Road following his appointment as Permanent Way Inspector. Her first jobs were in retail, working in the local newsagents and then Marks & Spencer. However, when the Blitz started, Elsie's father rented a house in Didcot and moved the family out of London, whilst he stayed in the Sandhurst Road house alone. The rented house was opposite Didcot railway station and not far from the Ordnance depot where

Elsie, who had always been good at figures, got a job in the wages department and worked there for the rest of the war. Didcot was only about a mile from Harwell and the single women, and some not so single, often came to the dances and parties at the base; and that is how, on the day that Lt Col Frank Bourne, the last British survivor of the battle at Rorke's Drift in 1879 slipped peacefully away from this life, the strands of fate brought Elsie and I together to start the rest of our lives.

The following few days were filled with very mixed feelings; we were very excited that the war with Germany was over but we also knew that the Japanese were not yet defeated and we thought about the lads who had not made it through, those who had died in the skies over Europe and elsewhere, together with those who hadn't even made it that far and had been killed whilst training.

Elsie and I spent as much time together as we could over the next few weeks because I knew that another posting was not going to be very long in coming. We made some lovely memories of our time in Oxfordshire. Whenever we could, we would get the train from Didcot and head off into the countryside that is the Vale of White Horse. Rationing was still in full force of course, even though the war with Germany was over, and indeed it continued for many years to come, with some things still being rationed in the 1950s. It made it a little difficult to get anything interesting for a picnic, but we managed well enough. Life was simpler then: our expectations were much lower than people's today and we were content with a lot less; on balance I know we were happier for it. Sometimes we would take the train into Oxford and go to a dance or to the pictures; it all depended upon how much time we had.

Even though we were still at war in the Far East, I began to notice a subtle change in attitude to my uniform from the public. Nothing very obvious and certainly not hostile, more a kind of indifference. Whereas in the dark days of the war, whenever I was in a pub and anyone found out that I was with Bomber Command, a drink would appear and I was everyone's friend, now people just turned away.

How fickle public opinion is, and in this case, as I came to understand, it was fuelled by the politicians in the run-up to the General Election held in July.

The Japanese maintained their strong resistance in the Pacific and even though, as with the Germans, the final outcome was inevitable, they would not surrender and intended to fight for every little island across that great ocean all the way back to gates of the Emperor's palace. Our own Far Eastern troops and the Americans both knew what fanatical fighters the Japanese were and it was clear to everyone that before the Rising Sun was finally vanquished, the cost in human life on both sides was going to be enormous. With that sobering thought in mind we now started the preparations for what was known as the Tiger Force, the British contingent to be sent out to the Far East to start the fight for those islands. Bomber Command would play an important role in this task, as once more, together with the USAAF, we would bomb the enemy ahead of the ground troops, cut the lines of communication and prevent reinforcements and supplies reaching the front line, wherever that happened to be.

In the event, ironically with the help of captured German scientists, the war in the Pacific was brought to a shattering conclusion with the dropping of the two atom bombs on Hiroshima and Nagasaki on 6th and 9th August: the world had changed forever. Six days later, the Japanese surrendered and the Second World War was finally over after almost six years. Whatever else resulted from the dropping of the atom bombs, two things are certain, tens of thousands of lives were saved which would have otherwise been lost on both sides relentlessly fighting across the myriad of Pacific islands. Moreover, it also provided for the speedy release of thousands more Allied prisoners of war who were being held by the Japanese in the most appalling of conditions imaginable. The FEPOW memorial at the National Arboretum, with its pictures and interviews with survivors, gives a harrowing glimpse into the barbarous treatment of these men. Many of those who did survive would not have done so had the war continued much longer.

With the war over, the gradual closing of Britain's airfields and wartime infrastructure, started after Germany's surrender, now accelerated, seemingly with indecent haste. It grieves me to think that the political and military bureaucracy thought so little of what we had achieved that out of 7,379 Lancasters made, only 26 survive today and only one Wellington was saved, and that only because it crashed into Loch Ness on a training flight. The personnel priority was to repatriate the POWs and then start to release those airmen who were not going to stay in the RAF.

Elsie and I had decided that we were right for each other and so I took her home to meet my mum and dad. I had already met her parents, simply because it was much easier to get in and out of London on a weekend pass, than it was up to Shrewsbury and back. Both my parents took to Elsie straight away, although I know that Mum felt that she was losing her only child for good. Dad was very pleased, saying that it was about time I settled down now that I was in my thirties. Thanks, Dad.

My first priority was to find work. I knew that I would have my demob pay but that would not last long and so I resolved to return to the TPO for the time being if I possibly could. There were a lot of chaps coming out of all the services looking for work, and there had also been a huge demographic change during the war in that women had taken on so many of the traditionally male jobs and were now highly skilled in them. Whilst most of these women gave up their jobs when they married or when their husbands returned, it all took a little time to settle down; there was no guarantee of a job for most men. The Labour Party had won the 1945 general election and Clement Atlee was now the Prime Minister; the Government might have changed but Britain was bankrupt and the challenges were innumerable.

I remembered that in November 1940, when I left the TPO to join the RAF, Egbert Ramsbottom had promised me my old job again if I came back from the war; it was time to call it in. I had talked it through with Elsie and we decided that although it wasn't very sociable, it paid well and would help to set us up until something better came along. So just before I left the RAF, I put on my best blue uniform with all my medal ribbons crisp and clean, and travelled to London to keep my appointment with my old TPO head supervisor. When I had arranged to see him, I was pleased to know that he remained in charge of the reinstated TPO, but more importantly, I was encouraged by the fact that he still remembered me and wanted to see me.

"Hello, Trevor," smiled Egbert's elderly and faithful secretary, with whom I had made the appointment. "How lovely to see you safely back from the war. My word, you do look dashing in your uniform; I wish I was thirty years younger," and she blushed at her own temerity.

"Hello, Miss Canter, it's nice to see you too. How are you?"
"Oh, much better now that the war is over. Mr Ramsbottom is expecting you, do go in please, Trevor."

"Come in." His familiar and fatherly voice answered my knock on the door. "Trevor, how good to see you. I was so pleased to know that you had made it through." He eased his bulky frame from his generously proportioned leather chair and came round from behind the equally generously proportioned oak desk to greet me with a firm handshake. As he did so I saw him swiftly take in the colours of my medal ribbons.
"Hello, Mr Ramsbottom. Thank you for seeing me."
"Delighted, Trevor. Tell me a little of what you got up to in the RAF." This wasn't idle curiosity but the interview for my old job. He waved me to the rather austere seat opposite his desk and returned to his own more comfortable one.

I very briefly ran through my service and was conscious that he was listening very intently to what I said. After I had finished, he looked at me hard and said, "If I'm not mistaken, Trevor, you are wearing the medal ribbon of the Distinguished Flying Cross, but you haven't mentioned it. When did you get it?"

"I was awarded it in 1944 for my service throughout two tours of operations in bombers."

"Any man who comes in here wearing a DFC can expect to be treated well. We owe you all a great debt, Trevor. I don't suppose you have an actual release date from the RAF, yet, but let Miss Canter know as soon as you can."

We chatted for a few more minutes about the war, about the 70,000 GPO workers who had joined up, the 3,800 who had not returned and the 400 who had been killed either in the Home Guard or on GPO duty, including when the Farringdon Road depot took a direct hit on 18th June 1943. We also talked about the changes which were beginning to emerge in the country, not least the new government, and the proposals for nationalisation of the railways.

"It'll be a sad day if ever they do, you know, Trevor; it will be the end of a great railway era in this country. I won't be part of it, though; I'm due for retirement next year." He gave a sad wistful smile and turned to gaze out of the window at the dark grey clouds which scudded across the sky as if hurrying to leave the city and its problems behind.

How right he was. Within twenty years, Dr Beeching and both the Conservative and Labour governments had decimated Britain's railways almost to the point of destruction. The cardinal sin committed by the British Railways Board, of which Beeching was the chairman, was to sell off the lines and the track beds; selling the land was unforgivable and today has come back to haunt us, constraining the expansion and development of a more efficient and vibrant railway network. Passenger numbers today are back to their late 1940s levels and yet the network is only half the size: little wonder it is congested.

And so on Thursday, 21st March 1946 I finally left the RAF and returned to the TPO. Elsie had already left the Ordnance depot at Didcot, secured a job in a shop and moved back to her parents' house in Sandhurst Road, where I joined her. Although it is now fashionable for unmarried couples to live together, immediately after the war it was often a case of simple necessity, so many houses had been destroyed by German bombing, especially in the cities, there were just not enough to go round.

The next few months were very hectic in the Minshall household as Elsie's four sisters had also met servicemen towards the end of the war and we were all getting married at about the same time. I was of course working away at night on the TPO, and so we continued to live in the Sandhurst Road house for a few weeks until we could find somewhere of our own. Despite the genuine warmth of her family, after a time we inevitably turned our thoughts to working more sociable hours and getting a home of our own and in due course we moved into 17 Aubert Road. We were married in the Islington Registry Office on the 17th May 1946 and our son Neville was born in September 1947.

Me visiting a friend's dog [Neville Bowyer collection]

The winter of 1946/47 was one of the most severe of the twentieth century and after the train got stuck on Shap Fell for several hours for the third time in a fortnight, on the worst occasion arriving in Carlisle thirteen hours and twenty-three minutes late, I knew that the shine had very definitely worn off the TPO. Strangely, though, it was not the snow, the wind, the tiredness, the boredom or the hunger which I remember most about those nights, but the cold. Had I remained in the RAF for another year, I would have most certainly been back in the air, this time helping to drop food supplies to isolated villages and feed to sheep and cattle stranded on the hill farms.

It was bitter, almost constant freezing temperatures all winter; the trackside collection and delivery apparatus was shut down for that fortnight and many rural services simply stopped because the roads were blocked with snow. When the heating in the carriages broke down it soon dropped well below freezing inside too and most of the men could barely move for the cold, and yet I hardly noticed it. All those nights sitting in the rear turret behind my Browning guns with the temperature plummeting to minus thirty, forty or fifty degrees centigrade had hardened me to it.

Snowfall on Shap Fell

After the great snow and the great freeze came the great thaw and the great flood and we had to struggle with more delayed services and long nights, often not arriving in Carlisle until mid-morning. Eventually, of course, the weather improved and everything got back to some sort of normality, even though rail nationalisation was looming and we didn't know how it would affect the TPO. Nevertheless, all the TPO teams had an official commendation from the Head Controller, Mr FG Fielder; but this was 1947 not 1936, I was that much older, no longer single and the war had aged me beyond my years; I had had enough of the cold and of working at night. It had been fun before the war, it had been well paid and it had been waiting for me when I returned, but it was time to leave the TPO.

I applied for a nine-to-five clerical post and if possible a transfer back to Shrewsbury, since the prospect of our getting a house in London was hopeless. Once more my DFC opened doors that would otherwise have been closed to me and within a few weeks I was desk bound. It took a little time getting used to because I had not worked in such circumstances since I had left the Farringdon Road sorting office to join the TPO in 1936. Even though I had taken a drop in wages, the post had its compensations and going home to bed each night instead of rocking up and down the west-coast line was definitely one of them.

Eighteen months later in 1949, my transfer to Shrewsbury came through and, together with my young family I moved back to Shrewsbury and into a new house in Springfield. My job now was working on the counter in the main post office at the top of Pride Hill; I was back in the very same building that I had stood in as that fourteen-year-old boy looking for his first job on Oak Apple Day, 1928; I had come full circle. As I walked into work on the first morning, I recalled the feelings I had had all those years ago, the expectation, the uncertainty, the excitement. How could I have possibly imagined what was ahead of me in the years that lay between those two first mornings?

With Elsie in the garden at Springfield [NB collection]

Immersed in such thoughts, I arrived at the staff entrance at the same time as a small, thin, elderly man with a very pale complexion, who walked with a slight stoop. "I don't think I know you, young man, do I?" his voice barely audible as I turned and looked at my questioner.

He wasn't as tall as I remembered him, he wore spectacles now, the Adam's apple was a little more pronounced and he had to look up when he spoke to me rather than down his pointed nose, but there was no mistaking him; it was the rake. I couldn't believe that he was still here. I suddenly felt very sorry for him.

"You do, Mr Polling, it's Trevor Bowyer, but you haven't seen me since 1933. I expect I have changed a bit since I was nineteen."

He peered up at me more intently. "Yes, so it is. We've been expecting you, Trevor. The London office said they were very sorry to lose you, but you've decided to come back home, have you?" By now we were inside the building and the relative quiet made it easier to hear him.

"Is Mr Stamp still here?" I asked him.

"Oh no, he retired a long time ago." That humourless thin smile was still there.

As I watched, he walked away from me towards that familiar office in which I had first been interviewed and I realised that he had succeeded Mr Stamp as Senior Supervisor. He opened, went through and closed the door behind him without the slightest sound. I smiled to myself; some things at least had not changed.

Counter work was alright but, for the most part, dull. It was, however, warm and dry, I had a seat, set breaks and some good chaps to work with. Around 1955 I had the chance to carry out relief work in small post offices across the county. This was more interesting simply because there were different places to go to and different people to meet. In the 1950s there were many more post offices than now, every small community had one and covering for the holidays and other absences of the postmasters was an integral part of the GPO administration.

Fishing with Neville at Atcham at the same spot I visited fifty years earlier [Neville Bowyer collection]

And later the same afternoon [Neville Bowyer collection]

By about 1960, I moved to a clerical post in the sorting office in Castle Gates, Shrewsbury, with responsibility for personnel and security, and then on to the television licensing detection team. Finally I moved to the best job of all; head of the stationery store in Butcher Row, at the back of the main post office. This was a particularly enjoyable position since not only was it an easy job, but I was effectively my own boss. I had an older assistant who, like me, enjoyed a beer or two. We would often lock the store and deliver the stationery orders to the sorting office in Castle Gates and then call into a pub for a couple on the way back.

On one occasion around 1971, we overran our lunch time somewhat and lingered a little longer than we had intended. The beer tasted particularly good, slipped down particularly easily and the company was particularly convivial; we got a little drunk, not hammered, just a little drunk. In due course we wandered back to the stationery store, opened up and put the kettle on. Within a few minutes the Head Postmaster arrived and after a short but rather terse conversation with me, announced, "Trevor, I consider that you are pissed and I think that it is a disgrace. You need to control yourself."

He was a man who, apart from being half my age, was very full of himself and tended to strut about the place making sure that everyone knew his position; the sort of person who would have very quickly been dropped from a bomber crew, probably through the escape hatch. I had not been brought up to be disrespectful to people but the beer rather loosened my tongue on this occasion and in reply, I borrowed a line from Winston Churchill,
"I am, but tomorrow I shall be sober, whilst you, Sir, will still be pissed with power. Please leave my offices, the kettle has boiled and it's time for tea."

I thought that my elderly assistant was going to choke from trying not to laugh, but it all had the desired effect; we never saw him in there again.

Enjoying a beer at the Christmas party 1971
[Neville Bowyer collection]

In 1967 Elsie and I had bought our own house on the new Sutton Farm housing development. Elsie had taken quite a while to settle in to the much quieter and slower pace of life in Shrewsbury, after the helter-skelter of London, but in time she did and during the 1960s and 1970s, two of her sisters moved up to Shrewsbury too. From the 1950s until she retired, Elsie worked for various catering businesses in the town, in particular Sidoli's in Barker Street, now the Bellstone restaurant, the Greyhound Café in Butcher Row, now a clothes shop and Carter's in Rousehill Bank. As she neared retirement, Elsie kept her hand in by doing casual waitress work at wedding receptions and a few hours in a florist shop.

Elsie very rarely used a bus to go into town, even when she went shopping, but instead preferred to go on her bicycle, which she did right up to her 80th birthday. She became quite a celebrity in her later years, cycling around the town, and locals who knew her would often call out, "How's your iron horse today, Elsie?" as she rode by, giving them a wave.

I retired at sixty in 1974 and was awarded the Imperial Service Medal by the GPO. This was not an automatic award on retirement; on the contrary, it was awarded very infrequently. I remain immensely proud of it because it represents a whole lifetime's achievement. I understand that I am one of only twelve people to have been awarded the Imperial Service Medal with the DFC post-nominals. I also know that the Head Postmaster couldn't have been too offended that afternoon, because he must have had a hand in the nomination process somewhere along the way; perhaps he had a sense of humour after all.

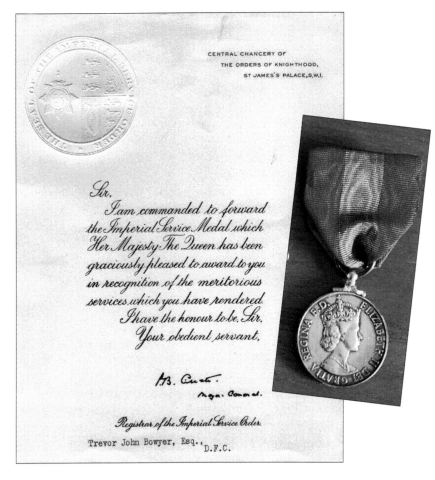

My Imperial Service Medal and citation
[Neville Bowyer collection]

Head Post Office

St. Mary's Street, Shrewsbury SY1 1AA

Telephone (0743) 4212 Giro Account 403 7014
Shrewsbury
From the Head Postmaster: B. W. Baxley

POST OFFICE

3 January 1974

Mr T J Bowyer
5 Stretton Close
Sutton Farm
SHREWSBURY
SY2 6BY

Dear Mr Bowyer

Now that your retirement from the Post Office is imminent, I am taking this opportunity of thanking you for your very long service with us in a number of localities and wishing you a very long, happy and healthy retirement. There will be a further opportunity of saying more about this when I present you with the ISW next week.

I don't know what you have lined up for your retirement but I believe it to be a period in which one should keep busy though without the compulsion of everyday working life. I do hope you will find plenty to do in particular of those things you most enjoy doing. I also hope that you will from time to time have pleasant memories of your working life with us.

Yours sincerely

Letter from the GPO 3rd January 1974 [NB collection]

I have enjoyed my retirement, which has been spent quietly and contentedly. It has given Elsie and me time together and we have both enjoyed good health. We have had time to visit many of the small towns around Shropshire and over the border into Wales. Elsie's time is spent looking for a bargain in all the local shops, whilst I develop my hobby of looking at the old churches and reading the history of the community told in the gravestones of the church yard.

Revisiting old haunts – the aptly named Bowyer Arms near Didcot [Neville Bowyer collection]

and Crewe Station [Neville Bowyer collection]

Now, thinking back over all those years and experiences, I remember with some amusement, the last time I flew in the RAF. There was very little flying taking place and as a Warrant Officer I was rather kicking my heels around the place, getting bored and waiting for the evening to come when I could go off duty and see Elsie.

Exactly a week into the peace, on a beautifully clear early summer day, I had just left the mess after lunch when I heard a familiar voice calling to me, "Trev, are you gainfully occupied at the moment, old chap?"

I turned around and as I expected was facing Flying Officer Cruickshank, AFC, six years my junior. "Well that depends upon what you've got in mind, Jimmy," I replied with a smile.

"Good lad. I'm fed up with all this mooching around here. Fancy a spin?" I had seen that grin before and knew that some prank or other was in his mind.

"God yes," I replied, "I haven't been up since February and anything to break this tedium."

"Right, get the crew together, Trev, we're going."

"Okay, right away, Jimmy."

Without any further ado I gathered together the usual suspects, and we met up in the locker room. Jimmy had sorted out the formalities and so, duly kitted out, we commandeered a jolly, fresh-faced young WAAF with a truck to take us out to a waiting Mitchell B25. We spent the next two and a quarter hours on what was euphemistically recorded as 'local flying'; in other words we were joyriding around the English countryside and out over the Irish Sea for no other purpose than the simple fun of flying. It was wonderful. No-one was out there trying to kill us, waiting to shoot us down; we were just six young men indulging in pure unadulterated, harmless pleasure. Up and down the country there were many crews doing much the same thing; there was no counselling, it probably wasn't even a word, and so this was our way of unwinding from the experiences we had been through. I don't suppose we would get away with it today; we would be castigated across the front pages of the tabloids, but then a great many things were different in 1945. Much has changed, not all of it for the better. Although I didn't plan it, that trip turned out to be the last time that I ever flew in an aircraft of any description and there have been very few occasions when I have enjoyed myself quite so much as I did that afternoon.

I had started my RAF career on 30th November 1940 as a raw recruit Aircraftman 2nd Class, I had survived fifty-nine bombing missions, two crash landings, my oxygen mask being shot off my face, and countless rounds of cannon, machine-gun fire and flak shells. I had been promoted to the rank of Warrant Officer, awarded the Distinguished Flying Cross, the 1939/45 Star, the much coveted Aircrew Europe Star, the Africa Star, the Defence Medal, the 1939/45 War Medal and the Imperial Service Medal; but most of all I had been a member of Bomber Command and I had come through it, part of a small group of men who had completed two operational tours. Life had been very, very good to me.

Dusk; and the shadows were growing deeper across the National Memorial. One by one the birds had fallen silent until, just as at Skellingthorpe, only a solitary song thrush could be heard, trying to deny the approaching darkness.

I had been here all day but now it was time for me to go too. As I watched the glow of the twilight slowly fade into the west, as I done so many times from my turret, it was the faces of the friends I had lost that drifted across my memory: the ones who, one night, hadn't come back, who hadn't made it to the peace that they had fought for. They were so young and yet at the time we hadn't really thought about it. But we were: I was young at thirty, but so many hadn't even made twenty-one, not old enough to vote, but old enough to die. I had seen death too close and too often and I had known immensely courageous men; not natural heroes, but ordinary young men who, despite their own fears, repeatedly climbed into an aircraft and flew out to face the most terrifying combat experiences imaginable, never knowing if it was to be the last time that they would do so. And for 55,573 of them it was. I have known what it means to be truly frightened, but I have also known true comradeship. I have seen the world change out of all recognition, some of it for better, some of it less so. But the most important part of my life has always been my wife and family, because so many people gave their lives so that we could live in freedom.

- Per Ardua Ad Astra -

A different sort of Spitfire. Me leaning on Neville's Triumph

THE AUTHOR

The author with Marshal of the Royal Air Force
Sir Michael Beetham, GCB,CBE,DFC,AFC,FRAeS,DL

Kenneth Ballantyne was born into a Forces family at Gibraltar Military Hospital in 1949. His father, an officer in the Royal Artillery, had served throughout the Second World War as had his mother who, at twenty-one had joined the First Aid Nursing Yeomanry [The Princess Royal's Volunteer Corps], whose centenary was celebrated in 2007.

Educated at schools across Europe, Scotland and England, Kenneth practiced as a solicitor for many years before retiring to combine his interest in writing with fund raising for the Severn Hospice in Shropshire, following the care given there to his late father-in-law. He established his own publishing business in order to put his first book into the shops. Other books have followed and he has also become involved in raising money for the Eden Valley Hospice in Cumbria and the Bomber Command Association.

Kenneth is an associate member of the Aircrew Association, No.50/61 Squadrons Association and No.210 [Flying Boat] Squadron Association. He has an enduring interest in the Royal Air Force and particularly collecting and recording the true stories and individual contributions of the men and women who served in it during World War Two providing a record for future generations.

Mural at Citadel Station, Carlisle

*The TPO platform at Citadel - our early
morning arrival point*

*My wife to be, Elsie Minshall on 8th November 1945
[Neville Bowyer]*

Me enjoying retirement in the 1970s [Neville Bowyer]

*Nose camera picture of an attack on
enemy ships in the Mediterranean [Ray Morris]*

*Date palms.
Seeking
forbidden
fruit!
[Ray
Morris]*

It ain't 'alf hot mum - 'the boys to entertain you'
[Ray Morris]

Ray Morris [left] & brother John who was Mentioned in
Dispatches [Ray Morris]

Blake Turner [2nd from right] relaxing in Cape Town before sailing for Freetown [Turner Family]

Last minute top up [Reg Payne]

Wheels going up skipper [Reg Payne]

Lincoln Cathedral waited for us at the end of the runway

Lancaster over Lincoln [Reg Payne]

First wave crossing the coast [Reg Payne]

Coned [Reg Payne]

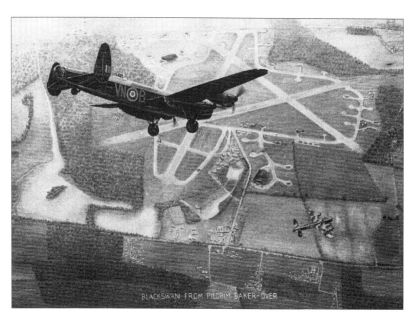

Black Swan from Pilgrim Baker - over [Reg Payne]

Bernard Fitch [3ʳᵈ from right] QR-S & crew [B Fitch]

*Ted Beswick [front left] & crew - no ops tonight
[Ted Beswick]*

*March 4th 1945 Bohlem mission James Flowers [2nd from
right][James Flowers]*

Taffy in the mid-upper turret [James Flowers]

James at his rear guns 1945 [James Flowers]

All kitted up and ready to go [James Flowers]

Arthur Harris with an aircrew. The public knew him as 'Bomber' Harris, but he was 'Butch' Harris to his crews

The last moments of Queenie [Reg Payne]

East Kirkby control tower near to where Queenie crashed

The NAAFI at East Kirkby

*Petwood House, Woodhall Spa. If you're going to
have an officers' mess, have a good one.
No.617 Squadron Officers' Mess*

The poigniant end of AJ-A and her crew piloted by Sqn Ldr 'Dinghy' Young DFC and Bar

Nos.50 & 61 Squadrons memorial at Birchwood...

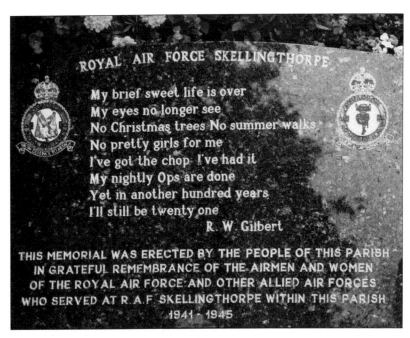

ROYAL AIR FORCE SKELLINGTHORPE

My brief sweet life is over
My eyes no longer see
No Christmas trees No summer walks
No pretty girls for me
I've got the chop I've had it
My nightly Ops are done
Yet in another hundred years
I'll still be twenty one
                    R. W. Gilbert

THIS MEMORIAL WAS ERECTED BY THE PEOPLE OF THIS PARISH
IN GRATEFUL REMEMBRANCE OF THE AIRMEN AND WOMEN
OF THE ROYAL AIR FORCE AND OTHER ALLIED AIR FORCES
WHO SERVED AT R.A.F. SKELLINGTHORPE WITHIN THIS PARISH
1941 - 1945

...and at Skellingthorpe Village Hall

W/Cdr Jimmie Flint, DFC,GM,DFM,AE

James, Eunice, Reg & Freda [James Flowers]

Bernard Fitch with Elaine Ballantyne and the author

The author at the controls of Lancaster NX 611 Just Jane

The crew of VN-B having fun over the
Lincolnshire countryside [Reg Payne]

Lancaster bomber NX 611 Just Jane

*Flypast by Lancaster PA 474 of the Battle of Britain
Memorial Flight at Skellingthorpe*

Gone But Not Forgotten. RAF stone at the
National Memorial Arboretum

The open space and tranquility at the
National Memorial Arboretum